Suspended Fictions

Suspended Fictions

Reading Novels by Manuel Puig

LUCILLE KERR

UNIVERSITY OF ILLINOIS PRESS
Urbana and Chicago

Publication of this work was supported in part by a grant
from the University of Southern California.

© 1987 by the Board of Trustees of the University of Illinois
Manufactured in the United States of America
C   5   4   3   2   1

This book is printed on acid-free paper.

Library of Congress Cataloging-in-Publication Data

Kerr, Lucille, 1946–
  Suspended fictions.

  Includes index.
  1. Puig, Manuel—Criticism and interpretation.
I. Title.
PQ7798.26.U4Z76   1987   863   86-1265
ISBN 0-252-01329-8 (alk. paper)

Contents

Preface

This book was begun, without my knowing it at the time, when I decided to write about *The Buenos Aires Affair*, Puig's *novela policial*. In working on that text, I saw that I couldn't talk about Puig's detective novel without considering some of the directions taken by modern fiction and, in addition, some of the critical responses to that body of writing. To talk about Puig's novel, for example, I had to think about the hierarchies of value implied by the idea of "high" and "low" forms of art; I had to acknowledge the possible inadequacy of some of the formal categories and critical vocabularies that might be used to describe or analyze works of narrative; and I had to recognize the potentially subversive models of reading that are now being proposed by contemporary "experimental" fiction. As I began to look more closely at other of Puig's novels, I realized that such issues inform his writing as a whole. I decided that a close reading of his work would not only provide a detailed analysis of how his fictions work, but would also help to uncover more systematically those sorts of questions. Moreover, I thought that a close reading of Puig's novels could show us how he has raised the kinds of issues that circulate not only in recent Spanish American narrative and modern fiction in general, but in modern critical theory as well. In writing this book I have become more conscious of how our theoretical and critical vocabularies make it possible for us to organize and undertake our readings. Puig's writing reminds us that those vocabularies always also limit what we can say; his fictions tell us that there is indeed a whole lot more that can be said. In fact,

Puig's writing seems to clarify and extend some of the theories that might be brought to bear on them. For instance, while the work of Bakhtin (his writings on parody and stylization), that of Foucault (his formulations about relations of power), and that of Barthes (his views on the figure of the author), among others, have helped in reading Puig, Puig's writing has also helped in reading those theoretical texts. In the course of working on this project, then, I have found that to read Puig is in some way to explore—now in explicit, now in implicit, terms—how we go about reading works of fiction and how those same works teach us how to read.

One of the critical issues with which I have had to deal early on, and on which Puig's writing has helped me to focus, is the question of how to write about a living author, how to work with a "work-in-progress." Though contemporary theory has shown us that the idea of the "complete" work is actually as much a fiction for the case of the author long dead as it is a self-evident fact for that of the author who still lives, I don't doubt that there are those who would feel uneasy about undertaking a study of a contemporary writer. I have found that, precisely by reading the work of Puig, we begin to see how works of modern fiction have pushed us to reconsider the principles according to which some critical, as well as literary, practices have become part of our canon. For example, Puig's writing puts into question the cultural and literary hierarchies that seem to determine not only the kinds of texts writers write and critics write about, but also how and when those texts are read. As my comments throughout this book (especially those in the last chapter) emphasize, Puig's writing has helped me to reconsider the notion of an author's "work," as well as the figure of the author itself, in such a way that the idea of a certifiably "closed" or "complete" work—and, consequently, the critical study predicated upon that notion—is put into quite a different light. In reading texts like those of Puig, we can begin to give some thought to how critical and literary practices become situated by the traditions and contexts in which they are formed. My study of Puig aims to raise that kind of question not only by talking about Puig's writing, but also by doing so at this point in time.

Puig began his career as a writer in the 1960s, after first taking a turn toward, but then moving away from, the world of filmmaking. He spent his childhood in General Villegas, a small provincial town in the

Argentine pampas, where he was born in December 1932 and later spent many an afternoon at the movies. He left General Villegas (it is very much like Coronel Vallejos, where both *La traición de Rita Hayworth* and *Boquitas pintadas* are mainly set) for Buenos Aires (the "big city"), where he attended both high school and university. (His third and fourth novels, *The Buenos Aires Affair* and *El beso de la mujer araña*, take place in the Argentine capital.) When he first left Argentina in 1956, it was to go to Rome, where he had decided to use a scholarship won from the Italian Institute of Buenos Aires. He wanted to study in Cinecittá and did in fact work there for a short time. As he tells it, however, the Cinecittá experience was a disappointing one. His idea of the film world, his expectations of what it would be like to work with important directors, were not the reality he actually lived. His own insecurities as a director's assistant undercut even further the little control he might have had in a setting where authority is everything, where directors are figures to be respected and revered. Puig then began writing screenplays, and from one of them he developed his first novel. Thus he moved from working on films to writing fiction. Between 1956 and 1967, Puig lived mainly in Europe and New York; in 1967 he returned to Argentina, where he remained until the early 1970s. When he again left the country, he went to Mexico (his fifth novel, *Pubis angelical*, is set there) for about two years. In 1976 he moved back to New York (*Maldición eterna a quien lea estas páginas* takes place in Greenwich Village), and then in the early 1980s he moved to Brazil (the setting for *Sangre de amor correspondido*).

The facts of Puig's biography (like those of any author's "life story," I think) are intriguing for a variety of reasons, not the least of which, perhaps, is that they might seem to explain the "influence" of film on his writing. But this isn't really what interests me. What does interest me is that Puig's professional shift from film to literature—or perhaps his description of it—also reveals and reinforces the politics of some of the maneuvers that inform his writing. The world of film is a kind of antagonstic, even though also attractive, beginning for Puig's novels. It is a contradictory, if also negative, origin for the work of an author who, by opposing himself to and yet also allying himself with a popular tradition, finally makes himself into a respected authority on the popular. Though Puig rejects the real world of filmmaking, if only because it seems to have rejected him, he incorporates into some of his fictions a number of figures and fantasies that appear to come directly from his favorite films. In moving away from an arena in which he could become no more than an assistant to a director and by succeeding in situating himself in another in which he himself is the privileged director and author of things, Puig both renounces and reappropriates the film world and fictions to which his name has become attached.

This ambivalent, dialectical move is characteristic of Puig's writing. It is the kind of move that generates much of the political thrust of Puig's work as a whole. For the political force of Puig's work resides not so much in the representation of a specific sociopolitical or cultural situation (though, indeed, some of his novels do appear to address directly some such situations) as in the development of a variety of textual relations and references to literary and cultural canons or contexts through which questions of power and authority are repeatedly raised. Through that simultaneous rejection of and return to the world of film, for example, Puig begins to establish his writing as a writing that reveres and resists particular literary or cultural models, that underwrites and undermines different, even opposing, systems of authority. The films he refashions according to his own authorial plans are only one of the forms of popular culture with which he works in this way. As Puig develops his dialogue with various literary, cultural, and even critical traditions, he also raises questions about the authority that such traditions wield and about how such authority becomes accepted or challenged. It is that aspect of his work that makes him such a political writer. Puig's writing suggests that we can't really talk about the politics of an author or the political nature of that author's texts without taking up the details of how those texts are made. Indeed, it may well be that only if we are willing to read very closely can we begin to understand what is political about a particular set of texts or a particular writer's enterprise.

My aim, then, in reading closely Puig's novels is to show not only how individual texts are put together, but also what Puig's writing as a whole is about. In doing this, I suspect that I may be led to repeat some of the plots of the novels over which I have also attempted to exercise some kind of control; for my dialogue with Puig is a "conversation" that must remain suspended, much like the fictions around which that dialogue has been created and the traditions of reading within or against which I myself have aimed to work.

A portion of Chapter 3 has appeared previously in *MLN*. I thank the editors of that journal for granting permission to use that material. Chapter 4 is an expanded and revised version of material previously published in Spanish in *Texto crítico*. I also acknowledge the generosity of the American Philosophical Society, whose support helped me to complete part of this study. My very special thanks go to the colleagues, friends, and family members—they know who they are—who encouraged and supported me throughout this project. Ann Lowry Weir, of the University of Illinois Press, made the usually burdensome publication process a pleasure with her enthusiasm for the project and her attentive overseeing of its completion.

1

The Imprimatur of Tradition: Politics, Parody, Puig

Among the writers whose work has called attention to the self-critical nature of much of contemporary Spanish American fiction, it is perhaps Manuel Puig (Argentina, b. 1932) who has shown how adventurous and radical that self-questioning can be.[1] Many of the Spanish Americans would remind us that their enterprise is generated partly by a desire to alter and disrupt the conventions of literature. In the work of Puig the complexities and contradictions of that critical project become most dramatic. Interestingly enough, though talk of the "death of the novel" subsided well before Puig's writing appeared on the international literary scene, questions about possible or even proper directions for fiction have lingered.[2] However, along with many of his Spanish American compatriots, Puig has shown that the writing of narrative fiction is not tied to forms that live and die, that the concerns of fiction writing are not only formal, but in many ways cultural and political as well. Together, these concerns give a special life to Puig's work.

Since the "rediscovery" of Latin America through the "boom" of Spanish American literature both within and outside its own borders, Puig and other Spanish American writers (e.g., Arenas, Cabrera Infante, Cortázar, Fuentes, García Márquez, Neruda, Paz, Sarduy, Vargas Llosa) have come to the attention of readers, writers, and critics from diverse cultures and traditions.[3] The expanded publication and translation of Spanish America's authors, as well as the international prizes awarded some of its best-known figures (e.g., Jorge Luis Borges

1

shared the Formentor/International Publishers' Prize with Samuel Beckett in 1961, and the Nobel Prize for Literature was awarded to Miguel Angel Asturias in 1967, Pablo Neruda in 1971, and Gabriel García Márquez in 1982), are signs of the increasing interest in a whole body of writing that appears to be emerging from the margins of Western literary history. Given its former colonial status and marginal position, it is remarkable that Latin American literature has received international recognition in the course of a few decades. In the case of the Spanish American novel or "new" narrative, the best-known and most widely disseminated group of works, this modern discovery does not, however, mark the closing of the gap between European and Latin American models, nor does it remove Latin American writing as a whole from an inherently political arena in which its status remains problematical.[4] Though recent historical events have brought this area to the forefront of North American and European concerns, Latin America is still geographically and culturally set apart from those centers of activity and power. But that distance and, therefore, difference from the "primary" models of culture may be precisely what give this "secondary" tradition its extraordinary potential.

Although founded upon European models—models that are at once familiar and foreign to the Spanish Americans themselves—contemporary Spanish American literature has sought to break away from their authority, if not to subvert entirely the hierarchy in which it has for so long been situated in a subordinate, "parasitic" position. The struggle against the original and dominant modes of European writing has caused the Spanish Americans to become further estranged, as it were, from that primary tradition. It is perhaps this strangeness that both attracts and puts off, inspires praise from and neglect by, critics inside and outside Latin America.[5] Not unlike some currents of modern criticism which have tried to work against the notion that critical writing is, and must be, subordinated to the literary texts upon which they rest, contemporary Spanish American literature has sought its independence from European models while also remaining in dialogue with them.[6] This struggle is at once literary, cultural, and political. As we know, literary history is as much the story of how and why certain texts, authors, or traditions become part of accepted canons as it is the recording of what those canons have been or now are. To be sure, some of the problems surrounding contemporary writing have as much to do with the positions from which that writing is viewed as with the objects of study themselves.[7]

We have some good examples of this situation in Spanish American fiction's rise to its new position and in the development of Puig's writing in relation to a variety of texts and traditions that surround his work. From the apparently "primitive" or "old" Spanish American novels of the first three decades or so of this century (for example, from Azuela's *Los de abajo* [1916] to Gallegos's *Doña Bárbara* [1929]) to the emergence of the more "creative" texts of the "new" novelists, a whole new tradition seems to have been inaugurated and to have matured in little over forty years.[8] The "boom" of Latin American literature as a whole has involved not only the commercial success but, more important, the artistic development of a diverse body of writing—a "revolutionary" writing. These texts have managed to build on the techniques of their European and North American predecessors and to create a language (in the widest sense of the term) all their own, a language that questions the notion of what is proper in and for literature, a language that "reinvents" Latin American reality as primary and authoritative.[9]

The modern enterprise of Spanish American fiction is indeed a critical one, and even before the "boom" this critical spirit is evident. From the early texts of Borges (perhaps the most European of the Spanish American writers, he is the writer whose eye has been fixed on European literature and philosophy for over fifty years now) to those of a novelist like Puig (perhaps one of the most "popular" of Spanish American writers, he is the writer whose eye, fixed as it is on various forms of popular culture, is engaged in a unique way by Spanish America's quotidian reality), the Spanish Americans have displayed a special interest in the problems of language and literature. In fact, the question of language is paramount for the Spanish Americans. It is important both for authors of texts that appear to return to "classical" (i.e., mimetic) forms of narration and representation (to name but two, for example, García Márquez's *Cien años de soledad* or Donoso's *Casa de campo*) and for writers whose radical experiments with narrative structure and technique erode the underpinnings of mimetic fiction (among others, Arenas's *El mundo alucinante*, Cabrera Infante's *Tres tristes tigres*, Sarduy's *Cobra*, Fuentes's *Terra nostra*, as well as much of Puig's work).

While the question of language is by no means entirely new with the Spanish Americans, their relation to it (exemplified and brought to a special limit by Puig) is perhaps different from that of European and North American writers. As writers who emerge from a culture and language born of an extended colonial experience, they are themselves perhaps somewhat estranged from the European languages that are (but are also not quite) their own. They would seem to come to their language from outside, from its margins. They would seem to try to free themselves from while binding themselves to it, to work against while also working within it. In the texts or, rather, languages of writers like Puig we are reminded of the Spanish Americans' battle, their dialogue, with various models of language. But, as Puig's work reveals so well, these models are themselves embattled networks of dialogues among the forms of discourse that comprise them, among the languages that make up Spanish American reality itself.[10]

In the writing of the Spanish American novelists the notion of a reality outside or, rather, independent of language is undermined repeatedly. Their work emphasizes that language is as much a reality in and of itself as it is the material out of which an illusion of reality is created. Even in the novels that seem to have the power to convince us of the reality of their fictions and to make us forget temporarily the artificial nature of their represented worlds, there is always a return to (or perhaps a reminder that we have never really left behind) the fact of textuality and the primacy of the language that makes up the individual text. In these novels it is difficult, if not impossible, to conceive of reality as separate from language. This is especially true of Puig's writing. In his work fictional reality emerges from the interplay of heterogeneous discourses through which a complicated and contradictory assessment is made of the languages from which that fiction is drawn. To be conscious of the historical, cultural, and artistic realities that are lived in the real world as well as in novels is, for the Spanish Americans, to be conscious of and engaged with language itself. Yet, as we know, only through and within language can those disparate but interdependent realities be examined at all. The text that attempts to represent reality as a network of languages and fictions can only do so by also uncovering the fictional supports of the text through which it seeks to present that same reality.

This paradox characterizes much of contemporary Spanish American

4

narrative. It is also intrinsic to reflexive literature in general and to the "novel as a self-conscious genre" in particular, the tradition to which writers like Puig have given new life.[11] Although it is, as we know, in the nature of literature to draw attention to itself as such, the novel is particularly well suited for revealing the fiction/reality interplay and authorial duplicity that inform this type of writing.[12] By making visible the unresolvable dialectic of their inherent "ontological doubleness," such works investigate the conditions of possibility for rethinking the categories of fiction and reality.[13] When we read novels that seem to fit this label, we see them as turning back on themselves to contemplate and "comment" upon their own status as literary texts and, moreover, to draw attention to the linguistic and structural underpinnings of those reflexive operations. They appear to turn in different directions at once, to intermix and superimpose the apparently polarized realms of fiction and reality, and to refer alternately and yet simultaneously to the interdependent but distinct spheres of fictional story and literary text.[14]

To engage in this kind of writing is to aid in the subversion of an established order, to undermine the priority of and the hierarchy supporting the privilege of mimetic fiction. Spanish American new narrative seems to be founded on just these sorts of principles. It is part of, but also leads the way within, the recent developments of significance in postmodern fiction. To assert, as does the self-conscious novel, that a fiction is indeed a fiction, a lie that masquerades as an unmediated truth, is to undercut the illusion of authenticity, the place of authority, that has for a long time been attached to mimetic fiction. The contemporary self-conscious novel would depose realist fiction from its place of preeminence. It would call into question the status of that type of novel as a primary mode of fiction and undermine the critical vocabulary and values that have persisted far beyond the nineteenth-century tradition from which they still seem to derive their power, even in the face of the literary developments of the past half-century or more (e.g., the work of Joyce, Faulkner, and the writers of the French *nouveau roman*, for example, as well as of the Spanish Americans).[15]

The Spanish Americans seem to have raised this type of fiction to a new and apparently more central position where—like the Spanish American tradition itself—it appears as a fresh, original (albeit "secondary") phenomenon. However, much like some of the materials with which the Spanish Americans, and particulary Puig, work, this type of fiction is in a sense all too familiar. It therefore bears within its most recent development something of a contradiction. From the European and North American vantage points, Spanish American fiction, somewhat exotic to begin with, might appear doubly strange and distant precisely because it returns to their own tradition something of what has been partially forgotten, if not also intermittently suppressed. With the Spanish American new novel, fiction writing returns with remarkable force to a reflexive mode that isn't really all that new. Although appearing to postdate and to exist in a secondary position with relation to realist fiction, the self-conscious novel can also be viewed as a more primary form which, "eclipsed" as it was by nineteenth-century realism, has once again asserted itself as a dominant mode of writing.[16]

The paradox of this play between old and new, primary and secondary, traditions and forms of fiction coincides with the nature of the texts produced by writers such as Puig. It is in the return to, and in the rediscovery and conservation of, the familiar but virtually forgotten and estranged art forms and languages formerly excluded from the realm of "Literature" that some of the Spanish Americans—particularly Puig—have proven themselves most radical.[17] This revolutionary quality of their work is heightened by the apparently parodic nature of their writing.[18] Parody has an intrinsically political character. It introduces what is, or what appears to be, strange or alien into the normal or authoritative. It is an essentially reflexive form of discourse that has played a significant role in the development of narrative fiction, from the writing of Cervantes to that of contemporary authors.[19]

In calling attention to and commenting upon a parodied genre, theme, or language from the canon, a parodying text always also directs attention to—sometimes even to parody—itself in a highly analytical and even evaluative manner. A parodic text refers to both a fictional world and the textual strategies and devices through which that particular fiction is sustained. It points to specific texts and forms of discourse upon which it is itself based. If the novel can be viewed as a kind of "mosaic" constructed through the interweaving and convergence of the many traditions within it, then the parodic text can be seen to underscore in a radical way its own intertextual quality.[20] Parody therefore also implicates the literary, cultural, and historical traditions to which a particular text might be related. A parodic novel—or one in which parody figures as a significant device—emphasizes the genre's fundamentally dialogic or polyphonic nature. It highlights aspects of textuality and demonstrates the basic openness and productivity of literary texts as a group.[21]

Reflexive fiction in general and parody in particular work within several frames of reference. The critical operations of both move in several directions at once. In each, attention is focused on a represented fiction and on the fact of textuality; in each, either a specific literary model or set of conventions is, so to speak, analyzed. While parody would seem to direct its gaze inward (toward features of the parodying text itself) after first looking outward (toward an original discourse, text, or tradition), reflexive fiction would appear to look outward (toward the conventions of the genre and its history) by first looking inward (toward its own status as a text and the interplay of represented reality and narrative technique). But there is actually a simultaneous interplay of critical "gazes" in both types of texts, and this interplay also serves to link, perhaps in the end to identify, these two forms of writing. Moreover, in each the superimposition of critical perspectives and operations undermines the possibility of locating an original "glance" or critical stance that would appear to generate the text as a whole. Both reflexive and parodic texts develop and display a basic duplicity or ambivalence that disallows the possibility of identifying a privileged verbal or visual position or a temporally or spatially original subject—a position or subject that we nevertheless seem to have to imagine and invoke in order to talk about these sorts of novels. Such texts are problematic precisely because their discourse cannot be immobilized or their "original" subjects located. Reflexive and parodic texts seem always to involve highly ordered yet uncontrollable turns between one critical point of view, or pole, and another.

This identification and interplay between reflexive writing and parody is precisely what characterizes so many of the Spanish American new novels and creates many of their radical possibilities, much of their political thrust. Puig's novels illustrate not only some of the ways in which the Spanish American enterprise as a whole has developed and revealed those connections to us, but also some of the problems entailed in reading this type of "experimental" fiction. To read Puig is to confront a set of texts that at once seem to take different positions in relation to the many kinds of models (i.e., languages, themes, genres) with which they work. His writing involves the combination of and confrontation among what appear to be radically different attitudes and aims. The problematic merger of various types of positions and opinions, as well as traditions and techniques, calls attention to the radical, critical, yet seductive nature of Puig's writing.

Puig has been regarded as the celebrator of popular culture and as its critic; as the regenerator of its languages, forms, and characters and as their detractor. His work is in fact a powerful blend of both these projects. His fictions are committed in unexpected and paradoxical ways to the very same cultural models, myths, and art forms they would often appear to judge. As such, his writing becomes a unique meeting-ground where various designs for power and pleasure are unveiled and tested, where a variety of dialogues, at once textual and fictional, political and erotic, are betrayed in a critically provocative way. In Puig's novels we see an extravagant convergence of diverse discourses, narrative devices, and cultural and artistic traditions toward which several kinds of positions appear to be taken. Each of his texts is therefore an intricate and complex network of "critical readings." One of the most intriguing features of that writing is the way that the heterogeneous "voices" and diverse narrative forms and techniques seem to harmonize while also doing battle with one another.[22] Puig undertakes a questioning of certain hierarchies of literary and critical practice precisely through this intermingling of literary, subliterary, and nonliterary forms, themes, and languages. His work calls attention to and implicitly comments upon the hierarchies of value that inform and generate artistic production and reception. The various alliances of traditions and techniques in Puig's work reveal a system of literary and cultural values against and yet within which his writing manages to work, a system that is at the same time regenerated and subverted.

For example, when Puig writes his own version of a serial novel (*Boquitas pintadas*) or a detective text (*The Buenos Aires Affair*); when he saturates a novel with sentimental cinematographic fantasies (*La traición de Rita Hayworth*) or plot summaries of romantic and melodramatic films (*El beso de la mujer araña*); or when he ventures to combine his own brand of science fiction with filmic as well as political fantasies (*Pubis angelical*), or to produce a novelistic fiction of every-day dialogue from a quasi-sociological inquiry (*Maldición eterna a quien lea estas páginas*), or to construct a small-town tale of erotic obsession from an encounter with its popular protagonist (*Sangre de amor correspondido*)—in these instances he would bring into the realm of "high" art, or "Literature," various "low" forms of art and culture and typically nonliterary modes of discourse.[23] When he inter-mixes the languages of popular songs, women's fashion magazines, advertising, soap opera, medicine, law, and religion in one text, or those of romantic fantasy, political rhetoric, religious ritual, and small-town gossip in another; when he plays with both the gaps and the links between fact and fiction, or scientific theory and narrative art, or pol-itics and sexuality; or when he displays with great virtuosity the nar-rative possibilities of immediate direct or hidden dialogue, interior monologue, omniscient narration in the third person, letters, diaries, school compositions, and official documents—the effects are, to say the least, dazzling, even subversive. Yet the discursive and narrative heterogeneity of Puig's work would belie the powerful and paradoxical strategies of his entire literary project, the simultaneously subversive and conservative nature of his writing.

In the first place, the discursive, narrative, and formal heterogene-ity of his work has a democratizing effect within each text. This het-erogeneity disallows the possibility of assigning more importance, or granting more authority, to one type of discourse or device than to another. In grafting together but also opposing so many different ge-neric, thematic, and discursive forms, Puig draws attention to the laws and assumptions that underwrite or privilege certain forms of culture and art, certain kinds of languages. Moreover, his writing appears to correct and upset the dominant modes, to confound a variety of textual and discursive hierarchies. By self-consciously rereading and rewrit-ing, reevaluating and recuperating a set of popular models (detective fiction and serial novels, for example) whose "low" positions are estab-lished by their perceived relation to what we call "high" art, Puig's writing proposes to liberate and legitimize various kinds of popular paradigms. These sorts of strategies constitute the democratic, or even "revolutionary," quality of his writing. Puig undermines the authority of "aesthetic" writing with other apparently less captivating forms. His writing overthrows the notion of the classically "beautiful" text, the text that, because of its "beauty," seems to hold us in its grasp. This overthrow of the regime of aesthetic (i.e., "artistic") domination, however, is accomplished by texts that are themselves captivating in their own strange and radical way. It is their strangeness that holds us in its power, even though that strangeness, of course, must itself soon turn into what is familiar.

This democratic and potentially radical movement of Puig's writing also seems to contradict itself, for his strategies have their own suppressive aims and effects. It is not only that his writing, in its political relation to the forms and traditions it seeks to question, would put down a good portion of prior literary and critical practice by putting in their place models of his own choosing. (This is, in a sense, what happens at every "new" stage of literary history.) It is also that within his novels it is not always clear exactly what (if any) model or language or figure is unequivocally supported. That is, the apparent assertion of equality among diverse narrative techniques, generic forms, and languages seems also to deny that same democracy. In Puig's novels the mechanisms that make possible this radical transvaluation, the strategies that undermine the possibility of hierarchically placing languages and forms and themes, also affect the models his texts would seem to want to raise to new positions. The potentially subversive aspect of his work is made possible by strategies whose display of ambivalence, whose turns in disparate directions, also call into question the radical aims of his work. Many of the models apparently elevated by his writing are also always deflated by it. Those that are seemingly accorded somewhat reduced positions are simultaneously invested with a great deal of power and prestige. Puig's novels are, in fact, models of instability, ambivalence. Their "shifty" nature impedes our efforts to resolve their complex turns.

These kinds of maneuvers and effects affirm the inevitable interconnections between the production of reflexive writing and "double-voiced" or "double-directed" discourse, some of whose similarities are noted already.[24] In fact, much of the perplexing nature of Puig's work derives from the ostensibly impossible interplay of two such forms of discourse—i.e., parody and stylization—in each text. The mobile, turning quality of Puig's novels is generated partly within the various meetings between these basically ambivalent operations. If we consider briefly the nature of these forms of discourse, we can begin to understand some of the categories in terms of which his novels have been read and described, categories whose further clarification would aid us in reading Puig's work as a whole.

As we know, a parody is generated through a particular kind of intertextual relation formed between a parodying and a parodied text.[25] The parodic relation implies the virtual union of and overlap between authorial and readerly functions—that is, the positions of producer or sender and of perceiver or receiver of the texts. The author of a parody is first a reader of and receiver for the model for the parody, and then a producer of the second and parodic discourse. The author of the parodied model and the reader of the parody do not necessarily play overlapping parts. The parody and its author, however, always represent a superimposition of textual roles. The parodist is thus the central, active participant in this "act of double literary communication"—a kind of ambivalent, yet neutral, speaker (or "voice") and listener (or "ear") whose double position, even attitude, characterizes the mode.[26] In appearing to take a position with respect to the parodied model, the parodist defines at least two positions between which his own voice repeatedly moves—two poles that are balanced against, even neutralized by, one another, though never entirely reduced to a univocal stance. Parody always implies and creates a critical doubling that is both discursive and textual in nature. He who listens to a previous discourse also speaks and calls attention to it within his own; he who reads the work of another also rewrites it as his own. Such a meeting of voices and texts creates (at least theoretically) a democratic superimposition. In such a union the voice, position, or text of each writer and reader, each speaker and listener, appears equally powerful.

Yet, when we consider parodic texts, we are actually accustomed to privileging one of the voices. We seem to "hear" a voice raise itself "above"—and thereby look down on while also playing with—the discourse or text that precedes, and thus authorizes and supports, it. Although modern criticism has in general dispensed with the question of intentionality, when confronting this kind of text we usually employ some notion of intention. That is, we implicitly consider the intention of the "voice" of or within the text, though not necessarily that of the empirical author.[27] While in some forms of double-directed discourse (e.g., stylization) the intentionality of the two speech acts may coincide, in parodic discourse they do not. In parody the author "intro-

11

duces a semantic direction into that word which is diametrically opposed to its original direction. The second voice, which has made its home in the other person's word, collides in a hostile fashion with the original owner and forces him to serve purposes diametrically opposed to his own. The word becomes the arena of conflict between two voices. Therefore the merging of voices . . . is impossible in parody."[28] We understand that many kinds of objects (i.e., genres, myths, languages, character types, etc.) can be parodied in varying degrees and for many reasons; that a fundamental and irresolvable doubleness, or ambivalence, characterizes the roles played by authors and readers and defines the internal structure of parodic discourse; and that a conflictual relation underlies any form of parody.[29]

The conflicting nature of this type of discursive meeting is precisely what separates parody from stylization, the other form of double-voiced discourse that we need to consider. Stylization is a "conditional word," a "conventionalized utterance," through which the stylistic devices or structures of a previous voice or text are reproduced, though from a distance. In this form of double-directed speech an author takes seriously and tries to be faithful to a prior speech act, without imitating exactly that model.[30] However, parody and stylization are fundamentally alike in that they are paradoxical and ambivalent types of utterances. Each represents the intersection of two speech acts whose distance and difference from one another are at once asserted and negated. In parody the distance, the duplicity, is exaggerated precisely because of the gap of intentionality that informs the relation between original and secondary utterances. This is not the case in stylization. Nonetheless, each is structured as a dialogic movement that is, by definition, irreducible to either of its discursive or textual poles. As the terms "double-voiced" and "double-directed" remind us, such texts are models of mobility. They turn in two directions and "speak" from two positions; they represent two styles, two voices, two subjects, all at the same time.[31]

When we read this type of fiction, we must try to sort out the relationships among these multiple voices and directions. Our position as reader seems to become as problematic as that of the text we work to understand. Like reflexive fiction, stylizing and parodic texts also call attention to the act of reading and the process of interpretation, as well as to the models with which they themselves work, through the dialectical turns they take between mutually exclusive but superimposed frames of reference. It is all but impossible to stabilize conceptually and resolve into univocal form the plurality of directions and voices that support this kind of writing. Such a text is at once a single and a double utterance—an utterance that folds back on itself through its commentary on another text or discourse that is, curiously enough, both prior to and simultaneous with, both outside and within, itself. These are precisely the types of problems entailed in reading Puig, whose novels are at once parodic and stylizing in nature, whose dialogue with a variety of discursive and textual forms is, in the end, impossible to reduce to or identify with only one or another position. It could be argued that this mobile, turning quality of his writing is precisely what makes possible the critical transvaluations represented by his work to date. The possibility of reading Puig's strategies in different, apparently contradictory, ways at once allows us to posit and expose the seductively political effects of his writing.

Let us take first the case of parody or, rather, the possibility of reading Puig's work as essentially parodic. If we posit for the moment the superior force of one of the voices within a parody—that is, the greater power of the discourse derived from and, to a degree, emulative of another anterior to it—it is possible to demonstrate how Puig's writing produces a transvaluation of certain linguistic and literary forms. Although we must acknowledge a simultaneous idealization and criticism of an original within the parodying text or discourse (this is in fact what we could call the fundamental "paradox of parody"), the model discourse nevertheless seems to be placed in a position subordinate to the secondary text, and thus to be devalued by the act of parody itself.[32] Even though the high position of the parodied model is acknowledged by the energy used to direct attention to and play with it, the original, "serious" text is divested of its power through parody's inversionary mechanisms. When we read a parody as an inherently critical form of discourse, we recognize that it has the power to upset established literary and aesthetic orders, to invert and subvert the discursive and textual hierarchies supporting "artistic," canonic systems.

To read Puig's novels as parodic is to recognize and privilege the carnivalesque inversions they seem to generate.[33] According to this reading, it would be possible to show how the radical transvaluations of discourses and genres, for example, are tied to the political structure of parody itself. In the critical "suppression" of one voice by another, the positions held by specific forms of writing are shifted, and the value (or lack of value) accorded to them is changed. The parodic inversions created by Puig's writing could be said to reevaluate historically devalued (i.e., potentially repressed) forms by generating inversions of those already inverted models. If in the production of a parody the position of the original discourse is inverted and its authority, or lack thereof, is undermined, then Puig's novels could be read as producing a carnivalesque reversal whereby an inverted (i.e., already devalued or "lowered") object is turned upside down and thus raised "up" (i.e., implicitly revalued). Through such maneuvers the position of what is originally "below" (what is virtually suppressed or kept "down"—that is, the forms of "low" art, language, and culture with which Puig works) would be reversed through the mechanisms of parody. That which is originally devalued would be (re)valued; that which is "low" would be raised "high." The effects of such operations on the materials used by Puig are indeed significant. As the terms underscored here (i.e., "high" and "low") remind us, the question of value is itself originally attached to the very models with which he plays. It informs our general perception and critical evaluation of them. If we were to read Puig's novels as essentially parodic, then, we would see that the inversionary and subversive tactics inherent in parody would serve to reevaluate in a radical way the subliterary genres, themes, and languages, as well as the nonliterary forms of popular culture, with which his writing is so dramatically engaged.

If, on the other hand, we were to read Puig's novels as complex networks of stylizing operations, his writing would not necessarily lose its radical thrust. In fact, it would—in another way—retain it. Stylization has the same kind of power to change the value of the repudiated models with which Puig works and to arrive at (through a different, apparently opposing, route) that same type of transvaluation. Puig's writing also seems to ask to be read as a direct effort to recover and revalue an array of devalued models whose positions are also upended by the more or less democratic thrust of stylization in his work. That is, if we were to read the relation between his texts and their popular models as that of a stylization, we would have to read their exchange, their "dialogue," as an interchange between equals. According to the structure of stylization, neither voice or discourse would be situated in a privileged position. Oddly enough, an inversion of the status of the popular originals—that is, a raising "up" from their originally "low" position—would also be produced by the democratic mechanisms of stylization. The stylizing discourse would appear to treat the original, "serious" discourse as having a status equal to, perhaps even higher than, itself. In not being looked down upon but instead being treated as on a par with the second discourse, the "low" model would be raised "up" at least to the level of the text generating the stylization. To view Puig's novels as examples of stylization would therefore mean to read them as efforts to bring value (back) to—precisely because they would not seek to devalue—the original forms of popular art, language, and culture reworked in them.

Puig's novels not only raise the question about which of these apparently mutually exclusive readings is possible; they also cause one to wonder whether any such determination can be made, whether his writing can be pinned down to a single, albeit discursively ambivalent, position.[34] The difficulty of deciding the aims and effects of his novels arises not only from the inherently dialogic and dialectical structure of both parody and stylization, but also, maybe principally, from the combination and superimposition of disparate models and contradictory operations within them. Puig's writing implicates each of these mutually exclusive, but nonetheless related, forms of discourse in the other, revealing the complexity of both his narrative texts and the theoretical categories in terms of which it seems appropriate to read them. Puig's novels reveal the difficulty of establishing absolute limits between these two forms of double-voiced/double-directed discourse and, consequently, the impossibility of characterizing—that is, domesticating—his writing in terms of only one position or the other. In fact, his writing produces a dialectic of stylized parodies and parodic stylizations—doubly "dialogized hybrids"—that, to complicate things even further, are themselves both juxtaposed and superimposed throughout his novels.[35]

Reading Puig's work therefore entails dealing with the shifting and dialectical patterns that characterize his type of reflexive writing. The reflexive quality of his work has much to do with the way his writing calls attention to and questions the adequacy of the critical vocabulary and theoretical categories now available to us for reading works of fiction; indeed, it has as much to do with that as with the way his novels are able to draw us into their fictions while also making us aware of the strategies employed for our seduction. His writing calls into question the possibility of fixing, of understanding in an entirely systematic and stable manner, precisely what it is that we call "reflexive" fiction (or any of the variety of synonyms now in use). It reveals our current terminology's inadequacy for describing his work. Puig's texts challenge the descriptive power of modernist and postmodernist vocabularies and force us to consider not just what, but also how, we read—through which theoretical categories, critical positions, and cultural systems we both receive and perceive works of literature.

The readings that follow attempt to consider these issues by exploring the basically ambivalent and dialectical structures of relations, the "shifty" and turning movements, that characterize what goes on in each novel's fiction and text alike (i.e., among characters, between reader and author, and among some of the texts and traditions to which each seems to refer). These readings try to follow and turn with, to disentangle and expose, the relationships that support each textual and fictional network—to make sense of them as discrete yet interconnected works.[36] In trying to deal with the complexity of those networks of discursive, thematic, and structural relations, these discussions emphasize what is specific to, even idiosyncratic about, Puig's writing. But they also implicitly assume that, in pushing us to examine that complexity, Puig's work leads us to consider how contemporary writing raises questions about a variety of matters that are at once literary, cultural, and political in nature. Puig's novels offer us models for reading and returning to other texts and traditions, both "conventional" and "experimental," both "high" and "low," and the critical and literary practices through which we have learned to perceive and evaluate them. In the provocative juxtaposition of distinct narrative models and cultural myths, and in the revelation of the political nature of all sorts of textual relations, Puig's work sets up a strategic array of confrontations that raise questions about the nature and history of literature and criticism. Such questions may lead us in the future to consider as well the cultures in which those enterprises have thus far been developed.

16

NOTES

1. At the time of this writing Puig's novels include the following: *La traición de Rita Hayworth* (1968), *Boquitas pintadas* (1969), *The Buenos Aires Affair* (1973), *El beso de la mujer araña* (1976), *Pubis angelical* (1979), *Maldición eterna a quien lea estas páginas* (1980), and *Sangre de amor correspondido* (1982). With *Bajo un manto de estrellas: Pieza en dos actos; El beso de la mujer araña: Adaptación escénica realizada por el autor* (1983) he has moved into the field of drama as well. See the chapters that follow for information about editions of these works in Spanish and English.

2. See, for example, John Barth's much talked about article, "The Literature of Exhaustion," *Atlantic Monthly* August 1967: 29–34, and his follow-up comments in "The Literature of Replenishment," *Atlantic Monthly* January 1980: 65–71. Significantly, Robert Alter, who in his *Partial Magic: The Novel as a Self-Conscious Genre* (Berkeley: U of California P, 1975) refutes Barth's original notions (see the chapter entitled "The Inexhaustible Genre"), cites Puig's work as proof of the "continuing of the genre" in his review of the English translation of *The Buenos Aires Affair* (*New York Times Book Review* 5 September 1976: 4).

3. For discussions of the "boom" from different angles, see Emir Rodríguez Monegal, *El Boom de la novela latinoamericana* (Caracas: Tiempo Nuevo, 1972); José Donoso, *Historia personal del "boom"* (Barcelona: Anagrama 1972); Hernán Vidal, *Literatura hispanoamericana e ideología liberal: surgimiento y crisis* (Buenos Aires: Hispamérica, 1976); and David Viñas et al., *Más allá del boom: literatura y mercado* (Mexico City: Marcha, 1981). While many of the Latin Americans have only recently been "discovered" by North American and European readers, as early as the 1960s Borges had already come to the attention of a number of French critics (e.g., Blanchot, Genette, Ricardou, Macherey, and Foucault). See Emir Rodríguez Monegal's "Borges and La Nouvelle Critique," *Diacritics* 2.2 (1972): 27–34, for a discussion of the French readings of Borges. The question of the reinvention and rediscovery of America has pervaded Latin American thought since its beginnings; that such a project has continued and itself been recovered in contemporary literature should therefore not surprise us. See Carlos Fuentes, *La nueva novela hispanoamericana* (Mexico City: Joaquín Mortiz, 1969), and Roberto González Echevarría, *Alejo Carpentier: The Pilgrim at Home* (Ithaca: Cornell UP, 1977) 15–30, for comments on these issues.

4. The distinction between "new" and "new new" narrative is most likely derived from that between the French *nouveau roman* of the 1950s and the *nouveau nouveau roman* of the 1960s and '70s. These terms have been applied to the Spanish American context in order to define what perhaps no longer

seem to be clearly distinguishable groups of writers. In *Books Abroad* 44.1 (1970)—a special issue devoted to the Latin American novel—the distinctions between the "old" and the "new" generations of writers are outlined by both Mario Vargas Llosa ("The Latin American Novel Today: An Introduction" 7–12) and Emir Rodríguez Monegal ("The New Latin American Novel" 45–50). See also Rodríguez Monegal's "The New Latin American Novelists," *Tri-Quarterly* 13–14 (1968–69): 13–32, and, for a more extensive discussion, his *El Boom de la novela latinoamericana*.

5. See *Mundo nuevo* 28 (1968) and 33 (1969) for a series of articles that debate the quality and importance of the "new" novel(ist)s of the early part of the "boom."

6. In his preface to *Literature and Society: Selected Papers from the English Institute, 1978*, ed. Edward W. Said (Baltimore: Johns Hopkins UP, 1980), Edward Said draws attention to this shift in the relation between criticism and literature. In "A Literature of Foundations" (1961), trans. Lysander Kemp, *Tri-Quarterly* 13–14 (1968–69): 7–12, Octavio Paz gives a poetic reading of the process by which Spanish American literature has acquired its independence from, but still retains its kinship with, the Spanish tradition. That tradition is the "tree" from which Spanish American literature first emerges as a new "branch," but from which it nevertheless frees itself, developing into a new "trunk" or "tree" with a life all its own.

7. See *Critical Inquiry* 10.1 (1983)—the special issue entitled "Canons"— for a variety of approaches to these and related questions. We might note here that, although as a group the Spanish Americans are regarded as being on the cutting edge of contemporary fiction, they are on the whole conspicuously absent from studies that could properly direct attention to them. Though the Hispanic tradition is referred to in the repeated mention of Cervantes and Borges as seminal figures in the development of the modern novel and reflexive writing, the discussions of postmodern fiction that relate quite closely to points addressed in this study focus on European and North American writers (those of the "primary" tradition) while only briefly mentioning, or leaving aside entirely, the Spanish Americans (the "secondary" tradition). For example, of the studies mentioned below in note 14, only that of Hutcheon makes significant mention of Spanish American fiction. (Spires's book on modern Spanish fiction initiates a corrective move with regard to the other branch of the Hispanic tradition.)

8. See Mario Vargas Llosa, "Novela primitiva y novela de creación," *Revista de la Universidad de México* 23.10 (1969): 29–36, for a discussion of the Spanish American novel in terms of these categories, whose underlying evaluative assumptions have already been put into question. The principal booklength studies and essay collections that deal with one or both phases of that devel-

opment include the following: Fernando Alegría, *Historia de la novela hispanoamericana* (Mexico City: Andrea, 1965); John S. Brushwood, *The Spanish American Novel: A Twentieth-Century Survey* (Austin: U of Texas P, 1975); Jean Franco, *An Introduction to Spanish-American Literature* (New York: Cambridge UP, 1969); Carlos Fuentes, *La nueva novela hispanoamericana*; Zunilda Gertel, *La novela hispanoamericana* (Buenos Aires: Columba, 1970); Cedomil Goić, *Historia de la novela hispanoamericana* (Valparaíso: Ediciones Universitarias, 1972); Jorge Lafforgue, ed., *Nueva novela latinoamericana*, 2 vols. (Buenos Aires: Paidós, 1969 and 1972); Juan Loveluck, ed., *La novela hispanoamericana*, 4th ed. (Santiago: Ed. Universitaria, 1969); Emir Rodríguez Monegal, *Narradores de esta América*, 2 vols. (Buenos Aires: Alfa Argentina, 1974 and 1976); Luis Alberto Sánchez, *Proceso y contenido de la novela hispano-americana*, 2nd ed. (Madrid: Gredos, 1968); Ivan Schulman et al., *Coloquio sobre la novela hispanoamericana* (Mexico City: Fondo de Cultura Económica, 1967); and Alberto Zum Felde, *Indice crítico de la literatura hispanoamericana: La narrativa* (Mexico City: Guaranía, 1959).

9. These comments draw on Emir Rodríguez Monegal's "A Revolutionary Writing," *Mundus Artium* 3.3 (1970): 6–11; see also his "El retorno de las carabelas," *Revista de la Universidad de México* 25.6 (1971): 1–4, for another version under the section entitled "escritura revolucionaria."

10. This refers to the notion of dialogue developed by Mikhail Bakhtin. Future mention of this and related terms draws on his *Problems of Dostoevsky's Poetics* (1929), trans. R. W. Rotsel (Ann Arbor: Ardis, 1973) (hereafter cited as *Dostoevsky's Poetics*), and *The Dialogic Imagination: Four Essays* (1933–75), trans. Caryl Emerson and Michael Holquist, ed. Michael Holquist (Austin: U of Texas P, 1981).

11. See Alter, *Partial Magic*.

12. See Edward W. Said, "Molestation and Authority in Narrative Fiction," in *Aspects of Narrative: Selected Papers from the English Institute*, ed. J. Hillis Miller (New York: Columbia UP, 1971) 47–68, regarding the authorial duplicity that characterizes all narrative fiction. This material is revised and incorporated also into his *Beginnings: Intention and Method* (Baltimore: Johns Hopkins UP, 1975) 81–100.

13. Alter refers to the "ontological doubleness of language in Cervantes" and emphasizes the dialectical, unstable quality of self-conscious fiction as a whole (*Partial Magic* 11, 15, 20–21, 81, 171, 187). See also Mikhail Bakhtin, "L'énoncé dans le roman," *Langages* 12 (1969): 126–32, for comments on the inherently reflexive, because dialogic, nature of novelistic discourse.

14. These comments by no means pretend to be a complete review of the definitions and descriptions of this form of writing. Besides Alter's *Partial Magic*, a number of studies try to deal with reflexive writing in detail, as well

as with related developments in contemporary fiction. They include the following: Michael Boyd, *The Reflexive Novel: Fiction as Critique* (Lewisburg: Bucknell UP; London: Associated U Presses, 1983); Christopher Butler, *After the Wake: An Essay on the Contemporary Avant-Garde* (Oxford: Clarendon P, 1980); Linda Hutcheon, *Narcissistic Narrative: The Metafictional Paradox* (Waterloo, Ontario: Wilfrid Laurier UP, 1980); Robert C. Spires, *Beyond the Metafictional Mode: Directions in the Modern Spanish Novel* (Lexington: UP of Kentucky, 1984); and Alan Wilde, *Horizons of Assent: Modernism, Postmodernism, and the Ironic Imagination* (Baltimore: Johns Hopkins UP, 1981). The recent proliferation of these kinds of studies points, I think, not only to the return and predominance of reflexive fiction in contemporary letters but also to the problems confronting us when we try to figure out how to talk about such texts. Writers like Puig can be described, it seems, in terms of this category, for this is the sort of notion that critics use to talk about certain types of strange texts. What we discover, however, and what the renewed interest in this kind of writing signals, is that these notions are not fully adequate to the strangeness, the complexities, of modern writing (especially Spanish American fiction).

15. See Alain Robbe-Grillet, *For a New Novel: Essays on Fiction* (1963), trans. Richard Howard (New York: Grove P, 1965), for comments on the gap between the work of many modern critics, whose vocabulary and methodology is grounded in the era of "realistic" fiction, and that of contemporary writers, whose work questions and tries to subvert the basic assumptions of that tradition; see especially his chapter "On Several Obsolete Notions." See Edward W. Said, "Contemporary Fiction and Criticism," *Tri-Quarterly* 33 (1975): 231–56, for a discussion of related issues, and Matei Calinescu, *Faces of Modernity: Avant-Garde, Decadence, Kitsch* (Bloomington: Indiana UP, 1977), for comments on the properties and politics of modern art, in relation to which the Spanish Americans could also be read.

16. See Alter's chapters on "The Self-Conscious Novel in Eclipse" and "The Modernist Revival of Self-Conscious Fiction," in *Partial Magic*.

17. For some views on how contemporary Latin American literature has recovered and reworked a variety of cultural traditions, see the essays by Alegría, de Campos, Fernández Retamar, Jitrik, Rodríguez Monegal, and Sarduy in *América latina en su literatura*, ed. César Fernández Moreno (Mexico City: Siglo XXI, 1972). In "Tradición y renovación," in that same volume, Rodríguez Monegal points out the paradoxical movements informing the recent developments in Latin American literature and singles out Puig's work as exemplary of the "rescate de formas olvidadas" (145–46). In "El folletín rescatado," *Revista de la Universidad de México* 27.2 (1972): 25–35 (hereafter cited as "Folletín"), he also focuses on that aspect of Puig's work in his inter-

view with the author. See Alicia Borinsky, "Castration: Artifices; Notes on the Writing of Manuel Puig," *Georgia Review* 29 (1975): 95–114, for comments on Puig's challenge to the category of "Literature" and his negation of the hierarchies of discourse supported by many other Spanish American novelists. (This article has also appeared as "Castración y lujos: la escritura de Manuel Puig," *Revista iberoamericana* 41 [1975]: 29–45.)

. 18. See Jean Franco, "La parodie, le grotesque et le carnavalesque: Quelques conceptions du personnage dans le roman latino-américain," trans. Anne-Marie Métailié, in *Idéologies, littérature et société en Amérique latine* (Brussels: U of Brussels, 1974) 57–66 (hereafter cited as "La parodie"), for comments on the political (i.e., parodic and subversive) nature of the Latin American novel and its relation to European literary models and traditions.

19. For comments on the critical nature of literary parody as an analytical and evaluative operation and on the history and definitions of the term itself, see, for example, Henry K. Markiewicz, "On the Definitions of Literary Parody," *To Honor Roman Jakobson, Janua Linguarum*, Serie Maior, 32 (The Hague: Mouton, 1967) 2: 1264–72; J. G. Riewald, "Parody as Criticism," *Neophilologus* 50 (1966): 125–48; Tuvia Shlonsky, "Literary Parody: Remarks on its Method and Functions," and Ulrich Weisstein, "Parody, Travesty, and Burlesque: Imitations with a Vengeance," both in *Proceedings of the IVth Congress of the International Comparative Literature Association* (The Hague: Mouton, 1969) 797–801, 802–11. The distinction between parody and other related forms is made by Linda Hutcheon, "Ironie, satire, parodie: Une approche pragmatique de l'ironie," *Poétique* 46 (1981): 140–55; the self-critical and reflexive nature of parody is stressed by G. D. Kiremidjian, "The Aesthetics of Parody," *Journal of Aesthetics and Art Criticism* 28 (1969): 231–42; and the importance of parody in the development of self-conscious fiction is stressed by Alter throughout *Partial Magic*. Two books that develop many related points and lines of thought regarding parody and/or reflexive writing came to my attention too late for inclusion here: Margaret A. Rose, *Parody/Meta-Fiction: An Analysis of Parody as a Critical Mirror to the Writing and Reception of Fiction* (London: Croom Helm, 1979), and Linda Hutcheon, *A Theory of Parody: The Teachings of Twentieth-Century Art Forms* (New York: Methuen, 1985).

20. See Julia Kristeva, "Bakhtine, le mot, le dialogue et le roman," *Critique* 239 (1967): 438–65 (hereafter cited as "Bakhtine"). Her detailed discussion of intertextuality is in *Le texte du roman: Approche sémiologique d'une structure discursive transformationelle* (The Hague: Mouton, 1976) 138–76. Kristeva's comments take up and expand upon Bakhtin's theory of the novel as a dialogic system of intersecting languages, voices, and traditions, developed in his *Dostoevsky's Poetics* and "L'énoncé dans le roman."

21. See Kristeva, *Le texte du roman* 176, for comments on the novel's intrinsically "polyphonic" and "polygraphic" nature. See Sanda Golopentia-Eretescu, "Grammaire de la parodie," *Cahiers de Linguistique Théorique et Appliquée* 6 (1969): 167–81 (esp. 181) on parody's exemplary quality as described above.

22. In "Problèmes de la structuration du texte," [Tel Quel] *Théorie d'ensemble* (Paris: Seuil, 1968) 299, Julia Kristeva asserts that this kind of harmonization and neutralization of opposing and intersecting discourses is characteristic of literature as a whole. Puig's writing draws attention to that complex process.

23. See John G. Cawelti, *Adventure, Mystery, and Romance: Formula Stories as Art and Popular Culture* (Chicago: U of Chicago P, 1976) 319–29, for a bibliography dealing with "high" and "low" art, mass culture, and forms of popular literature.

24. According to Bakhtin (*Dostoevsky's Poetics* 153) in this type of discourse "the word has a double-directedness—it is directed both toward the object of speech, like an ordinary word, and toward *another word*, toward *another person's speech*." For another version in English of his discussion of this type of "word" or discourse, see "Discourse Typology in Prose," trans. Richard Balthazar and I. R. Titunik, in *Readings in Russian Poetics: Formalist and Structuralist Views*, ed. Ladislav Matejka and Krystyna Pomoroska (Cambridge: MIT P, 1971) 176–96.

25. Golopentia-Eretescu, "Grammaire de la parodie," 167.

26. Ibid., 170; see also 168 for a table summarizing all the possible relationships, as well as overlaps, among the roles played by readers and authors of parodied and parodying texts.

27. Cf. W. K. Wimsatt and Monroe C. Beardsley, "The Intentional Fallacy" (1946), in W. K. Wimsatt, *The Verbal Icon: Studies in the Meaning of Poetry* (Lexington: UP of Kentucky, 1954) 3–18; and Bakhtin, *Dostoevsky's Poetics* 160–62.

28. Bakhtin, *Dostoevsky's Poetics* 160.

29. Bakhtin observes that "the parodistic word can be extremely diverse. Another person's style can be parodied as a style; another person's social-typical or individual-characterological manner of seeing, thinking and speaking can be parodied. Furthermore, parody can be more, or less, deep: one can parody only superficial verbal forms, or one can parody the deepest principles of the other person's word. Furthermore, the parodistic word itself can be employed by the author in various ways: parody can be an end in itself (the literary parody as a genre, for example), but it can also serve other, positive purposes . . ." (ibid., 160–61). See also Golopentia-Eretescu, "Gram-

maire de la parodie" 172–73; Shlonsky, "Literary Parody" 801; and Markiewicz, "On the Definitions of Literary Parody" 1269–71.

30. Bakhtin, *Dostoevsky's Poetics* 157. "Conditional word" is taken from
this text, and "conventionalized utterance" is from the other translation cited
in note 24. The term "double-directed" is used in the sense given it in the
passage cited in note 29; cf. the description of stylization as a "single-directed"
word and parody as a "hetero-directed," "double-accented" word on 164–65.

31. See Bakhtin, "From the Prehistory of Novelistic Discourse," in *The
Dialogic Imagination* 75–76.

32. See Mikhail Bakhtin, *Rabelais and His World* (1940), trans. Hélène
Iswolsky (Cambridge: MIT P, 1968), for comments on the simultaneously "re-
generating" and "degrading" character of parody as a carnivalesque form. See
Severo Sarduy, "Notas a las notas a las notas ... : A propósito de Manuel Puig,"
Revista iberoamericana 37 (1971): 555–67 (hereafter cited as "Notas"), for an
application of Bakhtin's terms to Puig's writing.

33. See Franco, "La parodie," for related observations on modern Spanish
American fiction. See the following for discussion of the related notions of
carnival and parody, dialogic and polyphonic texts, and the inversionary, ambivalent mechanisms that characterize them: Kristeva, *Le texte du roman*
162–76, "Bakhtine" 441–49; David Hayman, "Au-delà de Bakhtine: Pour une
mécanique des modes," *Poétique* 13 (1973): 76–94; Laurent Jenny, "Le discours du carnaval," *Littérature* 16 (1974): 19–36; Z. Nelly Martínez, "El carnaval, el diálogo y la novela polifónica," *Hispamérica* 17 (1977): 3–21; and
Emir Rodríguez Monegal, "Carnaval/Antropofagia/Parodia," *Revista iberoamericana* 45 (1979): 401–12.

34. This view of the notion of undecidability or indeterminacy draws on
Barbara Johnson's comments in "The Frame of Reference: Poe, Lacan, Der-
rida," in *The Critical Difference: Essays in the Contemporary Rhetoric of
Reading* (Baltimore: Johns Hopkins UP, 1981) 146.

35. This term is taken from Bakhtin's "Discourse in the Novel" (1934–35),
in *The Dialogic Imagination* 301–5 and 363–64. See also Christine Brooke-
Rose's comments on "metafiction and surfiction" in *A Rhetoric of the Unreal:
Studies in Narrative and Structure, Especially of the Fantastic* (Cambridge:
Cambridge UP, 1981) 364–89.

36. The term "reading" is here used in the sense it is given by Tzvetan
Todorov in "How to Read?" (1969), in *The Poetics of Prose* (1971), trans. Rich-
ard Howard (Ithaca: Cornell UP, 1977) 234–45. The term "disentangle" is
used by Roland Barthes in opposition to the idea of "deciphering" a text, in
"The Death of the Author" (1968), in *Image-Music-Text*, trans. Stephen Heath
(New York: Hill and Wang, 1977) 147.

2

A Familiar Romance:
La traición de Rita Hayworth

Puig's first novel, *La traición de Rita Hayworth*, tells a story of life in a provincial Argentine town (Coronel Vallejos, the site of action as well in *Boquitas pintadas*) during the 1930s and 1940s.[1] The narrative gives an account of the lives of a particular family[2] in that town: Berto and Mita (the parents) and Toto (their son). Their story, however, is fragmentary. We do not know and cannot learn all there is, or all we might think we need, to know about these characters. The fragmentary nature of that story derives from the fragmentary nature of the novel's text, which is made up of sixteen monologues and dialogues that correspond to its sixteen chapters.[3] In those chapters individual subjects take turns speaking and writing about themselves, the people they know, and the town's everyday world. As they move among and within the novel's separate narrative units, they displace each other as subjective sources of the fiction.

La traición de Rita Hayworth is a typically postmodern text, for there is no privileged narrator upon whom the reader can rely for complete information, nor is there an authoritative discourse or figure to whom we can turn for something like an objective, final truth regarding its fiction. The reading difficulties created by this absence of an organizing, potentially omniscient, mediator who could filter and interpret all the discursive performances in the text are significant but not impossible obstacles. Clearly, this narrative technique requires that the reader work to make connections among the chapters and the characters—in a way, to take the place of the missing narrator. However, when compared with the more complex narrative structures and strategies of some of Puig's later novels, *La traición de Rita Hayworth* might seem to be a more manageable text from which a tale, though incomplete, can be extracted in a more or less linear fashion. Even though there is one significant disjunction between its story and its plot (the temporal inversion of the last chapter, to which we will return later), the narrative unfolds in a generally chronological order from the early 1930s to the late '40s.[4]

Toto, apparently, is the novel's protagonist. He is the character to whom most attention is given in both the novel's text and fiction. He is the subject who both speaks (Chapters III and V) and writes (Chapter XIII), as well as the character who is spoken about, more than anyone else. As the novel shifts from representations of spoken discourse (the monologues and dialogues of Chapters I-XI) to written texts "authored" by a variety of characters (Chapters XII-XVI), it presents what appears to be the formative stages of an artist's—that is, a writer's—(auto)biography.[5] The chronicle of that future artist's early years, as well as the depiction of the environment in which he is formed, begins in 1933, the year of his birth, and ends in 1948, the last year in which anyone engages in discursive activity in the novel. The story of Toto is also the story of the lives of his family, his neighbors, his friends, and his classmates, all of whom live in the provinces, on the edges of culture, where nothing of importance ever seems to happen. Toto spends his early years in Coronel Vallejos with his familiy—his parents, Mita and Berto, and his cousin Héctor. (Héctor, the son of his father's brother Jaime, comes to live with them just after Toto is born.) When he is thirteen, he goes off to boarding school in another provincial town. While growing up in Coronel Vallejos, Toto is virtually an only child. Héctor occupies a rather marginal position within the family, and, although Mita and Berto have another child two years after losing their second son in 1943 (he is only a few days old when he dies), Toto remains the center of attention. Overly fearful of his father but desirous of his affection, Toto appears to take Mita, with whom he shares a passion for the movies, as his intellectual, cultural and, perhaps, sexual model. Immersed in the world of fiction, film, and fashion, he is the very antithesis of Berto and Héctor, two handsome "macho" figures of authority about whom Toto is ambivalent and from whom he himself elicits contradictory reactions. Toto's status at boarding school—the Colegio George Washington, where he is nominated as best student in 1947—is not unlike his position at home; his academic success and perfect behavior set him apart from those in whom he alternately inspires both admiration and resentment.

We learn about Toto and Coronel Vallejos sometimes directly from him, in his spoken and written monologues, and sometimes obliquely, from the novel's other speaking and writing subjects. For example, in addition to providing a portrait of herself as a widow, mother, and working woman, Mita's friend Choli comments upon scenes that represent Toto's, as well as Mita's, relationship with Berto (Chapter IV). When Delia, Mita's neighbor, speaks in Chapter VII, she provides not only a view of her own plight as a small-town "spinster," but also an inside view of Mita and her family. And when, in Chapter XI, Cobito delivers his interior monologue while awaiting the return of his classmates to the Colegio George Washington one Sunday evening, he tells us as much about Toto's position and life at the school as he does about his own. Toto's childhood is charted through the novel's forward movement. What we learn about him, however, is that he doesn't really change all that much as he gets older. Though his monologues progress in a linear fashion, showing in linguistic terms how Toto matures (his "growth" is displayed by the progression from the language he produces as a six year old in Chapter III to the prose he writes as an adolescent in Chapter XIII), they also possess a circular, repetitive quality. They reveal the fantasies and real events, the imaginary and historical scenarios, that construct his inner world and psychical reality.[6] As we read Toto's chapters and follow him to each new stage, we actually see him always turning back, reimagining, reinventing, and reliving the same "dramas." In his mental and artistic wanderings he reveals himself to be an inherently ambivalent subject whose psychical experience is grounded in contradictory roles and relations. The novel's other characters are not unlike him in this respect. Toto is difficult to pin down to one opinion, one attitude, one desire, because he is a dialectic of opinions, attitudes, and desires.

Toto is the fiction's exemplary character. His story is a model of the stories of those who surround him in *La traición de Rita Hayworth*. Like Toto's, none of those stories is a progressive chain of scenes and relations through which each character moves or can be seen to change over time. Each subject presents a potentially repetitive, even regressive, web of real and imagined scenes through which all their performances interconnect with and, in some ways, seem to repeat one another. Moreover, Toto and, thus, the other subjects who come to sound like him in their own chapters return us to the exemplary, titular figure who appears first and last in the text. Rita Hayworth hovers over the whole novel in a seductive and treacherous manner, now turning one way, now another. In order to move on with Toto and the rest of the text, we first need to return with him to its title, which initially draws our attention to certain thematic and structural models. We see in that title a graphic and powerful representation of the problematic turns made both by the novel's fictional characters and by its narrative text.

As a separate, but connected, written unit of the novel, the title has a crucial and also curious relation to its text. Certain issues are raised by any such heading because of its complex relation to its "body"—titles, as we know, appear to precede, float above, and follow their "bodies"; they help us to read, but are also themselves read through, their texts. Puig's title embodies a paradoxical movement that both aids and impedes our reading of the novel. The title sets up a reading, an interpretation, that it also undercuts. It is precisely through its dialectical, reflexive moves that this title offers a way of understanding some of the connections among the novel's fictional and textual figures, as well as the relations between its narrative structure and thematic material.

What we notice first, perhaps, is the name "Rita Hayworth." That name connects the novel with another form of fiction (that is, with film) through which it also establishes its dependence on and dialogue with the world of popular culture. The name seems to pull us in several directions at once. It takes us toward the fictional text that is about to unfold and that turns out to be saturated with fantasies based on films. But it also pushes us outside the novel, toward the extra-textual reality from which that name comes. The Rita Hayworth named in the title seems to occupy at least two positions and pertain to two distinct spheres at the same time. She contradicts yet complements the contexts within which she is simultaneously situated.

Rita Hayworth is also turned into a model of instability by the dialectical movement of the title's grammar. In the phrase "La traición de Rita Hayworth" the preposition *de* functions as a double genitive which, at the level of grammar, has an irresolvable dual value. "Rita Hayworth" is both agent and recipient of "la traición," both subject (betrayer) and object (the one betrayed) of treachery. The title's grammar establishes within the figure of Rita Hayworth an irreducible difference, a thematic as well as grammatical opposition, that identifies her. To fix Rita Hayworth in either of these roles is to read her in only one context; it is to interpret away the mobile quality that characterizes her appearance.[7] While the "truth" of Rita Hayworth's double identity is displayed by the title, her other appearances within the novel seem to cover it up. However, we also discover that her presence is in a way felt and her performance repeated by the fictional characters and textual figures who support and follow her every move both within and beyond the thematic arena (i.e., that of betrayal) that she brings to our attention right from the start.[8] In fact, Rita Hayworth takes us back to Toto, the character to whom she is mainly attached and upon whom she is dependent for her major appearance in the novel. If we look at Toto's representation of Rita Hayworth, following its consequences in both fiction and text, we begin to get some sense of how text and title are at odds even as they are at one with each other, and how certain characters (our exemplary cases are Toto and Berto) bring into view the sorts of problematic relations that, in the end, appear to inform much of the novel.

Rita Hayworth makes her first treacherous appearance in Chapter V ("Toto, 1942"). Here, within the interior monologue of nine-year-old Toto (we later learn that his full name is José L. Casals [244]), we see Rita Hayworth as she appears in *Sangre y arena* (*Blood and Sand*, 1941) opposite Tyrone Power.[9] In relating his father's and his own reactions to the film, Toto reveals what are for him, as well as for us, significant details: ". . . y salíamos del cine caminando y papá decía que le gustaba Rita Hayworth más que ninguna artista, y a mí me empieza a gustar más que ninguna también, a papá le gusta cuando le hacía 'toro, toro' a Tyrone Power, él arrodillado como un bobo y ella de ropa transparente que se veía el corpiño, y se le acercaba para jugar al toro, pero se reía de él, que al final lo deja. Y a veces pone cara de mala, es una artista linda pero que hace traiciones" ["... and we were walking out of the moviehouse and Dad said he liked Rita Hayworth better than any other actress, and I'm starting to like her better than any other too, Dad likes when she did 'toro, toro' to Tyrone Power, him kneeling like an idiot and her with a transparent dress that you could see her bra through and she came right up close to him to play toro, but she was laughing at him, and in the end she leaves him. And sometimes she looks wicked, she's a pretty actress but she's always betraying somebody"] (82). This first mention of Rita Hayworth in the text (she is subsequently named in connection with this film on 83 and 109) seems to give us a chance to begin to interpret the novel's title. The role Rita Hayworth plays here is that of the seductive subject of betrayal ("hace traiciones"). But, as we know, the apparent stabilization of the movie star in the position of the betraying subject is itself already betrayed by the title, where she is accorded another, contradictory, role. Her powers of seduction nevertheless seem to predominate in this chapter. Her appearance as the powerful embodiment of betrayal in Toto's discourse might easily lead us away from the problematic identity already revealed in the title. It might allow this figure to turn us toward a fiction of stability—a kind of treacherous stability—that is not without its own power in Puig's novel.

The critical nature of this model of seduction and betrayal is revealed in the rest of Toto's description of the same afternoon. Through his account of their viewing of *Sangre y arena* there develops a parallel situation in another sort of familiar (because familial) romance. In Toto's description of Berto's virtual abandonment and betrayal of him, as well as in his representation of his own shifting perceptions of and reactions to that scene, we see an immediate reenactment of this relational model. The inherently unstable, dialectical quality of the Rita Hayworth role seems to be erased by Toto, however, as he ignores its reality while also unknowingly revealing its force. In this dramatic familial moment the suppression of that instability in one subject (Berto) seems to elicit conflicting responses from the other (Toto). That Toto is betrayed by Berto and that Berto seems to be made to follow in the footsteps of Rita Hayworth is clear from Toto's version of the scenes following their film outing. His description of them reveals a complex structure of imitative desires through which each also turns around the position of the other.[10] At first, instead of criticizing and distancing himself from the film his son fears he will dislike ("A papá no le va a gustar, ay qué miedo, no le va a gustar, y ¡sí! muchísimo, que salió contento de haber ido . . ." ["Dad's not going to like it, oo how scary, he's not going to like it, and yes! a lot, he walked out glad that he had come . . . "] [82]), Berto seems to appropriate the objects originally admired by Toto, the very images in which Toto asserts that his father is uninterested. Berto not only declares Rita Hayworth his favorite actress but also underscores his attraction to the key scene between her and Tyrone Power—the scene wherein she emerges in Toto's discourse as the powerful and seductive betrayer of the one who desires her.

Although it seems that Toto is the one originally interested in the film and its figures, his account of his father's reactions also inverts the order of things. It places Toto's desires in a contingent relation to those of his father. It seems to be precisely because of his father's interest in the scene between Rita Hayworth and Tyrone Power (especially Berto's attraction to Rita Hayworth) that Toto not only directs his own attention to those objects, but also delights in describing the appearance and actions of that same seductive subject of betrayal. Berto appears to take from Toto a desire that his son here presents also as having been copied from him. Although this circular model of imitation, through which the origins of desire are impossible to locate, would confound these two subjects, the identification with, as well as attraction to, the treacherous object of desire (or even her imitators) seems mostly to place Berto and Toto in opposing positions on that afternoon. What emerges from this complex interchange is not only the imitation of desires, but also the desire for and denial of the original subjects whose desires seem to have been imitated. Toto's version of this afternoon presents Berto's momentary flirtation with and final rejection of his son's world. Berto's attraction to Rita Hayworth at once reveals and produces his imitation of her treacherous maneuvers, through which he is identified with the subject to whom he is attracted but whom he nevertheless finally seems to reject.

Rita Hayworth is the star whose performance with Tyrone Power becomes, in Toto's description, the model of Berto's with Toto. As Toto tells it, Berto's "abandonment" of his son after they leave the theater is perceived as just such a rejection. Instead of going with Mita and Toto to a cafe, Berto invites some of his employees, whom they meet after leaving the theater, to listen to a sports broadcast at their home (83). The invitation to the men is perceived as just that kind of rejection of Toto and, by implication, of his world of film and fiction. This world is perceived by Berto, it seems, as "feminine." Identified with

Mita and shared by Toto, it is placed in opposition to the "masculine" world of sports and work shared by Berto and his men, and by others such as Héctor. Although Berto's seduction into the world of film and fantasy by both Toto and Rita Hayworth is certified through his apparent promise to repeat the afternoon with his wife and son (". . . 'ahora voy a venir siempre con ustedes al cine' . . ." [". . . 'Now I'm going to the movies with you all the time' . . . "] [82]), Toto finally recognizes his father's subsequent betrayal in his breach of promise ("Y después no volvió más a ir al cine, que dice que aunque vaya se le pasan por delante todas las cuentas del negocio con los pagarés y los vencimientos y no ve la cinta" ["And he never went to the movies again, because he says even if he goes the store bills and IOUs and deadlines are staring him in the face and he can't see the movie"] [83]). What we begin to see here, then, is both the reduction of Rita Hayworth to one of her roles (that of the seductive subject of betrayal) and the implicit identification of Berto with her within Toto's discourse.

The distillation of roles and identities that appears to dominate this instance of discourse is also connected to a sense of instability that its speaking subject cannot help revealing as his monologue progresses. This instability of attitude also mirrors from the other side, as it were, the shifts in the objects he admires. The mobility within the thematic register of Toto's discourse is bolstered by and intertwined with the linguistic and narrative turns that characterize not only this discursive instance, but also his preceding performance as a younger speaking subject (Chapter III) and the later display of his abilities as a writer (Chapter XIII). In Chapter V his monologue moves between the present time of his own narration and that of the scene at the movies, for example, conflating into one temporal frame the thoughts and actions from each register. It also shifts between representations of Toto as actor in and spectator of the various scenes that he, as discursive subject and verbal "translator," reconstructs in his monologue. As Toto shifts among those opposing positions, thereby appearing to occupy them simultaneously, so must the other entities about whom he speaks do likewise. As Toto's position moves among levels of framing and framed actions, among film scenes and those from his own present and past reality, and between different levels of discourse and action, his monologue appears to do two contradictory things at once. It conflates distinct scenes and subjects of betrayal so as to offer fixed images of

Berto/Rita Hayworth and Toto/Tyrone Power. However, it also reveals that there is a narrative and, oddly enough, thematic mobility upon which those seemingly stabilized images are based.

Curiously enough, even though it is in Toto's discourse that the implicit and powerful connection between Berto and Rita Hayworth as betraying subjects is constructed, Toto also seems to attempt a denial of Berto's role as such. Even though Toto's own memory of the scene after the movie acknowledges Berto's move toward and choice of the other men over his son (". . . lo empecé a tironear a papá pero agarró para donde estaban ellos . . ." [". . . I began to pull Dad away but he went over to them . . ."] [83]), in a subsequent comment he appears to shift responsibility for his ruined afternoon from Berto to those other men (". . . escuchaban la pelea y nada más que hablar de la pelea y esos tontos por la pelea no fueron a ver a la noche *Sangre y arena* que si íbamos con papá a la confitería hubiese sido lo más fantástico que hay . . ." [". . . listen to the fight and talk talk talk about the fight and because of the fight those jerks didn't see *Blood and Sand* and if we had gone with Dad to the café, it would have been so great . . ."] [83]). That shift seems to signal an operation internal to Toto the speaking subject. And while it changes Berto's position (it begins to lift the blame from him and to unhinge his link with Rita Hayworth), it does not seem to alter entirely Toto's. Although Toto here assumes a more active, but only discursive, role as accusing subject (he cannot here punish, but can only judge), a role that has its own force in these passages, he also remains the object of betrayal by the father, in relation to whom he displays his shifting perceptions and positions. The association between Berto and Rita Hayworth seems to hold up throughout this monologue and, necessarily, to carry with it a representation of Toto as innocent, but also ambivalent, object of betrayal, a victim not unlike the "muchacho bueno" (83) played by Tyrone Power. While Toto virtually acknowledges Berto's role and indirectly represents his own potentially violent reaction to it, he is at the same time the subject who desires the company of his father, whose "cara linda" can be linked with, perhaps in Toto's version of things only equaled by, that of Rita Hayworth, "la más linda de todas" ["the most beautiful of all"] (83).

In this monologue, then, Rita Hayworth acquires a power, a position, that has significance both for the novel's fiction and for its text.

Her powers are played out in various ways. *Sangre y arena*, itself metonymically reduced to the Rita Hayworth/Tyrone Power relationship, or even to the figure of Rita Hayworth herself, becomes emblematic of historically consecutive but discursively concentric scenes through which the characters' roles and relationships go on turning. This kind of dialectic is played out in all of Toto's monologues. These structures of relations seem to characterize everyone's performance in Coronel Vallejos as well. In these film and family relationships certain figures seem to be fixed in roles whose unclear origins would actually betray their own fixity. The possibility of seeing the mobility that supports those thematic oppositions (oppositions that, paradoxically, are also eroded by the novel's end) is already present in other registers of the monologue. The text would in one register establish a dominant model in which Berto and Toto are fixed, as is Rita Hayworth; in others it would belie the ambiguous turns that describe the movie star's double position in the novel's title and, eventually, both Toto's and Berto's positions in the novel as a whole. These scenes, then, also begin to betray a movement that returns us to the title—the title whose meaning those same scenes initially seem to fix.

These scenes are important also because they begin to highlight what happens in family relationships, relationships that are revealed not only by Toto's monologue but also by those of the novel's other subjects. In the representation of the real and fantasized interaction between father(s) and son(s), or more generally between parent(s) and child(ren), *La traición de Rita Hayworth* constructs both an unchanging model of power relations into which the characters are inserted and a fluid movement of figures among fixed roles that determine those models.[11] It is precisely in the representation of the relations among Toto's family members that the futility of such attempts to fix identities is demonstrated. The univocal representation of Berto as powerful paternal figure of authority and that of Toto as powerless filial object of rejection or impending violence turn out to be fictions, half-truths that would, for a time at least, obliterate other contradictory versions of these same figures. When we reach the novel's last chapter—"Carta de Berto, 1933"—we see that Berto presents himself in a radically different manner than do the other subjects who surround him in the fiction. He finally affirms, in a different way than does his son, his own connection to his favorite movie star. Formerly presented by those who know him as the domineering father and spouse, as the betrayer whose potential violence often governs the actions of others around him (besides Toto's descriptions of Berto in Chapters III and V, see also Choli's comments in IV and Mita's in VIII), Berto here portrays himself in the opposite role—as the object of betrayal by other subjects over whose actions he, as son, younger brother, and even husband, seems to have had no control.

Berto's letter to his brother is both a protest against and a recognition of the position in which he, also a victim of familial plots, has been cast by design. Although he would verbally reassert his powers through his intermittent angry utterances and then physically dramatize the violence of his stance by destroying the letter itself (he tears it up, we are told, in Chapter II [28]), Berto cannot control or erase the text, the structure of relations, in and from which he has been produced. This familial character cannot break up or rewrite the familiar networks and plots that in one way or another have bound him. Berto's letter to his older brother reveals a pattern of repeated betrayals suffered by him as the youngest and least powerful member of one family (the one in which he grew up) and as the oldest and most powerful member of another (the one he now heads as he writes his letter).

Indeed, betrayal is the dominant motif of Berto's letter to Jaime. He seems to reassert what Toto's monologue also begins to demonstrate: to be or to see oneself as the victim of betrayal by those to whom one is also deeply attached is to become the subject of an irresolvable ambivalence toward those same figures. They, in turn, are themselves bound to others in the same way. Moreover, read together, the texts of the father and the son seem to cast all those who look like or function as parents (especially fathers) as victimizers and all those who are presented as children (especially sons) as victims. But, since each subject's identity cannot be reduced to a single exclusive role, Toto and Berto also reveal that their apparent stabilization in any of the monologues is but a fiction in which each of them would like to believe, even when their own actions or attitudes would betray another truth. If we read Berto's letter together with the passages from Toto's first 1942 monologue, we see each appear to be fixed in a place that turns out to be only one of the several places in which he may be situated. That juxtaposition reveals the oscillations internal to both the "fixed" subject and/or object of betrayal, as well as the shifts between the poles or identities in which each would seem to be stabilized at specific points in the text.

Berto's letter is that of a subject who seeks to engage in a virtual dialogue with the brother who has so often, we learn in that same letter, disappointed and abandoned him. (For example, Jaime took Berto out of school when he was fifteen so that he could work in Jaime's factory; but when Jaime suddenly decided to sell the factory and leave behind his younger brother, Berto had to support himself and his mother, instead of returning to school [see 298–99]. At the time when Berto writes his letter, he has again been deserted by Jaime, who, now residing in Spain, has left his son Héctor in Berto's care [see 292, 298].) His epistle is an attempt to make contact with the fraternal interlocutor who has refused to write to him (the letter begins: "Querido hermano: Aunque sin tener ninguna tuya a la que contestar, me pongo a escribirte esperando que estés bien . . ." ["Dear brother: Although I still don't have any letter of yours to answer, I'm writing with the hope that all is well with you . . . "] [292; see also 298]). It is also a potentially violent rejection of Jaime as the head of the family from which he comes and to which he is, of course, still intimately connected. Jaime seems to have functioned as both fraternal and paternal figure of authority for Berto; he seems to have had the power and position, usually associated with father figures, to determine the course of Berto's life. (No mention is made of their father, although it seems that Jaime has had to take his place as owner and operator of their factory; it is perhaps only upon his father's death or disappearance that Jaime accedes to that position of authority.)

Although Berto seems to have had to accept Jaime's authority and position, in the 1933 letter he finally asserts his resistance. Berto's text ends with his refusal to pardon his brother for the crimes of betrayal and abandonment committed against him, the innocent victim, in both the past and the present. Interestingly enough, this refusal forms part of an ending in which Berto's oscillating, unstable sentiments are also brought into the open. The aggressive resistance to his brother is mixed with expressions of affection and declarations of concern for his brother's own situation: "Si no te importó sacarme del colegio cuando era un chico, y eso no te lo puedo perdonar, y total se te antojó cerrar la fábrica después y quedé en la vía, trato de pensar que sos lo único que tengo, mi hermano mayor, lo único que me queda, y vos también tendrás tus razones por todo lo que hiciste, pero por más que trato no te puedo perdonar, Jaime, no te puedo perdonar . . ." ["Why, if it didn't matter whether or not you took me out of school when I was a boy, which I can never forgive you for, and anyway, afterwards you suddenly had the inspiration to close the factory and there I was, out in the rain. I repeat to myself that you're the only one I have, my big brother, the only one I have left, and I say to myself too that you must have your own reasons for what you did, but no matter how hard I try I can't forgive you, Jaime, I cannot forgive you . . . "] (299).

As he presents himself, then, Berto is a powerless object of his older brother's maneuvers. Nonetheless, he also begins to offer his private resistance to the figure and the family under whose control he views himself as continuing to operate. While his version of himself seems to fix his identity as a son who is also an object of betrayal, the letter reveals some of his powers as well. It acknowledges his status as father and potential subject of treachery and unveils his shifting responses to family figures to whom he is inextricably bound. The letter begins with a polite, apparently sincere address to the brother whose silence Berto attempts to overcome; it ends with a series of angry, forceful utterances and a final negation of the letter itself: "¿Y a qué me voy a gastar un centavo en escribirte, para que no me contestes, como a la otra carta? No sé para qué te escribo si no te importa nada de mí, y creo que nunca te importó, Jaime, estoy lleno de veneno hoy, y no te voy a mandar esta carta me parece, no te quiero amargar, vos también tendrás tus problemas con la salud de tu mujer. Pero te cuento todo esto para que tengas mis noticias, aunque sean malas ¿no esperás carta mía? ¿no te importa recibir mis noticias? ¿verdad? . . . Esta carta va al tacho de la basura, para vos no pienso gastar un centavo en estampillas" ["And what for? so that you won't answer, like with the other letter? I don't know why I write you, you don't care about me, and I don't think you ever cared about me, Jaime, I'm full of bile today, and I don't think I want to send you this letter, I don't want to upset you, you must have your problems too, with your wife's health. But I'm telling you all this because it's the only news I have to offer, even though it's bad news, don't you expect a letter from me? It doesn't matter if you don't get any news from me, right? . . . This letter is going into the wastepaper basket, I wouldn't spend a cent on stamps for you"] (299). The end of Berto's letter in a shifting blend of utterances reveals that he is both patently vulnerable and potentially violent. It contains a plea for support from and an accusation of betrayal by the family figure who also seems to matter most to him (cf. 297, where Berto shifts his position vis-à-vis Mita, as he describes to Jaime, cast there as his confidant, another type of domestic betrayal).

Berto's letter presents a subject who continues to turn around and return to thematic positions that work in dialectical relation to one another. This movement cannot be interrupted, it seems, except through some sort of violent rupture from within, much like the text that conveys its turns. The end of his letter therefore doesn't really close things off. It merely seems to suspend the story and the text in which it is produced. In a way, this letter seems to certify that no end is really possible here. That the text seems to stop with a kind of non-ending and that this letter is indeed not the end of the story that is told are significant features of the novel, whose own dialogue is colored by the way Berto's virtual dialogue with his brother cannot really be closed. As noted, Berto's letter (and thus the novel itself) ends with a potentially violent refusal to underwrite further ("esta carta va al tacho de la basura") a dialogue with an interlocutor whose absence that letter also asserts in its efforts to recuperate and keep him alive ("sos lo único que tengo, mi hermano mayor, lo único que me queda"). Neither the plea for recognition nor the ultimate rejection of the interlocutor toward whom that gesture is made has any force outside the discourse of the writing subject himself. Berto's final promise, not unlike the text within which it is stated, has a curious status. The promise to destroy the letter is a promise made only to the subject himself, even though it appears as directed to another. That promise, if kept, would deny the possibility of seeing any signs of its having been made. To perform the act named by the promise would be to efface the text, the instance of discourse, that it represents.

Of special interest here is the fact that the novel's text manages to assert and yet deny the power, or even the reality, of that promise through what appears to be a Rita-Hayworth-like maneuver. The temporal inversion through which this letter is presented to us manages to circumvent that affirmed reality and to undercut the desires and position of this apparently final figure of authority. The destruction of the 1933 letter in Chapter II, well ahead of the appearance of the letter's text in Chapter XVI, seems to render ineffective and virtually powerless the vow of negation and closure with which Berto's text ends. The "new" information about Berto provided in the novel's last chapter is not the only thing that matters here. Of equal importance are the means by which his final image is constructed and, moreover, how that textual maneuver returns him to the novel's titular figure, whose initial position is buttressed further through Berto's final appearance. Berto's turning image at the novel's end depends as much on that textual manipulation as on the movements of his thematic position. When we read Berto's letter in terms of both the thematic network and the textual scheme that finally makes it come into view, we see his image altered (that is, inverted from that of paternal subject to that of filial/fraternal/spousal object of betrayal) at the same time that we see in him and his text a model of alterity, a model that returns us to Rita Hayworth, the title's own turning figure. Moreover, as we perceive the shifting movements of this familial figure of authority, we realize that he is himself supported and, as it were, fathered by another figure who moves in the text in much the same way that Berto does in the fiction.

By finally speaking in his own voice and name, Berto would resituate himself within the various fictions of Coronel Vallejos and within the families through which he is earlier represented. His discourse would seem to uncover a suppressed "truth"—that of his own story, that of his role as a figure at an opposite pole from the one with which he seems to be identified in Toto's monologue. However authoritative his rewritten version of himself seems to be, its authority and finality are undercut by the narrative maneuvers through which it is revealed and by the textual position it is accorded. At the very moment when a new version of Berto is presented, we also see the text erode the possibility of privileging that revision. In the inversionary move whereby the reader is first deprived of and then provided with what appears to be significant information about Berto, the text's own treacherous designs are brought into the open. Through this design both authorial and readerly figures wind up playing roles not unlike those defining the fictive entities around whom they hover and, of course, the titular figure to whom they are critically linked.

Berto turns out to be a different kind of character from what he first appears to be. By virtue of the contradictory image finally projected by him, he reveals his own connections not to Toto's but to the title's

Rita Hayworth. Of importance as well is the fact that the very process by which the "truth" is uncovered in Puig's novel is also the movement by which the possibility of fixing truth is undermined. It is precisely in that last place that Berto—the authority on himself, as well as the principal figure of authority for Toto and Mita—calls into question, while also certifying, the authority of other figures who surround him and whose own precarious position his epistolary performance helps to disclose. Moreover, the figure whose powers seem to matter most at the novel's end is perhaps not really Berto after all, but the textual authority who is also unveiled through Berto's performance. As noted, the place where this seemingly final version of Berto's role and position is disclosed is itself the sign of the textual and temporal inversion through which that other "paternal" figure—the text's author— emerges with such force. The end of the novel is the place where we can also see how the attraction to and power of Rita Hayworth seem to permeate not only the design in, but also the design(er) of, the text we read.[12]

The authorial subject's controlling presence is most clearly and forcefully asserted by the temporal inversion of the text of Berto's letter. That letter is taken from its "proper" place at the novel's beginning (had it been placed chronologically, it would have appeared within or next to Chapter II, wherein we learn of its composition and destruction) and situated at its end, where it stands out as "improperly" placed. Given the conventional uses of temporal inversion, the repositioning of Berto's letter would suggest that the story being told is a kind of puzzle whose solution, already known to the authorial mediator, must be deferred until this final moment of the text. We recognize of course that the structural play employed in *La traición de Rita Hayworth* is that of mystery fiction.[13] Although Puig's novel is clearly not a detective novel (we will have to wait for *The Buenos Aires Affair* to see his version of that popular form), some of its thematic concerns, as well as its narrative play, do recall and refer to that model. Here questions of guilt, crime, and punishment, developed around dramas of familial conflict in which betrayal is a dominant motif, and connected (especially in Toto's discourse) with oedipal and primal scenarios, arise repeatedly in the fiction. In fact, everyone seems to be cast as some kind of criminal and/or victim—Berto's case begins to demonstrate this. Everyone in *La traición de Rita Hayworth* is implicated in just those sorts of mysteries. They are mysteries whose resolutions, nevertheless, are impossible to formulate. These endings, supposedly designed to reveal what we think we need to know, instead remind us that such knowledge is either unnecessary or impossible to acquire. Moreover, here it seems that such solutions are designed to remain hidden.[14]

In Puig's novel the fiction of mystery is coincident with or, rather, created by the fiction of a closing solution. The illusion of closure for both story and text is generated by the illusion of a gap. This gap is signaled by the textual displacement of Berto's letter. His position is thus marked by a temporal structure that informs not only his image of authority, but also that of the novel's implied author. Indeed, this ending returns us to several questions about the kind of authority on which the text rests. By definition, temporal inversion disrupts chronology by placing that which comes "before" after that which comes "after." It graphically represents how a cause also seems to be created by its own effects. It underlines how an origin or source may be imagined as such "after the fact" of the effects that point back to it but which, nevertheless, also precede it.[15] Berto's letter is both anterior and posterior to the novel's "main body": since it is a kind of originary text within the story but the ultimate text of the novel's plot, it occupies two contradictory positions at once. In the act of conjuring by the authorial manipulator—the "saving" of the letter already (Chapter II) but also not yet (Chapter XVI) torn up by Berto—the epistolary text's artificial status is both affirmed and denied by Berto's powerful "voice."

The peculiar status of this final text is not unlike that of the authorial strategist who reveals both that text, or Berto's voice, and himself through it. Its status is also not much different from the positions of the paternal figures who write that text (as an author) and write within it (as a character). Although each would appear finally to locate himself within a specific structure that is at once textual and familial, we realize that it is really in the nature of each to keep turning away from and then toward those privileged positions. The truth that each would reveal (not only the existence of that authority and, thus, the solution to the question of his own identity, but also the instability of his own powers) turns out to be both elusive and illusory. The "fathers" of and in the text are also always its "sons." Those images must, of necessity, keep turning. When we read the final chapter, then, we see those authors, or authorities, temporarily located in positions which, as the revelations of Berto's letter aptly emphasize, are not what they first, or even finally, seem to be. In the interplay of voices and images throughout the novel, as well as at its end, we see that the authority of each paternal figure is simultaneously asserted and denied. Their voices are suppressed by the discourse of others (by all those who speak throughout the novel); at the same time, it is in or through the discourse of those other subjects that the power of these two authorities is represented. The truth of the authority of each is grounded as much in the absence of his own discourse (the absence of the voice of an author or narrator; the absence of the voice of Berto) as it is in its final disclosure in Chapter XVI, where Berto is finally "heard" and "seen," and the author is finally "seen" and "heard." Through one father's (the authorial figure's) move to permit another (Berto) finally to speak, to overcome the suppression of his "true" image (an image of apparent powerlessness that is, curiously enough, also authorized by this other textual authority) by all the voices that precede him in the text, the truth of the familial, or filial, relations informing each is also uncovered.

This situation is not so final for either of these figures. The author cannot be fixed before, after, or even within his own text. The father cannot be located merely in the family he now heads or in a single position in it. There is no single or true status or role for either of them in the families or the texts within which they move. The ending that might seem to provide a closing, stable solution reminds us that its truth is neither determinate nor entirely truthful. Berto's letter and the novel's ending return us to the complex stories and contradictory moves located both behind and ahead of them. The progression toward what appears to be a future forces us to turn back to a past where even that temporal distinction is called into question. Like the dialectical turns taken by Rita Hayworth, the ending of the novel suspends the question of how to identify these characters and how to situate all the texts that present them. This literal and figurative return by the text to what has already happened, to what has been said and seen before, works against the notion of fictional progression and challenges our reading of the novel as a movement toward stable closure.

The figure of Rita Hayworth—the figure that turns between opposing positions, the figure that resists identification in one or another role—is the figure whose moves insinuate themselves throughout the entire novel, not just in Toto's monologue, where she appears, and in the letter by Berto, who is finally identified with her in that titular (as opposed to filmic) role. As its fragments of discourse are accumulated, the novel turns into a series of repetitions, a synchrony of oscillating, dialectical patterns and relationships both among the characters who perform as its prime subjects and within the discourse they produce. Like the movie star of the title, these subjects are alike and yet different from each other, sometimes because of the differences within themselves. Like the novel's title, we can read their discursive performances now one way, now another. Not only the fictional characters, in their roles as discursive and thematic subjects or objects, but also the language of individual texts shift positions according to similar patterns. They raise questions about their own identity and, consequently, about the identity of the novel as a whole. Let us turn first to some features of the characters' discourse as well as of the texts that present them and then to the thematic details of the novel's fictional world (particularly that of Toto, its organizing figure) in order to see how the issue of identity is raised according to this kind of pattern and how the figure of Rita Hayworth appears to return throughout text and fiction alike.

The first signs of identity are of course provided by the chapter headings that name, and sometimes situate temporally or spatially, their own subjects.[16] Each heading serves first to introduce and then to present a character as a subject whose discourse represents that entity both by characterizing it and by differentiating it from other subjects who are similarly identified and distinguished by their own utterances. The speaking or "thinking" and writing subjects identify themselves with and through specific lexicons and themes that are internal to their own discourse, yet typical of the cultural traditions and linguistic forms that precede and surround them within the fiction or outside the novel. The differential, as well as unifying, values of the discourse of each character cannot be missed. For instance, it would be difficult to confuse the violent gangster-movie language of Cobito in Chapter XI with the exaggerated, sentimental rhetoric of Esther's diary entries from Chapter XIV. Cobito: "Hay que darles muerte a estos hijos de puta, ni uno se va a escapar cuando lleguen a la ratonera, el garaje maldito infectado de malhechores, en la vereda caerán y no

van a tener tiempo de esconderse detrás del kiosco, turros degenera-
dos, van a aprender lo que es traicionar a Joe el implacable, un balazo
en una gamba (así no caminan más), otro en la mano (así largan la
pistola) y ya están indefensos . . ." ["I'm going to murder those bastards, not a single one of them's going to get away when they step into
the mousehole, that fucking garage crawling with criminals, they'll fall
on the sidewalk, no time to sneak behind the newsstand, the lousy
bastards, you'll learn what it is to fink out on Deadly Joe, one bullet
in the leg (and they won't run), a second in the hand (and they'll drop
their guns), they've had it . . . "] (196). Esther: "Tendría que estar
contenta y no lo estoy, una pena que no es honda pero es pena quiere
anidar en mi pecho. ¿Será la luz mortecina de este crepúsculo de domingo? Ya se va el domingo, con su bagaje de doradas promesas, y las
promesas no cumplidas ... de noche no brillan más, como mi broche
de lata. La 'E' de Esther, la llevo prendida al pecho" ["I should be
happy and I am not. Sorrow, not deep but still sorrow, wishes to nest
in my bosom. Could it be the fading light of this Sunday twilight?
Sunday is already going, with its array of golden but unfulfilled promises ... at night they shine no more, like my tin brooch. The 'E' for
Esther I carry pinned to my bosom"] (218).

It would be easy to distinguish the pseudo-intellectual thematics
and language of Herminia's notebook pages in Chapter XV from the
fashion and movie magazine motifs and phrases that pervade Choli's
discourse in Chapter IV. Herminia: "Nada de lo que he leído sobre los
sueños me satisface plenamente. Todas las suposiciones de los espiri-
tistas y astrólogos baratos son completamente inatendibles y las inter-
pretaciones de Sigmund Freud, por lo poco que me ha llegado de él,
me suenan un poco acomodaticias, cataloga todo de modo de confirmar
sus teorías. Modestamente se me ocurre que todo es mucho más com-
plicado de lo que ellos pretenden, aunque algún significado debe haber en el soñar" ["Nothing of what I've read on dreams fully satisfies
me. All the assumptions of spiritists and cheap astrologers are to be
completely ignored and Sigmund Freud's interpretations, from the
little that has come to my attention, sound a little too contrived for my
taste; everything is so neatly catalogued to fit into his theories. My
humble opinion is that it's much more complicated than he thinks,
although dreams must have some meaning"] (270–71). Choli: "—Una
buena base de crema en la cara y casi sin colorete (es mejor pálida,

más interesante) y después mucha sombra en los ojos que da el misterio de la mirada y cosmético renegrido en las pestañas. ¿Sabés una
cosa? todos los peinados de Mecha Ortiz me quedan bien. No hay
artista que me guste más, entre las argentinas" ["—A good base of
pancake on the face and almost no rouge (it's better pale, more interesting) and then a lot of eye shadow which gives you the mysterious
look, and of course mascara for the lashes. You know something? all of
Mecha Ortiz's hairdos look good on me. There isn't an actress I like
better in Argentine movies"] (54).

Likewise, it is precisely because each subject generates and is generated by his/her own idiolect that we can posit something like a con-
tinuum of personality, an identification between subjects of distinct
instances of discourse.[17] Although they represent disparate biographical moments, Toto's three monologues (Chapters III, V, and XIII)
share sufficient stylistic and thematic features so as to create the image
of a single subject. We are therefore able to perceive those texts as
having been produced by the same entity. Similarly, having "heard"
Cobito's monologue in Chapter XI, we see him give himself away linguistically in the "Anónimo dirigido al regente del internado del Colegio 'George Washington', 1947" of Chapter XIV. That is, Cobito's discourse already serves to identify and characterize him in Chapter XI
of the novel, where he speaks "openly" or in his own name. Consequently, he can be recognized as the author of the anonymous letter
in his second discursive performance. His name, suppressed by him
in his letter and by the novel's author, cannot avoid inscribing itself
within and between the lines of his subsequent discourse.

There is, however, a paradox inherent in the way in which at least
nominal identity is granted to each character. Even though a contin-
uum of personality or an image of a psychologically identifiable entity
may seem to establish itself as we move from text to text (the case of
Toto is apposite here), the fragmentary nature of the whole novel also
undermines such an image. The temporal and spatial gaps among
chapters and discursive performances could be read as proof of the
impossibility of stabilizing any individual subject or perceiving it as
entirely identical to itself. For instance, the Toto who speaks in Chapter III (1939) is, in linguistic terms, not the same as the discursive
subject of Chapter V (1942) or of Chapter XIII (1947). Although the
proper name "Toto," replaced by the pronoun "I" (the sign of the dis-

cursive subject), and the psychological entity it designates are the same in each instance, the situations of discourse are not. Indeed, the text emphasizes the temporal gaps between linguistic performances and their subjects.

These similar but clearly separate representations of the fictional entity called "Toto" would remind us that the means by which the image of a stable referent is created would also prove that, in moving from one situation of discourse to another and revealing itself in or through each one, that subject must keep differing from itself. If we acknowledge that the characters are also linguistic and textual subjects as well as thematically determined entities, we can better perceive and understand the various networks of turns and shifts that both define and differentiate them. The image of each character, apparently whole and "real" within the fiction, is in fact created out of a series of shifts in his/her linguistic and narrative positions. These shifts undermine the notion of a unified and stable subject, just as the maneuvers within the fiction erode that of an uncontradictory and unchanging character. When we read these characters, then, we are also faced with the problem of trying to understand how seemingly unified subjects contradict and differ from themselves in several ways at once.[18] Because each turns out to be a mobile subject who may be opposed to and then identified with others who also "speak" or "write" in the novel, they all seem to share the same positions from which each seems to turn away and yet in which each seems to be rooted. It is worth considering the linguistic properties and roles defining each. They are interconnected with and emblematic of the narrative functions and positions of these fictive entities and of the textual figures that turn around them.

A fundamental identity shared by Puig's speaking and writing characters is, of course, a discursive one. Each functions as a subject of discourse and, by definition, is thus posited in grammatical and pronominal positions that are identical to those of other subjects. That first-person pronoun is the property shared but not entirely owned by an individual subject: each can be read as linguistically identical to any other subject who says "I," but never as entirely identical with the pronoun itself.[19] The reality referred to by the first-person pronoun is the "reality of discourse." The pronoun "I" marks "'the individual who utters the present instance of discourse containing the linguistic instance *I.*'"[20] As we turn from text to text, we see that the one who speaks in one monologue can, and often does, become the one spoken to or about in another. Moreover, each discursive subject functions as a kind of narrator and mediator of the direct or indirect speech of other characters who, in turn, play similar roles in their own chapters.

Each speaking and writing subject in *La traición de Rita Hayworth* shares with others the capacity "to posit himself as 'subject.'" Each is capable of entering into relations of correlation and opposition with the other discursive subjects, objects, referents.[21] Since the text turns from one primary speaking or writing subject to another (no contiguous chapters are produced by the same subject), each character is alternately and yet simultaneously represented as a "person" (I/you)—that is, as present to the instance of discourse—or as a "non-person" (he or she)—that is, as absent from, but perhaps referred to in, a discursive situation.[22] The identities established in these discursive shifts are, moreover, further complicated by the temporal complexities of the texts within and among which those turns are orchestrated. The subject of enunciation in a particular text may juxtapose memories and fantasies in which s/he also becomes one of the objects of the utterance about whom s/he speaks or writes. And, within the remembered or imagined scenes of action, the discourse produced by those same characters may be represented either directly or indirectly. These representations of unmediated discourse actually signal a variety of mediating operations through which the characters (who are thus at once identifiable in grammatical, discursive, or narrative, as well as thematic, terms) are represented.

If we were to follow each entity's turns throughout the novel, or even within a single chapter, we could chart a path of shifts through which that character's univocal position, his or her stability, would be rendered questionable, if not entirely negated. In its representation of direct dialogue (the very model of any discursive situation), the novel's first chapter provides a good example of such movements. This immediate direct dialogue takes place at Mita's parents' house in La Plata in 1933. It underscores the potential of each grammatical position to be "occupied" by different referents and reveals the alternating movement by which each character may shift among distinct positions, thereby duplicating and differing from the roles of other subjects.[23] Here Mita's mother, father, two sisters (Clara and Adela), a niece, and a neighbor (Violeta) both alternate and coincide with one another as referents for the pronouns "yo" ["I"] and "tú" ["you"] (the signs of "person"), while Mita, Berto, and Toto, who are absent from the discursive situation, are marked by third-person pronouns (signs of "non-person"). In this chapter we see both the correlation of personality signaled by the opposition between persons present ("I" and "you") and those absent ("he" and "she") from the instance of discourse, and the correlation of subjectivity displayed in the relationships among the interlocutors.

In "En casa de los padres de Mita, La Plata 1933" the cases of Adela and Violeta represent the significant movements. One shifts from a brief role as "non-person" outside the dialogue to that of an interlocutor within it, while the other is first represented in a correlation of subjectivity with Mita's mother, sister, and the other speaking subjects, and then as a "non-person" referred to by those who remain in the dialogic exchange. That is, Adela, who is implicitly referred to as "ella" ["she"] immediately before making her entrance on page 16 ("—Pero Adela no podría haber estudiado con la vista tan mala") ["—But Adela couldn't have studied with such poor eyesight"], becomes a "person," grammatically a first person, when she enters the house and the dialogue itself ("—Estoy rendida del cansancio") ["—I am completely worn out"] and begins to shift between the two positions of subjectivity ("I" and "you"). Violeta, who is first a speaking and listening subject in the dialogue, is transformed into a "non-person" when, once she leaves the house (13), she can only be named as a "she" by those who remain as subjects of the dialogue ("—Abuelita, ¿por qué Violeta se pinta los ojos de negro?") ["—Grandma, why does Violeta put black around her eyes?"].

Both Adela and Violeta alternately share the same linguistic position of "non-person" with each other and with Mita, Berto, and Toto and the position of "person" with those who are posited only in terms of their discursive subjectivity. The move to other chapters signals the same kind of shift both within individual texts and throughout the novel as a whole. As different characters become primary subjects, the plurality of grammatical and linguistic positions which can be occupied by a single character, as well as the multiplicity of referents marked by any pronoun of "person" or "non-person," are emphasized. Each character alternately usurps and shares the discursive position of other characters in the novel. Each pronominal and grammatical indicator represents the serial or simultaneous superimposition of referents "behind" or "beneath" it.

In the novel's "written" monologues the links between discursive roles and narrative relations are emphasized. Those chapters are examples of how the mobility of textual, as well as fictional, figures is implied by the whole novel. The first of them—"Diario de Esther, 1947"—reveals unwittingly both the narrative hierarchy and the structuring fiction behind both "spoken" and "written" texts. It underlines the complex superimposition of roles that any one text or any one fictional or textual image represents. In all but one of the other written texts (Toto's composition) an apparently stable set of discursive relations is displayed. That is, each of the writing subjects remains fixed in a correlation of subjectivity with either implied or represented readers and/or interlocutors within either a primary instance of discourse or a secondary (i.e., represented) speech act. If the writer, who also functions as a narrator, shares any linguistic position with another in his or her own discourse, it is because the characters not present to the situation of discourse are represented within the utterance as speaking subjects. They therefore appear to move from a position of "non-person" to that of "person." Esther's diary shows us that when a writing subject posits him or herself as an "other," in an opposing personal position, s/he would render visible the superimposition of narrative roles that his/her discourse initally serves to cover up and would uncover another network within which his/her position may turn. This revelation reminds us of the textual figures who hover around, but who are also identified with, the various participants in the novel's discursive and narrative turns.

When Esther—the writing subject who names Toto, Héctor, and others as characters in her narrative, and who "transcribes" several dialogues between herself and them—refers to herself in the third person in her own diary ("Y Esther la taimada le dice a Casals . . ." ["And sly Esther says to Casals . . . "] [230]), she discloses that the person named in or by the discourse is not identical with the one who produces it. This discursive difference works to emphasize as well a narrative relation supporting the text, a relation between the text as represented enunciation or narration and the text as narrative utterance. As we know, in first-person narration a pronominal overlap impedes the perception of the distinction and, thus, the narrative hierarchies implicit in this or any narrative text. In Esther's text, when the pronoun "ella" ["she"] is implicitly substituted for the pronoun "yo" ["I"], which otherwise (that is, up until and after this moment in her writing) refers to or designates Esther, her diary unveils what appear to be indissoluble textual strata. The gap between Esther as "I" and Esther as "she" is identical with the one that separates the subject of enunciation from the subject of the utterance in any narrative, even a first-person text. But in the rest of Esther's diary, as in the other texts that follow it, these two subjects are conflated and potentially confused because the "I" who says "I" in that instance of discourse (the writing of the diary) overlaps with the "I" represented in both the scenes and dialogues described in Esther's utterance.

This momentary pronominal slippage emphasizes the complex temporality of the diary text and the plurality of narrative frames within and among which all the characters continue to move. Esther's diary text marks the significant turn from represented speech to writing. It betrays not only the fictional narrator-author's, but also the reader's, fluctuating positions. In these last chapters, in fact, we might see the parallel oscillations developed for the reader in, as well as the reader of, this text. If in the earlier chapters the image of the reader is implied as the specular opposite of the implied author, the signs of whom are presented by textual and structural features already noted, these last five "written" chapters disclose that only through the act of reading can the fiction, however naturalized, be perceived and understood. They would remind us that any narrator's "I"—the pronoun that masks the "I" of a more authoritative textual subject, the authorial figure or narrator, "behind" or "beneath" it—also points to and implies the "you" of the interlocutor (listener or narratee) and, through him or her, the reader.[24] In this succession of "written" texts the figure of the novel's reader is also uncovered and veiled. Each text in question either names or assumes a receiver-reader of the text within the fiction, even if that addressee is no more than a projection of the character-writer as an "other" in virtual dialogue with him or herself.[25] The reader's place is therefore exposed as a place "belonging" to him or her, but it also seems to be filled by various fictive surrogates who alternately and successively replace one another.

The positions of the reader are perhaps as complex and unstable as those of the novel's speaker-narrators. The reader, who is "present" and situated in the position of the text's general addressee, depends on, even reflects or identifies with, both the narrative and the fictional entities with which s/he engages in virtual dialogue and to which s/he responds or reacts.[26] As we know, because of the potential identification with the characters themselves or with the first- or second-person pronouns that alternately represent them, the reader may be made to "experience" the linguistic (pronominal or grammatical) shifts and overlaps developed throughout the novel. In playing the role implied by the text, s/he would also occupy both the position of general addressee and that of interlocutor, narratee, or reader—positions that are either implicit or explicit. When we become witnesses to or eavesdroppers on a dialogue within which the characters themselves say "I" and "you," we are potentially cast as "non-persons" and reminded of the reader's external position and absence from the discursive situation. The reader's place in Puig's novel is problematic but also emblematic. The linguistic and narrative turns internal to the narrative text also call attention to the proliferation of and dialectical movements among readerly positions. These positions are developed with and superimposed on the image of stability simultaneously created by the reader's role as general addressee.

The novel's epistolary texts provide particularly instructive examples of the plurality of positions accorded to its reader. Berto's letter, for instance, underlines how, while maintaining an apparently stable distance from the letter, Puig's reader cannot but be drawn into and move with it. In reading a text that seems already to have been torn up, but that nevertheless is both rewritten and re-presented before our eyes, we are forced to usurp the place of the fictional addressee (Jaime) who never receives the letter. At the same time, however, we would seem to have to coincide with and see through the eyes (also the "I"s—as subject of the utterance and of the enunciation) of its writer.[27] The reader is cast alternately and simultaneously as an implicit "person" and "non-person" in relation to the letter which displays an otherwise stable linguistic and narrative structure (that of the letter itself, as a virtual dialogue between Berto and Jaime; that of the novel's text, as a virtual dialogue between author and reader).

The proliferation of discursive performances in Puig's first novel creates a mobile ground upon which fictional and textual figures seem to turn, and within which they appear to be different from but also similar to one another. This proliferation of appearances undermines the image of stable difference or sameness that the text also seems to establish. The problem of the links and distinctions among fictive and textual characters, as well as between the two groups, cannot be resolved, because the identifications and distinctions among them are set up both within and between figures who turn in several registers at once. This is the problem that arises when we consider the position or status of the entire text—its own "identity"—within an intertextual network of relations. In *La traición de Rita Hayworth* the question of whether or not it is possible to talk about anything like a stable identity or a univocal position is also raised around the novel as a whole.

To progress from chapter to chapter in *La traición de Rita Hayworth* is to perceive and receive consecutively a heterogeneous array of styles, voices, and vocabularies that individualize the novel's subjects. The novel utilizes and refers to a variety of languages that are, nonetheless, related to one another through their common frame of reference—that is, the worlds of popular culture and everyday provincial life. As mentioned above, Chapter XI provides Cobito's verbal self-transformation into a gangster-movie "heavy"; Chapter XII reveals Esther's sentimental "dear diary" prose intermixed with Peronist rhetoric; Chapter IX includes Héctor's stylized version of a radio sportscaster describing a soccer game; and Chapter I presents the trivial conversation of an afternoon gathering of a family and friends in La Plata. In addition, in Delia's chapter (VII) the text is filled with the speaker's "soap-opera" descriptions of small-town romance and domestic life; in Paquita's (X) we "hear" an adolescent girl's Saturday morning ramblings about sin, guilt, love, and sex before she goes in to confession; and in Mita's (VIII) the voice is that of a mother and wife who attempts, unsuccessfully it seems, to reconcile herself to the death of her child, whose image keeps her awake and engaged in her monologue.

The proliferation of voices and languages has what we might call a critical effect in the novel. We cannot but become aware of the differences between one mode of discourse and another, or even between the techniques used to create them. We cannot but begin to consider the relations among these forms of language and the models from which they are derived. By having to readjust continually to textually new but contextually familiar modes of discourse, while also trying to draw anecdotal information from them, the reader is forced to become aware of the text itself. The novel's formal and discursive heterogeneity helps to create and point out its reflexive qualities. While it would allow us to learn something about each character through his/her language, the novel also reminds us that the style or form each uses is part of a performance derived from and critically connected to a popular tradition to whose development that same character also makes his/her contribution.

Each voice and/or language is at once engaged in a dialogue with an "original," as well as interacting with all the other voices, styles, and subjects that construct the novel. However, each dialogue is itself based on the meeting of other "conversations" also developed within it. The popular forms of language used within the fiction are themselves appropriated from models—speakers, voices, languages—to which the characters connect themselves at a distance. For example, when Héctor appropriates the style and vocabulary (thereby borrowing the voice) of a sportscaster, or when Cobito takes on the language and tone of a Hollywood gangster, we may discern several levels of dialogue, several kinds of distances, implied by their discourse. We may perceive an exchange between the character's "real" voice and the one he appropriates within the fiction, as well as another parallel and analogous exchange between an authorial voice, discourse, or text and that of the cultural model and context to which it refers. These virtual dialogues are, as we know, inherently dialectical and ambivalent forms of discourse. That is, they are double-valued, double-voiced, and double-directed. The "audible" or "visible" voice or discourse implicitly refers to and yet contains within itself the other whose place it takes, the one that is and yet is not there to be "heard" or "seen."

In fact, Puig's novel demonstrates the absence of, or the impossibility of discovering, an original or authentic voice for any of the novel's characters or for its authorial figure. Each fictional character seems neither to have possessed nor to have formulated his/her own language. The languages displayed in the speech or writing of each subject represent a mixture of voices that seem to be "borrowed" from other subjects and contexts with which they appear to desire to identify themselves.[28] The subjects' performances remind us repeatedly of their distance from themselves, of their alienation. They also implicitly call into question the possibility of ever "seeing" or "hearing" a purely "original," non-textualized performance in either the fictional world of Coronel Vallejos or the text of Puig's novel.[29] When Héctor, Cobito, and Esther, for example, reproduce the languages that also produce them, each is engaged in what seems to be a "sincere" linguistic effort. That is, even though the distance between each of them and the formulaic models he or she appropriates is emphasized, each subject seems to believe in and desire to be at one with the original discourse. Each perceives reality, or pretends to live it for a moment, through that model. Each is doubled in conversation with him or herself, as well as with the appropriated language and the identity it constructs for its subject.

For instance, in one section of his monologue the seventeen-year-old Héctor projects himself both as a sports commentator and as a soccer hero who is seen through the eyes and presented by the voice of that same sportscaster: ". . . pero el trío no se mueve, señores radioyentes y espectadores de este encuentro sensacional en la bombonera boquense, con los hinchas del equipo millonario fuertemente alarmados por la repentina enfermedad del centrojá [the position played by Héctor; see 163], sustituido a último momento por un jugador desconocido para el público, y descubierto esta mañana en un potrero de la capital, sin experiencia profesional salvo pocas apariciones ante el público en un torneo infantil ... y es él, es él que entra en la cancha seguro de la victoria, con la esperanza invencible de sus escasos diecisiete abriles . . ." [". . . but the trio doesn't waver for a second, radio listeners of this sensational encounter in the Boca field, with the fans of the mighty team seriously alarmed by the sudden illness of its center half, substituted at the last minute by an unknown player, and discovered this morning in a vacant lot of the capital, no professional experience except a few appearances in a boy's tournament ... and that's him, that's him now entering the field sure of victory, with the invincible hope of his barely seventeen Aprils . . . "] (166).

This projection clearly points as much to another, prior and typical, discursive situation (that of all the broadcasts of soccer matches that Héctor himself has heard) as it does to his own (that of a teenage boy who fantasizes about his own "discovery" and heroic performance). Within this part of the fiction, then, Héctor's discourse represents an effort at stylization that itself harmonizes and conflicts with other voices within the text. In fact, this derived performance, this clearly appropriated style and voice, is juxtaposed with and connected to a variety of voices, some apparently more "authentic" than this one, within Héctor's own discourse. Héctor's voice shifts among, but also merges, disparate voices, such as that of the young "tough" or "macho" or even "Don Juan" whose overriding interest is in sexual conquest (see, for example, 157–58) and that of an adolescent boy who, "abandoned" by his parents, secretly desires some sort of familial protection (see 162–63) and that of the sportscaster.

Héctor's monologue, like others in Puig's novel, represents a network of voices and styles. All of those voices and styles identify him; none of them can be said to have more authenticity or authority than the others. Even the apparently more "authentic" voice (the more "authentic" because more private or veiled voice of the boy who reveals his "true" emotions and vulnerability, for example) is but one among several related but different styles and tones through which the significant turns within this subject are played out. Héctor's monologue nevertheless accomplishes a harmonious merger of styles that are derived in one way or another from "outside" the subject. They merge in his performance, oddly enough, even while they would also betray the character's "inauthenticity," the subject's difference from himself. But these internal dialogues overlap with another, broader exchange—the exchange between the authorial representation of the borrowed languages (i.e., the authorial version of, and the author's position with respect to the character's performance as, the sportscaster or adolescent "tough") and the cultural model on which they are based. The ambivalence of this second-level dialogue is determined both by its nature (that is, its inherent discursive doubleness) and the impossibility of detaching it from the dialogues within the fictional discourse. In fact, it seems that we cannot entirely resolve the nature of these overlapping dialogic exchanges.

Puig's text seems to represent either a series of shifts between, or a contradictory superimposition of, both parody and stylization. If it seems that Héctor's vulgar slang or sportscaster style, or Esther's Peronist rhetoric (e.g., 223–24) or confessional diary style (e.g., 218, 240), represent antagonistic meetings between an authorial "voice" and the ones it would re-present through his speech or her writing, then we will read their texts as parodies.[30] But if at the same time we accept that, in the fiction, each in some way also speaks for him/herself, as it were, by using the voice of another whom s/he would attempt to emulate, then we would have to read those texts as authorial parodies of their stylizations, or as the text's parodic stylizations of the models each subject would imitate. On the other hand, if the authorial position seems to signal instead an effort to represent the discourse that exists prior to the fictional text, in these apparently derived forms, then we will have to read them as efforts to reproduce faithfully what is already—even in the fictional text itself—represented as a "pure" stylization.

La traición de Rita Hayworth presents us with a set of texts for which it is difficult to make these kinds of determinations. Each text turns in different directions at once. Each chapter reveals the dialectical and therefore undecidable quality of its discourse, along with the unstable position of its subject. Each shows that the positions taken by fictive and authorial voices alike seem clearly to stake their own ground, yet to deny the possibility of immobilizing either that ground or those voices in a single position on it. Puig's novel seems repeatedly to highlight the dialectical structure of both types of "dialogized hybrids." It also reveals how the complexities of those textual forms can be compounded and multiplied by their apparent combination in different registers at once. The authorial voice or position in either type of double-directed speech is only visible, as it were, in the relation established between original and secondary discourses. That authorial voice is dialogically engaged with another voice or style with which it can also be identified. It keeps turning from one position or voice to another; it therefore cannot be fixed in one place.

Puig's novel is a dialogic network within which the authorial voice or image seems to have so many positions at once, and to situate itself in relation to so many other voices, discourses, and texts, that it seems to have no single position. It keeps turning in place, not unlike the novel itself, which appears to turn with equal force between parody and stylization. However, the text does not finally proclaim—or, rather, allow us to assert—the superior force of one of those forms of ambivalent discourse, or to identify one fixed textual or authorial position, or attitude or aim, supporting the novel. The novel seems instead to be both an alternation between and a superimposition of these two types of double-voiced discourse and disparate authorial designs.

La traición de Rita Hayworth is at once a set of (intentional or unintentional) parodies of originally stylized or (intentionally or unintentionally) parodic discourses and texts. At the same time, it is also a collection of stylizations of discourses and texts that are originally either (intentionally or unintentionally) parodic or stylized in nature. The novel turns from one possibility to the other. It appears to combine those contradictory possibilities with each of those turns, establishing in the process its reflexive quality. The moves between apparent assertions and negations of discursive position and textual identity call attention to the text as such, even while they also lure us into the fictional world of its subjects' verbal performances.

As noted earlier, the fiction moves around stories and subjects that seem to match in their own realm the textual turns taken by the novel. Puig's characters are models of ambivalence. As suggested in the discussion of Toto, Berto, and Rita Hayworth, they keep returning us to the novel's title and the pattern of opposing and identifying moves through which everyone can be interconnected. The dialectical moves that inform each character's discourse and through which each is identified with the others is not unlike the pattern supporting the appearance of the authorial figure, as described above. Precisely because each subject keeps shifting among, and thus alternatively or consecutively repeats, the same thematic positions, each appears not to move (i.e., to develop or change) at all. Toto, as we recall, is the emblem and elaboration of that pattern. He is the focal point to which everyone, including himself, keeps (re)turning throughout the novel. Like the movie star that he, his father, and even the authorial subject seem to admire so much, Toto's movements are what keep the text returning to certain structures and roles whose repetitions reinforce the novel's fragmentary, even static, quality. While the progression from chapter to chapter does take the story forward, it is circumscribed by a network of repetitions and returns. Much like the structural return orchestrated by the inversion of the final chapter, the turns within Toto's world always seem to involve a kind of regression—a turn back to a position or role already displayed in a scene whose originality is put into question by the text's inversionary procedures.

In *La traición de Rita Hayworth* the notion of development—that is, evolution or progress—is questioned both by the single appearances of subjects whose performances cannot afford us a view of their changes in or over time, and by the multiple performances of the protagonist whose discourse reveals not a departure from but a solidification of the relations and subjective structures through and in which he is first identified. While Toto's three monologues mark his linguistic growth from the age of six (Chapter III) to nine (Chapter V) and fourteen (Chapter XIII), they also reveal a set of psychical configurations to which he returns throughout his appearances. His monologues also disclose their own conditions of possibility and necessity, and these seem to be the conditions and needs that inform as well the discourse of other subjects. Discursive production seems to be predicated upon a situation of loss, a real or imagined sense of loss that is both uncovered and obscured by the novel's predominant narrative form, the monologue.[31]

The progression from first to last chapter of the novel constitutes a set of generalized representations of that contradictory effect. As we recall, it moves from direct dialogue in Chapters I and II (the 1933 conversation in Mita's parents' house, and the dialogue between the Casals' maids that same year) to the first monologue in Chapter III (Toto's first performance), to hidden dialogue in Chapter IV (the conversation between Choli and Mita in which the words of the latter are suppressed from the text), and back to the monologue form that dominates the rest of the novel, first in the form of speech (Chapters V-XI) and then in the form of writing (Chapters XII-XVI). Through this sequence the text gradually unveils the conditions that create the need for discursive production in this alienated provincial world. It emphasizes that it is primarily because each subject is alone (here this may also mean abandoned, or betrayed, or deceived) and lacks an interlocutor that his or her monologue is not only possible but also necessary. The situations in which the characters are presented as discursive subjects are those in which each seems in some way to (need to) undertake the recovery of a lost situation or entity. The fictive projects of some of the characters reveal their ambivalent positions with respect to specific objects and situations they seem to desire. The display of that desire for recovery might be read as the sign of the impossibility of the project to attain it. Each monologue becomes a play of desires that are impossible to satisfy, a design for power over a reality whose revision can be no more than a fictive construct.

The text's move from spoken dialogue to written monologue constitutes an apparent gradual suppression of the interlocutionary aspect of discourse. It represents the absence of an object of, and also another subject in, discourse, since the monologue, the principal narrative form allowed each subject, predominates. Yet, because of the intrinsically dialogic nature of the monologue form itself, each subject also can momentarily obscure or deny that reality, that situation of solitude or privation.[32] The instance of discourse both reveals the actual situation of each subject and seems to grant the potential for negating its reality. It is, of course, in the space of language that each one authors a powerful but fictive antidote for the very situation out of which his or her discourse arises, even though that same performance reminds us of each subject's powerlessness in the face of the lived reality. In Coronel Vallejos, moreover, the questions of loss and desire are linked not only with power but also with violence. These categories are often bound together in different registers at once.

Toto's monologues are important both because of the nature of the scenes authored through memory and fantasy by Toto himself and because of the discursive context, the "scenes" or situations, within or around which those monologues are produced. In Chapter III ("Toto, 1939") and the first part of V ("Toto, 1942") that context is the siesta hour. This daily ritual of Hispanic culture makes Toto's monologues possible and necessary and marks his discourse in several ways. It is perhaps the crucial contextual detail that allows us to posit something like an originating situation for his monologue, a situation whose thematics also permeate Toto's appearances throughout the novel and, through him, establish contact with other subjects.[33] The siesta is a bracketed or "dead" time during which the time of reality seems to stand still while the time of fantasy and fiction moves on. It is also an inherently dramatic and powerful time for Toto: it is a time that needs to be killed, and a time during which one tries to avoid being killed. The siesta hour is when Toto is left alone ("abandoned") to amuse himself quietly, lest he be punished by his father, while his parents nap together. During that afternoon hour Toto "loses" Mita to Berto, whose image as a violent and threatening figure emerges both from Toto's representation of his experience of fact and from his excursions into fantasy.

If in the second monologue Toto clearly states that his problem is indeed how to kill time and, implicitly, how to avoid his father's wrath

("¿Qué dibujo hago hasta las 3? El aburrimiento más grande es la siesta, y si pasa un avión papá se despierta, los gritos, mamá aprovecha y se levanta" ["What can I draw until three o'clock? Naptime is the biggest bore and if a plane flies over Dad wakes up, the shouting starts and it's Mom's chance to get up"] [69]), in the first he not only implies that but also vividly represents the emotional impact of the hour's real and potential scenarios ("¿Adónde te vas? [¿]ahora ya es hora de dormir la siesta? ¿adónde? hoy no tenés que trabajar en el hospital ¿adónde te vas, a hacer una torta? ¡Mami! no me dejes solo que quiero jugar otro rato ¿por qué no me hacés una torta? mamá no va a la cocina, va al dormitorio ¿a buscar el libro con todas las recetas? Papá la llamó y mamá tuvo que irse a dormir la siesta" ["Where are you going? Is it naptime already? Where? you don't have to work in the hospital today, where are you going? to bake a cake? Mommy! don't leave me alone, I want to play some more! why don't you bake me a cake? Mommy's not going into the kitchen, is she going into the bedroom to look for the recipe book? Daddy called her and Mommy had to go in to take a nap"] [36]; ". . . y yo una vez la desperté a mamá a la siesta porque me aburro y papá 'nunca te he pegado pero el día que te ponga la mano encima te deshago' y voy a pensar en la cinta que más me gustó porque mamá me dijo que pensara en una cinta para que no me aburriera a la siesta" [". . . and once I woke Mommy up during naptime because I'm bored and Daddy 'I never slapped you but the day I put my hands on you I'll break you in two' and I'm going to think about the movie I like the best because Mommy told me to think about a movie so I wouldn't get bored at naptime"] [37]).

These remembered yet seemingly present scenes of conflict, wherein paternal violence and maternal abandonment and betrayal seem inevitably linked, are potentially countered by Toto as well. The siesta is also the time of fantasized plenitude. In the first monologue, for example, Toto constructs, both for himself and for his fictional surrogates (e.g., a small canary, a dove, little boys, Shirley Temple, little fish), idyllic fictions of adventurous escape from threatening figures (e.g., a rabid cat, black buzzards, the "bad gypsy," an evil grandfather, carnivorous plants), as well as scenes of union and reunion with, or salvation by, various desired figures (e.g., Mita, Ginger Rogers). This essentially familial drama, enacted as it is by a variety of real and fictional entities through the metaphoric and metonymic displacements that constitute the logic of Toto's psychical reality and free-associative discourse, also has woven into it, already in his first performance, versions of a powerful and mysterious primal scene to which Toto's later monologues also return, always in connection with the scenarios of triangular conflict (e.g., see the superimposition of Toto's description of the game "siesta"—children imitating parents having sexual intercourse during naptime—with the underwater and murder mystery films seen at the afternoon movies [41–43]).

In its apparently random movements among these dramatic scenes Toto's first monologue sets up a repetitive narrative scheme and a pattern of closure that are evident also in the two monologues in Chapter V and the written essay in Chapter XIII. In the 1939 text the interweaving of scenes and events from different historical and fictional contexts, the move from scenarios of potential violence to visions of salvation, bring us to a final "happy ending": Toto, finally safe from danger and accompanied by Ginger Rogers, one of his favorite stars, becomes a character in his own version of the ending of a Fred Astaire/Ginger Rogers film, playing in the clouds where he and "la Ginger" float above reality (48). Likewise, in the 1942 chapter Toto ends the first monologue with another filmic happy scene: he concludes a fantasized romantic adventure film with a "happily-ever-after" finale for a young couple and their infant, whose escape to a tropical isle protects them from pursuit by the police for an unidentified crime (87). Superimposed upon this is his vision of two persons whose company he desires; Alicita, his favorite friend, is metonymically linked with his mother through references to Alicita's hair, which is decorated with ribbons that Toto has made for her, and to the colored threads of Mita's bedspread (88). Its second section ends with analogous fantasies: first, with a fantasy of paradisaical salvation for Toto himself and of infernal punishment for his adversaries (he fantasizes a "Final Judgment" revenge on Raúl García, an older boy who "steals" his friend Paqui from him in a real scene of conflict immediately prior to the monologue, and on Luisito, the boy to whom Toto "loses" Alicita at a party from which he flees just before the monologue, as well as a vision of himself saved by Alicita's uncle in "Paradise" [95–96]); and, finally, with a vision of union with his savior, who is also the supposed object of his friend Alicita's affections (Toto's fantasy of salvation for himself merges with his fantasy of incorporation into the body of Alicita's uncle [96]).

These parallel endings are but the momentary solutions, the fictive and ephemeral endings, to the same kinds of conflicts that inform the 1939 monologue. However, the 1942 chapter more clearly presents scenes from the immediate historical reality within which Toto's discourse is produced. These "happy endings" seem more explicitly grounded in the situation of discourse for which they, like the 1939 chapter, also seem to offer themselves as immediate antidotes. The first section of the 1942 text (69–88) presents Toto's interior monologue during the siesta hour on the day preceding the birthday party that provides the temporal frame of the second section (88–96). The first, and longer, monologue presents Toto while he entertains himself by drawing pictures of his favorite movie stars and scenes from films he has seen with Mita. At the same time, his free-associative discourse constructs a path through memories and thoughts about his family and friends, as well as fantasies based on movies that he "rewrites," incorporating into them a variety of real persons, including himself (see, e.g., 85–86). The monologue itself is the answer to the question Toto poses about how to fill the siesta while awaiting Mita's return, about how to escape the boredom and fears generated in and by the siesta ritual itself (69, cited above). To counter the former, he draws pictures; to diffuse the power of the latter, he constructs a network of fantasies of danger and salvation in which he is at once actor, spectator, and author.

The second 1942 monologue is produced around 7:00 P.M. the next day. Toto hides in the vestibule of his house, having left his friend's birthday party early. Although the differences between the six and the nine year old are marked linguistically (the 1942 text is more regular in its syntax and phrasing, more scriptural), in the second set of monologues their similarities, their seemingly unchanged identity, are also stressed. The 1942 chapter repeats the same types of scenarios, the same kind of obsessive return to scenes of conflict and resolution, the same sort of narrative and thematic patterns that dominate the 1947 essay in Chapter XIII. When we read these monologues in sequence, we see that a certain recognition of the limits of reality is more consciously inscribed within each text as Toto, the subject, matures. Yet, as his essay shows as well, the fantasy of overcoming material reality also persists as the foundation of this budding writer's activities.

As we remember, Toto's 1939 monologue, produced at the time of his parents' siesta, is authored as a kind of veil for and solution to his solitary situation. He would cover up this situation by filling it with memories and fantasies that also reinstate discursively the figure whose presence Toto has been denied—Mita, the mother who has left him for, but who has also been taken away by, his threatening paternal adversary. In that monologue Mita is presented by Toto both as a character about whom he speaks (as a "non-personal" object of his discourse) and as his fictive interlocutor (as a "personal" and potential subject whom he addresses as if she were present for his solitary mental meanderings; e.g., 33, 35). However, this reunion with his preferred interlocutor is, and must be, attenuated by the presence of, among others, Berto, the third party whose threatening presence Toto's monologue works unsuccessfully to ignore and efface. For Mita cannot be recuperated in isolation from the structures of relations in which she and Toto exist. Along with her must come Berto, as well as other real and fictional subjects in the scenarios they enact together. Toto's effort to rewrite reality turns out to prove the futility of such an attempted solution. Not only is it impossible for him to write a new script for their family drama and romance; he also seems bound endlessly to repeat the old one. This is precisely what his 1942 and 1947 monologues seem to do. Although they focus more and more on non-familial characters and even on entirely fictional figures, the scenes and stories they present are but repetitive elaborations and revisions of those that appear earlier in Toto's texts.

While they stand as distinct discursive moments, the two sections of Chapter V can be read as a unified sequence that uncovers the psychical and material realities of the nine year old. In the first section Toto acknowledges the reality of his siesta situation (that is, the absence of Mita and the need to fill—or kill—time with pictures and film fantasies). In the second his discourse further acknowledges the distance between the reality he works to cover up and the fictions he repeatedly and, it seems, finally (i.e., in the "happy ending") constructs to take its place. In the first section he merely awaits the end of the siesta hour, knowing that its end will signify the return of Mita. In the second, however, he anxiously wonders where she is and whether he will be reunited with her. As he hides in their foyer, reviewing in his mind the troubling events that immediately precede his monologue and fantasizing perfect solutions to the triangular dramas in which he has just participated with some of his friends, he returns to the problem of how to locate Mita.

Because the figure of Mita cannot be unhinged from that of Berto, Toto's query is also an acknowledgment of the impossibility of finding her again. It recognizes the necessity of facing Berto, the frightening figure whose punishment he awaits. Berto here plays the role of the father to whom Toto must confess his cowardly (even "girlish") behavior—Toto flees two scenes of conflict and comes home with his eyes red from crying, believing that he must explain, even though he wants to cover up, the facts that his father's demanding gaze is sure to see (89–90, 95). Toto casts him as the father from whom he needs to defend himself, as the figure from whom he also hides. Here Toto's desire to return to Mita (she is, he thinks, at the movies, the place of refuge where they usually go to together; see 88, 92) seems to come up against its denial, the fact of the impossibility of that return, as well as a potential reality that keeps threatening to take its (and her) place.

This kind of turning between the refusal and the recognition of reality also informs Toto's essay about his favorite movie, *The Great Waltz* (Chapter XIII).[34] Toto's sentimental version of the life of Johann Strauss ends with just this kind of double stance, with a vision of a paradisaical, dyadic (re)union that is also acknowledged as an ephemeral and fictive reality. In Toto's summary the protagonist returns to his wife after a perfect but brief romantic idyll with his lover (an opera singer named Carla). The Austrian emperor (the former Duke of Hagenbruhl, Carla's former lover and Johann's ex-rival) has granted him a virtual reunion with his lost love. At a public gathering in his honor Carla appears to Johann; she hovers over his adulating public in the form of a "visión transparente" (264). As the story is told by Toto, it becomes a reinscription of the other stories of desire and conflict that proliferate in his monologues. His version of the film is a story of recuperation and salvation—a story about how a fantasy, a fiction, may be transformed, if only temporarily, into a reality. It is, moreover, not only about the desire for the satisfaction of desire, but also about the obstacles which, in Toto's world and in Coronel Vallejos as a whole, inevitably thwart attempts to achieve those ends.

Read in relation to the 1939 and 1942 monologues, the 1947 composition turns out to be a more coherent version. For example, the aggressive, violent relation between the Duke (the victimizer of a younger and weaker rival) and Johann (the challenging subordinate) is but another version of Toto's representation of his potential and actual relation to Berto, or his conflict with Luisito or Raúl, as well as the relations among many of the fictive surrogates who appear in Toto's fantasies. The stylized, if not parodic, oedipal triangle formed by the Duke, Carla, and Johann, and from which emerges the harmonious but finally impossible dyad involving the latter two figures, is but a revision of, among others, the Berto-Mita-Toto or the Luisito-Alicita-Toto dramas. Toto's confused representation of a (perhaps primal) sexual scene involving Carla and the Duke (252–53) seems to link up with, and even to reinterpret, Toto's conflated fearful fantasies about the underwater film and the murder mystery. It is also linked to his descriptions of the siesta game played with his friend La Pocha and the scene of sexual play between Paquita and Raúl, to which he is prime witness (41–45, 92–94).

The repeated return to these types of scenes and relations throughout Toto's monologues leads us to take them as a kind of psycho-sexual biography of a subject whose identity remains problematic both for those who surround him in the fiction and for those who might try to read him from outside it. The monologues chronicle and catalogue the ways in which, first as the innocent child, then as the confused but partially informed boy, and finally as the knowledgable but incredulous adolescent, Toto deals with the fact of sexuality and sexual difference.[35] In the 1947 text the question of sexuality, having circulated as a latent or incipient problem in the earlier chapters, is now manifested as an organizing principle underlying the returns to the scenes and situations already noted.

While the 1939 and 1942 monologues wander about, linking memories and fantasies that (as we see "after the fact") disclose the psychosexual reality of the subject at different stages of his "development," the 1947 text is organized as a subjective interpretation. It is a disguised because "artistic" investigation of a single emblematic story of an essentially illicit, though romantic, sexual relation from its beginning to its end. Toto's narrative focuses on the details of the relation between the lovers and on the events that either promote or prevent it. Since the affair is an "illegal" one, the question of what legitimizes or prohibits this relationship (in addition to what originally constitutes it) circulates silently, though also visibly, in Toto's text. The lovers, whose relationship is both the constitutive reality and the fantasy of the adolescent's composition, are the most realized example of the many "perfect couples" about whom Toto invents stories. Moreover, they seem to be sexualized versions of an original family dyad (that of mother and son) which, in its domesticated form, appears as a discursive relation between interlocutors who take pleasure in being narrators and listeners for one another. (See 246, 250; see also descriptions of Mita and Toto, 138–41, and Toto and Raúl, 86, as well as the protagonists' entire dialogue in *El beso de la mujer araña*.)

This composition also reminds us that the apparent origins of Toto's version of the Hollywood film lie both in his psychical reality, as revealed in his previous monologues, and in the network of popular stories to be found not only in the practices of Hollywood but also in the theories of psychoanalysis. The presentation of Toto's memories and fantasies of paternal aggression and maternal abandonment, the representation of triangular dramas and idyllic dyads as their resolutions, the descriptions of scenes of sexual seduction and, or as, violence—all of these point to a set of psychoanlytic "scripts" through which we could read Toto and which, at the same time, become objects to be read. The insistence on the oedipal and primal scenarios throughout Toto's discourse reveals what are certainly some very powerful material dramas for Toto.

On one level, the essay is an unself-conscious, "realistic" representation of the "mind" of a fictional character in whose existence we might for a time suspend disbelief. Toto's composition is his own personal, stylized version of a film in which he, the narrating subject, believes and with which he also identifies. (See, for example, his repeated use of rhetorical questions about the characters' actions, and the way he writes himself into the composition as an interpreter-character who says "I" [252].) It seems, however, at the same time to parody genres on which it is based (i.e., the sentimental Hollywood film and the high school composition), and even, as noted above, to parody the theoretical paradigms through which the adolescent author as well as the essay might be read. In what becomes an exaggerated version of those models, Toto's essay calls attention to the emotional excesses of *The Great Waltz*, or films like it, to the discursive and narrative conventions of the high school essay, to the exemplary stories and scenes of psychoanalysis, and, in the end, to the subject of the essay itself. But precisely because that subject takes seriously and is not himself distanced from his own materials, and because, in reading his work, we might also be seduced by his complete identification with his characters and story, the potential for reading the text and Toto himself as parodies is undermined.

We must here reckon with a crucial paradox of Puig's writing, a paradox that lends a certain power to his work. Added to, or perhaps because of, the play between the text's "serious" and "playful" techniques, the play between stylization and parody (or the various combinations and superimpositions thereof), the novel distances itself from and studies critically the very same characters, stories, and scenes with which it also identifies so closely. As we read each monologue and "enter" the world of each subject, we may be further drawn into the psychical realities and cultural situations represented. At the same time, however, we may also perceive the critical, reflexive display of the typical (but distinct and individual) languages, voices, and texts of the novel's subjects. Puig's writing may lead us to read the text as artifice, yet to perceive through it a kind of "reality." We are therefore able to move from one reading to the other, while the text seems to resist our effort to determine whether it should be taken "seriously" or not, whether it is more one mode of writing than another. The progression toward a conclusive interpretive position is displaced by the text's turning motion which we, in our reading, must also follow.

The novel seems to take us to many such problematic moments when, in addition, the thematic roles and discursive and narrative functions of the principal characters are redefined or resituated. Again we can turn to Toto to see how this problem is raised by the novel's dialectical, ambivalent patterns and how the text thereby works against the notion of a stable identity for itself and against the image an unchanging "personality" for its fictional characters. Like Rita Hayworth and Berto, Toto shifts position in relation to other figures to whom he may also be related. (We already have the case of his relation to Berto partly described above.) He takes on what appear to be contradictory attitudes and roles in scenes, or dramas, whose thematics are remarkably similar to each other and to those that also dominate the monologues of the novel's other subjects. These shifts are orchestrated within Toto's fantasies and remembered or reported actions. They are presented not only in Toto's own chapters, but also in those of the other figures who surround him. In revealing themselves, these figures also reveal much about Toto and establish points of contact among them all.

For example, in his own monologues Toto, obsessed with two kinds of scenarios—one conflictual and infernal, the other harmonious and paradisaical—interprets real events and imagines fantasy dramas in which he, as well as some of his characters, alternate between opposing roles. In one scenario he may be the innocent object of violence of the apparent "criminal-sinner" who receives punishment from a hostile judge and authority and who is, nevertheless, also rescued by a benevolent savior. In another he may become either an active subject, whose potential for aggression not only matches but may even surpass that of his own real or imaginary victimizers, or the savior of another victim whose salvation would not be unlike his own. (See, for instance, Toto and his fictive surrogates as victimized by Berto, the "bad gypsy" et al., but saved by Mita or her surrogates, in Chapter III, and Toto as victim of Luisito, but also as judge and castigator of his own victimizer, as well as savior of Alicita, another of his rival's apparent victims, in Chapter V.)

In one story Toto may be at odds with and flee from a figure of apparent aggression, but in another he may turn out to be in harmony with and even drawn to, because he also desires, that same figure. (See, for instance, Toto's conflict with Raúl and his fantasies of their escape together, as a "couple," in Chapter V, and his fearful fantasies and attachment to Berto, or his imaginary surrogates, in both Chapters II and V.) In one scenario he may be witness to a dramatic event, but in another version he may turn out to be an actor in it. If in one drama he seems to be a main character, in another version he may be recast as either its author or its audience. (See, for instance, his shifts between the positions of authorial-narratorial figure outside and fictional character within both the film story he rewrites in Chapter XIII and the film fantasies he invents in Chapters III and V.)

As Toto moves through these positions and among these contradictory roles in his three monologues, his shifting responses and relations to other figures, both imaginary and real, are brought into view. It becomes almost impossible to fix his attitudes and positions, or even his "identity," in relation to those other entities. Moreover, those figures are made to turn just about as much as does he, the shifty subject through whom they are perceived and represented. This is precisely the kind of mobility that defines Toto as we come to view him through the eyes (and "I"s) of some of those other subjects around whom he turns. The facts relayed and the fantasies revealed by some of the other figures who speak or write in the novel seem to corroborate the oscillations produced by Toto's discourse and to highlight the same types of scenarios and relationships that Toto's monologues disclose.

Those reports present him either as the victim of some kind of attack (physical or verbal, real or imaginary) or as the agent of vindictive or jealous aggression. (See, for example, Choli's view of Toto under potential attack from Berto, in Chapter IV; Teté's fantasy of Toto drowning, in Chapter VI; Cobito's description of the attempted sexual assault on Toto by his schoolmates, in Chapter XI; Delia's revelations of Toto as verbal victim of Mita, in Chapter VII; and the anonymous, vengeful epistolary attack on him in the text of Chapter XIV. See also, for instance, Toto's fantasies of infernal punishment for his attackers at school and his verbal assault on Héctor, the "intruder" into his family, as described by Paquita in Chapter X; and his displaced physical attack on the family maid, an innocent victim of revenge, actually aimed at a dinner guest, as described by Delia, in Chapter VII.) These descriptions of Toto reveal that the position in which he is cast is, as often as not, the sign of the changing responses he provokes both in the agents of the aggressive actions directed against him and in the subjects of the verbal performances that describe him.

We cannot resolve the relations among those other subjects and Toto because we cannot determine absolutely their positions or opinions. Toto, the prime subject, is also an object of their ambivalence. The issue of conflicting and shifting responses is brought into the open by Herminia, who is the final discursive subject in the novel's story, though not in its text (we remember that Berto's 1933 letter follows Herminia's writings in Chapter XVI). Within Herminia's 1948 writings the thematics of ambivalence finally surface. In fact, they are openly addressed, significantly enough, in connection with the figure of Toto: Herminia observes that "Es notable cómo se pueden sentir cosas distintas por una misma persona o por una casa o por un lugar" ["It's remarkable that you can feel different things for the same person, or the same house or the same [place]"] and focuses on ". . . el caso de Toto para ilustrar lo que quiero decir" [". . . Toto's case . . . for illus-

trating what I mean"] (274). Her attempt to analyze Toto, to understand how he provokes disparate reactions, succeeds only in raising
the issue (". . . yo siento por él respectivamente rabia, cariño o indi-
ferencia" [". . . I . . . feel anger, affection or indifference for [him]"]
[278]), not in resolving it. At one point she seems to come to some
conclusion about his problematic "identity," i.e., his apparently ambivalent sexuality: ". . . Toto cada vez me hace recordar más a ese anti-
pático invertido [a professor at the Conservatory], está muy afeminado
de modales. Que Dios me perdone el mal pensamiento pero los veo
muy parecidos, aunque no le deseo esa desgracia . . ." [". . . Toto reminds me more and more of that unfriendly homosexual, he's very
effeminate in his ways. May God forgive me for such thoughts but
they look so much alike to me, and I don't in the least wish that mis-
fortune on him . . ."] (290). It is a conclusion that certifies the contradictions inherent in Toto, who is the object of a study that also forms
part of a self-analysis of its own ambivalent writing subject.

Not without reason does Herminia's self-interrogation focus on Toto,
the character who is most like her in Coronel Vallejos. Their discursive
relation, for example, would bear this out. Herminia reveals that, at
the time when she writes, each of them is the preferred, and perhaps
the only important, interlocutor of the other. For Toto, Herminia is "la
excepción." He explains to her that ". . . no sale con nadie, no es amigo
de nadie en Vallejos . . . porque no tiene nada de qué hablar con
nadie" ["He doesn't go out with anybody, he's not friends with anybody
in Vallejos, he says, because there's nothing he can talk about with
these people"] (274). Her text also proves that Toto is as important for
her as she apparently is for him, since her notebook pages are filled
with descriptions of and critical comments on their daily dialogues. By
virtue of their apparent distance and difference from the provincial
population of Coronel Vallejos, the "budding-artist-homosexual" and
the "spinster-piano-teacher-intellectual" share with each other the
marginal positions and perspectives of essentially solitary, even alienated, subjects.

Precisely this kind of position seems connected with the production
of discourse throughout much of the novel. As noted above, most of
the monologues are grounded in situations of loss or isolation and/or
positions of ambivalence—situations and positions that appear tied to
events or scenarios not unlike those that dominate Toto's monologues.

Many of the other characters are also concerned with questions of abandonment and betrayal (e.g., Delia, Héctor, Cobito, Teté, Esther) and themes of "crime/sin" and "punishment" (e.g., Mita, Teté, Paquita, Esther), or with scenes of violence (e.g., Héctor, Cobito, Paquita, Mita) or romance and sex (e.g., Delia, Choli, Paquita, Héctor, Esther). Like Toto, moreover, many of them appear to try to resolve their individual dilemmas through fantasy or fiction. And, like his, their monologues also call into question the possibility of their own success.

All the "solutions" offered by these subjects also point to the irresolvable, problematic situations out of which their fictions emerge. Such solutions include scenarios that all of these figures would author in order to "save" either themselves or another figure. Héctor fantasizes being a soccer hero who, in saving his team, also saves himself from obscurity—and, more immediately, from having to return to boarding school, the reality he must face ten days after his monologue in Chapter IX: "Héctor, verano 1944." Mita dreams of escape to a fictive paradise either with her newborn son, dead some five or six months in reality but resurrected in her fantasy, or with Toto, who helps her to recover from that loss through their daily "flights" into the world of film, in Chapter VIII: "Mita, invierno 1943." Some solutions involve scenes through which the subject would appear to win the object of his/her desire, sometimes by "killing off" a rival. Teté's fantasy of seeing Mita drown Toto in the bathtub would allow her to appropriate Mita as a substitute for her own sick mother, whose death she already imagines with considerable guilt, because she believes that her mother's illness originated in the moment of her own birth, in Chapter VI: "Teté, invierno 1942." Esther's search for a "savior" is obvious in her fantasies about Héctor, the object of her adolescent desire, whom she plots unsuccessfully to possess through the help of Toto; she worships Héctor's image, virtually sacrificing herself to her romantic enterprise by betraying her familial and political responsibilities, in Chapter XII: "Diario de Esther, 1947."

Others appear as dramas of intrigue, revenge, or romance in which an individual would "star" or through which s/he would virtually control the outcome of that same drama (e.g., Choli's version of herself as a "mysterious," intriguing woman in the romantic scenes from her life as a widow, a life she makes into a narrative more filmic than factual as

70

she talks to Mita in Chapter IV: "Diálogo de Choli con Mita, 1941"; Paquita's Saturday morning pre-confession memories and fantasies of romantic sexual scenes for which she is either the real or virtual protagonist, a protagonist whose performance she takes great pleasure in remembering even as she imagines the punishment it will bring, in Chapter X: "Paquita, invierno 1945"; or Cobito's verbal or physical assaults on the victims whose "elimination" in scenes of filmic or factual violence would ensure his own status as a powerful and favored subject, the real or imagined betrayal of whom must automatically bring disaster to those who would possess what he wants for himself or who would seem to plot against him, in Chapters XI and XIV, "Cobito, primavera 1946" and "Anónimo dirigido al regente del internado del Colegio 'George Washington', 1947," respectively).

At the end of each monologue each subject seems to return, or remain bound, to the material facts of his or her own life story. For example, Mita remains the mother who cannot recover, or recover from, her loss despite the films and fantasies in which she tries to take refuge. Delia must go on as the small-town woman betrayed by her own desire and destined to a solitary existence on the margins of the family units she scrutinizes in Coronel Vallejos (Chapter VII: "Delia, verano 1943"). And Héctor, the disappointed adolescent boy apparently abandoned by various family members, seems to continue to mask some of his desires with his violent language and his Don Juan posture. Each performance reveals contradictions, certain irresolvable but not incomprehensible issues, at the heart of the "identity" of each subject. The ambivalence and undecidability that seem to characterize the novel's subjects appear to originate in their own stories, yet also in the stories of others. This is most visible in everyone's relation to Toto. His presence, noted by everyone in the novel, serves as a yardstick by which to measure the positions of those around him. He circulates within their chapters not only as an object for description but also as a kind of reflector about whom none of his readers can come to any stable conclusion. This interpretive issue moves around all the novel's characters but, as we have seen, most forcefully and critically around Toto, the figure who seems to matter most to almost everyone in fiction and text alike.

When that issue is finally addressed in the fiction by Herminia's critical confessions in Chapter XV, we see another subject whose own position is problematic, even as we recognize that fact in her overt discussion of Toto, the novel's exemplary subject. Moreover, it is there that we see the text turn toward some kind of resolution, only to return us to some of the novel's initial questions. At the novel's end we see that a variety of problems remain unresolved, even though the novel also suggests that we have seen their solutions. Through the temporal and thematic inversions of Berto's letter (Chapter XVI) and the textual and thematic confessions of Herminia's writings (Chapter XV), the novel finally uncovers some "secrets" whose revelation does not, in the end, solve very much. What is revealed about the text itself, about each character and subject, only returns us to the "truth" that we first see in its title. What is revealed at the end connects with what we also learn about the star of the title, the figure whose precise position, whose exact identity, resists reduction, turning as it does till the end. What is finally revealed near and at the novel's end is also what we have already seen. And what we have already seen is the figure of a return—a return to figures at once titular and textual, fictional and real, who circulate throughout Puig's novel and (in some ways, as we shall see) prepare us for what is to come.

NOTES

1. Manuel Puig, *La traición de Rita Hayworth* (Buenos Aires: Jorge Alvarez, 1968; Buenos Aires: Sudamericana, 1970; Barcelona: Seix Barral, 1971, 1976; Havana: Casa de las Américas, 1983). All quotations are from the Seix Barral 1976 "edición definitiva"; page references appear parenthetically within the text. The novel has been translated as *Betrayed by Rita Hayworth*, trans. Suzanne Jill Levine (New York: E. P. Dutton, 1971). Unless otherwise noted, English quotations are from this edition. Puig finished writing the novel in 1965; in December it was a finalist in the Seix Barral Biblioteca Breve competition. However, because of censorship problems, he failed in his attempts to publish it then in Spain, Mexico, and Argentina. Although Gallimard agreed to publish the French translation in 1965 and *Mundo nuevo* published two chapters in 1967, the complete novel did not appear in Spanish until "a small publishing house [i.e., Jorge Alvarez] took the risk of publishing [it]," as Puig tells it in "Growing Up at the Movies: A Chronology," *Review* 4–5 (1971–72): 51 (hereafter cited as "Chronology"). See Emir Rodríguez Monegal, "A Literary Myth Exploded," also in *Review* 4–5 (1971–72): 56–64 (hereafter cited as "Myth"; first published as "*La traición de Rita Hayworth,*

una tarea de desmitificación," *Imagen* 34 [1968]: 4–6), for an assessment of the censorship situation (61).

2. The allusion to Freudian models in my chapter title, "A Familiar Romance," is, of course, intended. See Sigmund Freud, "Family Romances" (1909 [1908]), *The Standard Edition* (London: Hogarth Press, 1959): 235–41, for his discussion of the principal stages in the "neurotic's family romance." My aim here is to address a variety of the novel's interconnected features and not to focus systematically on this model, though implict and intermittent reference is made to it.

3. The titles of and the narrative forms used in the novel's chapters are as follows: Part One: I—"En casa de los padres de Mita, La Plata 1933" ["Mita's Parents' Place, La Plata, 1933"] (unmediated, direct dialogue); II—"En casa de Berto, Vallejos 1933" ["At Berto's, Vallejos, 1933"] (unmediated, direct dialogue); III—"Toto, 1939" (interior monologue); IV—"Diálogo de Choli con Mita, 1941" ["Choli's Conversation with Mita, 1941"] (hidden dialogue); V— "Toto, 1942" (interior monologue); VI—"Teté, invierno 1942" ["Teté, Winter, 1942"] (interior monologue); VII—"Delia, verano 1943" ["Delia, Summer, 1943"] (interior monologue); VIII—"Mita, invierno 1943" ["Mita, Winter, 1943"] (interior monologue). Part Two: IX—"Héctor, verano 1944" ["Héctor, Summer, 1944"] (interior monologue); X—"Paquita, invierno 1945" ["Paquita, Winter, 1945"] (interior monologue); XI—"Cobito, primavera 1946" ["Cobito, Spring, 1946"] (interior monologue); XII—"Diario de Esther, 1947" ["Esther's Diary, 1947"] (written diary pages); XIII—"Concurso anual de composiciones literarias *Tema libre*: 'La película que más me gustó', por José L. Casals, 2.° año nacional, Div. B" ["Annual Literary Essay Competition Free Subject: 'The Movie I Liked Best' by José L. Casals, Sophomore, Section B"] (written composition); XIV—"Anónimo dirigido al regente del internado del colegio 'George Washington', 1947" ["Anonymous Note Sent to the Dean of Students of George Washington High School, 1947"] (written letter); XV—"Cuaderno de pensamientos de Herminia, 1948" ["Herminia's Commonplace Book, 1948"] (written notebook pages); XVI—"Carta de Berto, 1933" ["Berto's Letter, 1933"] (written letter). See Jonathan Tittler, "*Betrayed by Rita Hayworth*: The Androgynous Text," *Narrative Irony in the Contemporary Spanish American Novel* (Ithaca: Cornell UP, 1984) 78–100, for a reading of the novel as a set of narrative units (dialogues, interior monologues, represented writings) that produce different forms of narrative irony, as well as for several points of concurrence with and difference from this study (hereafter cited as "Androgynous Text"). See also Raúl Bueno Chávez, "Sobre la enunciación narrativa: de la teoría a la crítica y viceversa (a propósito de la novelística de M. Puig)," *Hispamérica* 32 (1982): 35–47, for discussion of Puig's narrative technique in part of this novel (esp. 35–43).

4. Temporal deformation or inversion is one of the signs of the transformation of "story" (*fabula* or *fable*: events in their normal or natural chronological order) into "plot" (*sjužet/siuzhet* or *sujet*: the reordered presentation of story events). Basic discussions and applications of these terms include the following: Victor Shklovsky, "Sterne's *Tristram Shandy*: Stylistic Commentary" (1921) and Boris Tomashevsky, "Thematics" (1925), both in *Russian Formalist Criticism: Four Essays*, ed. and trans. Lee T. Lemon and Marion J. Reis (Lincoln: U of Nebraska P, 1965) 25–57 and 61–95, respectively; Victor Shklovsky, "The Mystery Novel: Dickens' *Little Dorrit*" (1925), in *Readings in Russian Poetics* 220–26; P. N. Medvedev/M. M. Bakhtin, *The Formal Method in Literary Scholarship: A Critical Introduction to Sociological Poetics* (1928), trans. Albert J. Wehrle (Baltimore: Johns Hopkins UP, 1978).

5. Puig informs us of the autobiographical details included in the novel in the following interviews: Katherine A. Bouman, "Manuel Puig at the University of Missouri-Columbia," *American Hispanist* 2.7 (1977): 11–12; Ronald Christ, "An Interview with Manuel Puig," *Partisan Review* 44 (1977): 52–61 (hereafter cited as "Interview"); Rodríguez Monegal, "Folletín"; Saúl Sosnowski, "Entrevista [a Manuel Puig]," *Hispamérica* 3 (1973): 69–80 (hereafter cited as "Entrevista"); and Danubio Torres Fierro, "Conversación con Manuel Puig: La redención de la cursilería," *Eco* 28 (1975): 507–15 (hereafter cited as "Conversación"). The most detailed account of the connections between this first novel and Puig's own story is provided in "Chronology." For example, there Puig reveals the following details, which coincide almost exactly with the facts of Toto's life: Puig was born in December 1932 in General Villegas, and between the ages of three and four he "started going to the movies almost every day at six o'clock"; in 1940 he began grammar school and was considered the "best pupil in the class after the second week"; his "life was great" until 1943, when his younger brother, just a baby, died and when "a fifteen-year-old boy tried to rape" him—consequently, he "stopped growing physically for three years"; in 1946 he started boarding school in Buenos Aires ("It was awful; the children cruel. I missed my mother tremendously") and was able to compensate for his unhappiness through the films he saw each Sunday (49). We can easily read Coronel Vallejos as a thin disguise for General Villegas; it is clear that Toto's birth in 1933 (December 1932 comes rather close, of course), as well as his obsession with the movies and film stars, his position in school, and his attachment to his mother recall the facts of Puig's early years. Moreover, the novel tells of the death of the family's second son (Chapter VIII), some schoolmates' attempts to molest Toto (Chapters VI, IX, and XI), and Toto's apparently retarded physical growth (Chapter VII). In addition, Mita, a pharmacist, and Berto, a struggling businessman, resemble Puig's description of his parents: "Mother, a city girl working as a chemist at the country

hospital, her first assignment after graduation; father of local origin, just starting his business [in 1932]" (49).

6. The distinction between "psychical" and "historical" or "material" reality made here and elsewhere in this study follows from Freud's use of those terms in *Moses and Monotheism* (1937–39).

7. The title of the English version—*Betrayed by Rita Hayworth*—privileges the *de* as a subject genitive, according to the interpretation that most speakers of Spanish would be likely to give this word. However, in so doing it erases the other position, equally valid at the level of grammar, and thereby suppresses the image of Rita Hayworth as recipient—as opposed to agent— of the treacherous action. See also Tittler, "Androgynous Text" 80, note 5.

8. For discussions of the notion of betrayal in the novel, see the following: Ricardo Piglia, "Clase media: cuerpo y destino (Una lectura de *La traición de Rita Hayworth* de Manuel Puig)," in *Nueva novela latinoamericana* 2: 350–62; Alfred J. Mac Adam, "Manuel Puig: Things as They Are," *Modern Latin American Narratives: The Dreams of Reason* (Chicago: U of Chicago P, 1977) 91–101, 130–31 (hereafter cited as "Things"); Marta Morello Frosch, "The New Art of Narrating Films," *Review* 4–5 (1971–72): 52–55 (hereafter cited as "Narrating Films"; also published as *"La traición de Rita Hayworth* o el arte nuevo de narrar películas," *Sin nombre* 1.4 [1971]: 77–82); and David R. Southard, "Betrayed by Manuel Puig: Reader Deception and Anti-Climax in His Novels," *Latin American Literary Review* 4.9 (1976): 22–28.

9. The Hollywood film referred to by Toto is a 1941 version of *Sangre y arena* (1908), the Vicente Blasco Ibáñez (Spain, 1867–1928) novel set in the world of bullfighting. The 1922 version starred Rudolph Valentino, while the 1941 film had Rita Hayworth, Tyrone Power, and Linda Darnell in the main roles. See Leslie Halliwell, *The Filmgoer's Companion*, 6th ed. (New York: Avon, 1976) 81.

10. The comments on the structures of desire informing the relationships among Puig's characters draw on René Girard's discussion of triangular and mimetic desire in both *Deceit, Desire and the Novel: Self and Other in Literary Structures* (1961), trans. Yvonne Freccero (Baltimore: Johns Hopkins UP, 1965) and "Myth and Ritual in Shakespeare: *A Midsummer Night's Dream*," in *Textual Strategies: Perspectives in Post-Structuralist Criticism*, ed. Josué V. Harari (Ithaca: Cornell UP, 1979) 189–212.

11. Cf. Mac Adam, "Manuel Puig's Chronicles of Provincial Life," *Revista hispánica moderna* 36 (1970–71): 50–65 (hereafter cited as "Chronicles"; also published as "Las crónicas de Manuel Puig," *Cuadernos hispanoamericanos* 274 [1973]: 84–107), and "Things" 91–96. Mac Adam's reading of the father/ son conflict appears to accept the stabilization of identities suggested by Toto's chapter, while Piglia's ("Clase media" 358) does not. Piglia's reading of Toto

also as a betraying subject and the text as a dialectical movement comes closest to the position of this study. See also José Miguel Oviedo, "La doble exposición de Manuel Puig," *Eco* 31 (1977): 607–26 (esp. 611, on the Toto/Berto: Tyrone Power/Rita Hayworth model; hereafter cited as "Exposición").

12. The last chapter is, of course, not the only place where the figure of the author emerges in the novel. There are indeed various signs of such authority inscribed throughout the text. For example, its chapter divisions and headings, by definition, serve as authorial indicators not only because they mark the presence of a subject who has the power to cut and combine texts in order to construct the novel, but also because they here provide nominal and temporal information from "above" the fiction, information to which the reader would otherwise have virtually no access. See note 5.

13. In "Myth" 59–60, Rodríguez Monegal connects Puig's manipulation of the novel's chapters to the techniques of detective fiction; in "Betrayed by Manuel Puig" 22–23, Southard reads this device in relation to the reader's role in the text. For Puig's description of the authorial strategy represented by this temporal inversion, see Christ, "Interview" 53–54, and Sosnowski, "Entrevista" 72.

14. See also Rodríguez Monegal, "Myth" 60.

15. Because of its temporal inversion, Puig's novel reveals the fictionality of its own apparently original scenes, since it operates in terms of a model of causality that privileges the notion of retroactive determination. This type of deferral of an interpretation is not unlike the relations and operations signalled by Freud's term *Nachträglichkeit* (or *après-coup*). On this notion of temporality or causality, see J. Laplanche and J.-B. Pontalis, "Deferred Action (*Nachträglichkeit, Après-coup*)" (1967), trans. Peter Kussell and Jeffrey Mehlman, *Yale French Studies* 48: *French Freud: Structural Studies in Psychoanalysis* (1972): 182–86. On some of the textual problems inherent in this model of temporality, see David Carroll, "Freud and the Myth of the Origin," *New Literary History* 6 (1975): 513–28.

16. See note 5 to compare headings of, for example, Chapters I, III, IX, and XV.

17. Since they are presented as discursive subjects, the novel's narrator-characters are constituted only in and by language. They therefore occupy simultaneously the positions of producer and product of represented discourse. See Emile Benvensite, *Problems in General Linguistics* (1966), trans. Mary Elizabeth Meek (Coral Gables: U of Miami P, 1971) 226–27 (hereafter cited as *Linguistics*).

18. Although Puig's characters can be read in terms of the linguistic relations that define them, it seems nonetheless impossible, as well as impractical, to view them only as grammatical functions and therefore to dismiss the

referential images created by the text. See Jonathan Culler, *Structuralist Poetics: Structuralism, Linguistics and the Study of Literature* (Ithaca: Cornell UP, 1975) 230–38, for a review of structuralist efforts to deal with this aspect of narrative fiction and the basic differences between their theories and those of other critical traditions.

19. See Benveniste, *Linguistics* 218, 228.

20. Ibid., 218. See also his "Language and Human Experience," *Diogenes* 51 (1965): 1–12.

21. Benveniste, *Linguistics* 224. "The expressions of verbal person are . . . organized by two fixed correlations" which are "*the correlation of personality* opposing *I-you* persons to the non-person *he*" and "the *correlation of subjectivity* operating within the preceding and opposing *I* to *you*" (204).

22. According to Benveniste, the "he" is a "non-personal" form precisely because it designates the one absent from the instance of discourse for which the "I" and "you" are, by definition, present. The latter two pronouns therefore always function as signs of "person," while the former is always the sign of "non-person" (*Linguistics* 197–204, 217–22).

23. Puig's novel renders highly visible the kind of "circulation" of characters and pronouns that is inherent in narrative fiction itself; see Michel Butor, *Essais sur le roman* (Paris: Gallimard, 1969) 122.

24. See Gerald Prince, "Introduction to the Study of the Narratee" (1973), trans. Francis Mariner, in *Reader-Response Criticism: From Formalism to Post-Structuralism*, ed. Jane P. Tompkins (Baltimore: Johns Hopkins UP, 1980) 7–25, for a discussion of the relations among these terms.

25. Each written text seems to adhere to the conventions of its popular form. The two letters (that of Berto, in Chapter XVI, and the anonymous one by Cobito, in Chapter XIV) address the intended receivers directly as a "you." However, while Berto names Jaime throughout the represented letter, the identity of Cobito's assumed reader is supplied only in the chapter heading that precedes his text (265). The two examples of "private" writing—Esther's diary (Chapter XII) and Herminia's notebook (Chapter XV)—are intended only for the eyes of their writers. Thus Herminia names no addressee, and Esther posits either herself (e.g., 226, 231) or the diary (e.g., 237) as her fictive interlocutor, as the "tú" to whom she writes. Toto's composition (Chapter XIII), on the other hand, is intended for an unspecified readership and therefore does not address itself to any single named receiver.

26. See Wolfgang Iser, *The Act of Reading: A Theory of Aesthetic Response* (Baltimore: Johns Hopkins UP, 1978), on the "interaction" of reader and text.

27. See Janet Gurkin Altman, *Epistolarity: Approaches to a Form* (Columbus: Ohio State UP, 1982) 117–42, for a discussion of the temporal complexities inherent in epistolary fiction.

28. See also Morello Frosch, "Narrating Films" 52, and Rodríguez Monegal, "Myth" 62–64.

29. Puig recognizes that "in many cases [he] work[s] with alienated languages," and he questions as well the notion of an authentic language ("but then, what language is not alienated?"), in Christ, "Interview" 58. In his talk with Torres Fierro he emphasizes that "la cursilería" is a phenomenon that originates in first-generation Argentines; not having had "authentic" cultural models to follow at home, they had to invent their own languages. They therefore wound up using as their models the rhetorical and "unreal" languages of popular culture. The irony of this cultural reality, which Puig says he merely wants to represent for what it is in his novels, is that "el deseo de mejorar, de acceder a otro nivel . . . [y su] ideal de fineza y elegancia sólo los conducía[n] a la cursilería" ["the desire to improve, to advance to another level . . . [and their] ideal of refinement and elegance only led them to vulgarity"] ("Conversación" 508).

30. The politics informing the position taken by Esther's diary prose, or by the authorial "voice" it might also seem to betray, are further complicated by the fact that the figure and political system to which her discourse is also connected (i.e., Peron and Peronism) are drawn from Argentina's own political history. In Esther's reverence for romantic figures of authority—epitomized by and elevated to mythic proportions in the sentimental "portrait" of the nation's paternal savior, to whom subjects such as herself would willingly sacrifice themselves (see esp. 223–24, 240–42)—we might read Puig's critique both of this leader and of the authoritarian ideology supported by his followers. This potentially parodic attack on Peron(ism) could be taken as Puig's first (and perhaps necessarily oblique) "statement" about the historico-political realities of his own times. See also Chapter 4, note 28, and Chapter 5, note 3.

31. See Borinsky, "Castration: Artifices," for a discussion of *La traición de Rita Hayworth* in terms of "the notion of *loss* as the possibility for the existence of artifice" (99).

32. Jan Mukařovský emphasizes the intersubjectivity implicit in monologue, as well as the fundamental bonds between that form and dialogue, in "Two Studies of Dialogue" (1937, 1940), in *The Word and Verbal Art: Selected Essays*, trans. and ed. John Burbank and Peter Steiner (New Haven: Yale UP, 1977) 81–115.

33. References to the siesta hour are made by a number of characters besides Toto; they serve to keep its ritual scenes circulating in the novel. Besides Toto's returns to that kind of scene in Chapters III and V, see also the chapters of Choli (IV), Teté (VI), and Mita (VIII).

34. Toto's composition does not mention the film by name, but his retelling of the composer's story can be identified as the 1938 version of the life of

Johann Strauss, Jr. (1825–99), directed by Julian Duvivier (1896–1967) and starring Fernand Gravet and Luise Rainer; see Halliwell, *The Filmgoer's Companion* 233, 594. Toto's choice of this film, as well as others he either mentions by title or "rewrites" in his monologues, seems related to, if not actually determined by, Mita's film preferences as revealed in her monologue in Chapter VIII. Cf. Mita's description of the Viennese landscape (137–38) and both of their references to *The Great Ziegfeld* (1936) (40, 44, 76–78, 140–41, 154). Both Toto's and Mita's predilection for 1930s and 1940s Hollywood films of a certain variety (i.e., sentimental or romantic movies, as well as mysteries and musicals) is evidenced by Toto's mention of the following, for example, in his own monologues (Chapters III and V) or by the reports in the monologues of Teté (VI), Delia (VII), Cobito (XI), and Esther (XII): *Romeo and Juliet* (1936), *The Story of Irene and Vernon Castle* (1939), *In Old Chicago* (1938), *Weekend in Havana* (1941), *Intermezzo* (1939), *The Constant Nymph* (1944), *Roberta* (1934), *Spellbound* (1945), and *For Whom the Bell Tolls* (1943). Puig discusses his interest in and obsession with such films of that era in "Chronology," as well as in the interviews with Bouman, Christ, Sosnowski, and Torres Fierro. He also emphasized this fact in a personal interview (22, 25 January 1979). See Andrew Sarris, "Rerunning Puig and Cabrera Infante," *Review* 9 (1973): 46–48, for comments on Puig's use of film in this novel; see René Campos, "Las 'películas de mujeres' y *La traición de Rita Hayworth*," in *Literature and Popular Culture in the Hispanic World; A Symposium*, ed. Rose S. Minc (Gaithersburg, Md.: Montclair State College and Ediciones Hispamérica, 1981) 59–67, for comments about those films from another angle.

35. Piglia reads Toto's "innocence" as his willful forgetfulness and total rejection of sexuality, and he defines his overall project as one of sexual self-negation or censure; see his "Class media" 351–54. See Ilse Adriana Luraschi, "Donde se trata de la virginidad, otros milagros y demás razones de amor y sexo en dos textos de Manuel Puig, con todo sistema" (Primera Parte), *Hispanic Journal* 1.1 (1979): 63–70, for another perspective on the question of sexuality in the novel.

CHAPTER

3

A Succession of Popular Designs:
Boquitas pintadas

Boquitas pintadas, Puig's second novel, opens with a display of death—an obituary notice that announces the demise of Juan Carlos Etchepare, the small-time, small-town Don Juan who functions as both a seductive model and a model of seduction in this text.[1] This written verification of closure on the life of the novel's protagonist seems to offer us a sign of the finite nature of a text which might otherwise appear ready and able to go on forever. Along with the proliferation of distinct narrative and discursive forms within its pages, the generic model that the formal design of *Boquitas pintadas* is supposed to replicate—the serial(ized) novel (i.e., *folletín*) named in its subtitle—suggests a text potentially out of control, a text that might threaten to regenerate itself without end.[2] Yet *Boquitas pintadas* is in many ways a controlled text, one whose constituent parts seem to have been organized and articulated by an authorial figure whose own ludic performance and position are also brought to light by it. Within this meticulously ordered network we come to see a kind of "perfect match" between thematic material and structural machinery; it works to keep things open by turning them around. Moreover, this match discloses the image of an authority who, not unlike the novel's protagonist, seems to become caught in the act of plotting maneuvers that in the end may signal his own undoing.

Boquitas pintadas can be read as a play among discursive, thematic, and structural contracts that implicate not only the authority behind but also the literary and cultural traditions that surround the text. In this second novel the articulation of thematic and textual elements derived from diverse literary, subliterary, and nonliterary models makes the novel into a meeting-ground for discourses of both "high" and "low" origin. Like Puig's other novels, this one seems to present both parodic and stylized treatments of the generic, thematic, and linguistic paradigms to which it refers. Here Puig appears to identify with and to take seriously, but also to take a distance from and to scrutinize, the many texts and traditions that are brought together in the novel. This sentimental, even tragic, view of a world whose codes are both valorized and criticized is developed by a textual authority whose efforts to demystify parts of that reality are, we could argue, also betrayed by the seductive powers of those same objects of scrutiny. Not unlike *La traición de Rita Hayworth*, *Boquitas pintadas* constructs a network of dialogues from whose ground both authorial and readerly images, as well as the fictional characters around whom they revolve, emerge as problematical, mobile fictions. The positions of all those figures turn one way or another and resist being fixed in the end.

The issues raised by and the narrative methods used in that first novel are developed in a more complex and visible fashion in this second one. Coronel Vallejos again serves as the stage upon which Puig's dramatic rendering of small-town life is presented. The demystification of life in the provinces, begun through a "study" of one of its typical families in *La traición de Rita Hayworth*, is carried on and complicated in *Boquitas pintadas*. Given that the action of both novels takes place mainly in the same town in the 1930s and 1940s, and that the first basically tells a story about childhood and the second develops a tale of young adulthood, *Boquitas pintadas*'s story can be read as both continuing and coinciding with its predecessor. The two works appear to present, from different angles, parts of the same town chronicle through which all of the main characters are connected to one another.

While the move from *La traición de Rita Hayworth* to *Boquitas pintadas* seems to be a move from a familial to a societal framework and the scope of the second text would appear to be much broader than that of the first, we also see that the relationships among the characters in one text have points of contact with those in the other. Indeed, the mysteries of family relations are explored in the first and those that construct the later, yet still limited, network of small-town society are focused on in the second. The familiar romance of *La traición de Rita Hayworth* seems to have been reinscribed within, and yet expanded to encompass, the interconnected romances of *Boquitas pintadas*. The relationships lived or invented by Toto, his family and friends are regenerated in a series of romantic and criminal intrigues that are orchestrated around, as well as by, Juan Carlos Etchepare, the novel's protagonist. Juan Carlos, whose story is also the story of Coronel Vallejos, is a contradictory and complex figure. He represents both a critique of and a challenge to the Don Juan model. He is the organizing presence of a fiction in which seduction and betrayal, fantasy and disillusionment, are the structuring principles and experiences of its characters.

A complete chronological summary of this story would take us from 1935 in Coronel Vallejos to 1968 in Buenos Aires. Though significant attention is paid to the dates of the deaths of Juan Carlos (1947) and one of his girlfriends, Nené (1968), the episodes upon which the narrative text concentrates and which are presented as its most important events unfold mainly between 1935 and 1941, when all the characters live their entangled lives together. The story is presented as a network of interconnected and concurrently developed stories that can be only partially summarized. Because of its complexity, it cannot be represented or retold in the form of a single clearly linear narrative sequence. The tale deals with the lives and loves of the protagonist and several other characters from Coronel Vallejos. Juan Carlos, his family (his mother, Doña Leonor, and his sister, Celina), his best friend (Pancho), his girlfriends and lovers (Nené, Mabel, and Elsa DiCarlo), and his acquaintance (Raba) are the figures who matter most here. All of these characters' lives are linked in such a way that to tell the story of one is to tell the story of several, or perhaps even all the others. The story of Coronel Vallejos is a web of intertwining lives (here that means essentially the lies told, the loves won, and the losses suffered), constructed from the typical actions and activities that serve to fill up, and even kill, time in the provincial world of the era.

Boquitas pintadas is, however, not only a chronicle of life in the provinces. It is also a tale of romantic intrigues whose sentimental portraits and episodes, as well as dramatic maneuvers and turns, remind us that this text is also about other texts and, particularly, about forms of "high" and "low" art and culture. In episodes reminiscent of

Golden Age and nineteenth-century drama, as well as tragic-ironic tango sketches and episodic soap opera intrigues, Juan Carlos and his partners in romance and treachery become the points of convergence for all kinds of traditions and models with which the novel engages in dialogue. The novel's dealings with a literary legend or cultural myth (i.e., the Don Juan figure) and a specific form of popular art (i.e., the *folletín*) are of particular importance here. The development of those dialogues establishes a paradoxical but apparently perfect match between the various performances within and around the fiction.

It is evident from the first chapter—or, rather, installments; we should remember that the novel repeatedly asserts its generic origins in all sixteen chapter headings, where the word *entrega* appears—that the narrative techniques of the novel are also manipulative strategies deployed by an author whose relation to the reader is as significant as the relationships among its fictional characters.[3] Like some of Puig's other work, *Boquitas pintadas* is a complex and variegated text that presents several kinds of reading problems. These problems concern readerly interpretation as well as performance. The novel's text is composed through the juxtaposition, or virtual grafting together, of a set of anecdotally related but formally and discursively dissimilar texts.[4] Each of the novel's sixteen chapters appears as a collection of diverse narrative techniques and forms of discourse. Moreover, in many segments, or even whole chapters, there is little or no mediation by an organizing, privileged narrator. This novel represents well the narrative heterogeneity characteristic of Puig's work. Included in *Boquitas pintadas* are letters, diary entries, magazine and newspaper articles, official (legal, medical, police, and government) documents. In addition, there are interior monologues, dreams and stream-of-consciousness segments, hidden dialogues, immediate direct dialogues, and a variety of texts in which an undramatized omniscient narrator reports on the characters' actions and thoughts, or describes objects and places of significance within the fiction.

Given the fragmentary nature of the text and the intermittent appearance of an omniscient narrator within only some of its sections, there seems to be no position from which an immediately accessible narrative unity might be offered the reader. Rather, it is the reader's task to bridge the various gaps among separate texts and distinct modes of discourse, continually to shift perspective on and change his/

her relation to that text in order to follow and understand its movements—that is, in order to domesticate and control it.[5] Readers' abilities to understand, and thus master, the relationships among all of the
text's fragments also depend on their capacity for perceiving and overcoming the disjunctions between story and plot. These disjunctions
are created mainly by the temporal inversions and nominal, as well as
narrative, elisions that proliferate throughout the novel's pages. A
reading of *Boquitas pintadas* entails an engagement or dialogue with
a textual strategist who plays with, by also regulating, the reader's
desire for knowledge. That desire is periodically satisfied, yet sustained, by the narrative tactics deployed by two textual authorities
(i.e., the authorial figure and the narrating surrogate, the omniscient
narrator who intervenes only sporadically). Both of them control our
appropriation of the text by offering at once too much and too little
information about the novel's fictional events and characters. What will
be of particular interest here is that this play between authorial and
readerly desires, as well as performances, is connected in two significant ways with the story around which that relationship is developed.
The story of *Boquitas pintadas*, we remember, is a tale of romance and
mystery whose anecdotal complexity is, in its own way, equaled by the
complicated narrative structure and devices used to present it. And,
in their plays for power and pleasure, the novel's main characters offer
themselves as fictive analogues for the textual figures who appear to
hover over them on either "side" of the text.

In Puig's representation of Coronel Vallejos and its characters (and
especially in what could be called his "anatomy of the Don Juan/macho
syndrome") we see the development of a variety of plots aimed at
pleasure and power. These plots are typical of the popular forms of
culture from which the novel's episodes, characters, and languages
seem to be drawn; moreover, they represent (as Puig would assert) the
provincial reality dissected in it.[6] Those interconnections might be
discovered within the various plays with and around the question of
knowledge. The facts about the characters' secrets—their romantic,
and even criminal, entanglements—are disclosed in such a way that
we cannot put them all in place until we have completed the novel.
The revelation of important details is regulated so as to control our
access to the novel both as narrative structure and as fictional story.
We are only gradually shown and eventually, or finally, allowed to see

all the causes and consequences of the relations among the principal figures: Nené, Juan Carlos, Mabel, Pancho, and Raba. To work out the relationships interconnecting these principal characters would mean to diagram a set of parallel, yet crisscrossing, paths among them—paths that would remind us of the impossibility of sketching a neat diachronic account of their (inter)actions.

We cannot present that complex narrative pattern as a strict chronology of actions because it is actually a set of separate, but conjoined, relations among its actors. However, we can avail ourselves of the nominal sequence employed above (i.e., Nené, Juan Carlos, Mabel, Pancho, Raba) to chart a path through their relationships and to translate into a linear form the text's synchronic narrative web.[7] Through this series of names, the secret seductions and betrayals that inform the characters' movements are brought to light by the very order and grouping it overtly displays. Here we see the men surrounded by the women they desire and/or reject, and the women linked to the men they agree, or are forced, to love and/or leave.

We see Juan Carlos embraced, as it were, on one side by Nené. She is the girlfriend he tries but fails to seduce during their courtship in 1937 in Coronel Vallejos; she is the one who, in her own way, remains faithful to him until 1968, when she dies and the text ends. On the other side he is held by Mabel. She is his secret lover and partner in deception from 1935 to 1937; she is the girl who almost outdoes him at his own game when, in 1939, while Juan Carlos is away at a sanatorium, she takes up with his best friend. Pancho, Juan Carlos's friend, "student," and imitator (who also becomes his rival through his secret affair with Mabel) is flanked on one side by Raba, the servant girl he succeeds in seducing on 26 April 1937, but whom he quickly abandons after fathering her child, born on 27 January 1938; she is the one who avenges his various betrayals of her by murdering him on the night of 17 June 1939 as he leaves Mabel's bedroom. On the other side he is supported by Mabel, the girl who, having become his secret lover, operates as his accomplice in the betrayals of both Raba and Juan Carlos.

This brief description of the relationships among the main characters and the events that constitute the novel's story points up the difficulty of transforming the novel's plot (*sujet*) into story (*fable*). It reveals the real limits of an attempt to represent the characters' simultaneous re-

lations as a totally linear narrative.[8] In *Boquitas pintadas* we are reminded that to talk about story is to talk about the simultaneity of that
story's intertwined elements; to represent its story is to implicate its
plot. The story's complexity also suggests that to read this text is to see
how it both creates and fills in gaps of information. Through the exaggerated manipulation of structural and discursive forms, as well as
anecdotal details—the very elements that make difficult, of course,
the reader's perception of the text as a comprehensible chronology—
the promise of a solution for the complicated structure emerges. In
the reading process, the multi-directional nature of the story, as well
as the plot, is continually asserted, and the question of knowledge is
renewed (even though it is also intermittently resolved) throughout
the text.

Boquitas pintadas self-consciously underscores, and forces the
reader to recognize, that the process of reading and moving forward
in the text involves multiple activities that take us in many directions.
Puig's novel emphasizes that to read always means to look everywhere
at once. It is to process and select information to be retained or high-
lighted. It is to make, as well as to perceive, both syntagmatically and
paradigmatically, textual and anecdotal connections. It means to be
with, yet always behind and attempting to catch up with, or even to
move ahead of, the text that is all the while moving us along.[9] Our
acquisition of knowledge is both impeded and permitted through the
complex manipulation of diverse discursive and narrative forms and
the confusing presentation of anecdotal details. Such a text manages
to ensnare its readers in its complicated fictional network while also
displaying throughout its pages both the artificial nature of that story
and the artifice through which it is produced and represented.

When the differences between story and plot in *Boquitas pintadas*
are discerned, it becomes clear that the complexities of the one are
analogous to those of the other. In the temporal inversions through
which the disparity between the time of writing and/or narration and
the time of the story is disclosed, for example, we can see how the text
works to delay our perception of textual and fictional "truths." The
temporal plays are extended both across the entire text—that is,
throughout the inversion and rearrangement of the story's events
across the novel's sixteen chapters—and within smaller narrative units
(i.e., within individual chapters or chapter segments) through which,

moreover, the manipulation of individual texts repeats in microcosmic form the novel's larger patterns and strategic moves.[10]

The major temporal inversion through which *Boquitas pintadas*'s essentially anachronistic quality is developed is not unlike that of mystery fiction: it initially moves us back in time, instead of immediately and directly forward. The narrative text begins in 1947, when Juan Carlos dies and his obituary appears in a local paper. This text's appearance sets in motion the epistolary activity of one of his former girlfriends, Nené, who initiates a correspondence with Juan Carlos's family. Chapters I and II contain both the obituary notice and Nené's letters to Doña Leonor, Juan Carlos's mother. Chapters III through XII lead us back to all of the significant events and the complicated web of relations of the 1930s. In chapters composed of combinations of diverse narrative and discursive forms, mentioned earlier, the relationships among the principal characters—those among Juan Carlos and all his girlfriends, family members, and friends; those between Pancho and Mabel, or between Raba and Pancho, or among Nené, Mabel, Raba, and Celina—are developed and described. In Chapters XIII-XV the text moves us forward in time to the 1940s. Chapters XIII-XIV focus on scenes a few years after Nené's marriage and immediately preceding Mabel's; Chapter XV describes Juan Carlos's death, returning us to the temporal frame of the novel's first chapter. The last *entrega*, which can be read as an epilogue, jumps ahead some twenty years, to Nené's death in 1968, and gives us information about the situation and status of each character, dead or alive, at that time. Like several kinds of mystery texts, especially the detective genre (which Puig later rewrites in *The Buenos Aires Affair*, and to which the first two novels also pave the way), *Boquitas pintadas* traces a circular, as well as inverted, temporal route around scenes and reports of death as it winds its way through episodes of romantic and, finally, criminal intrigue.[11] The return to the fatal point of departure appears to signal something like a closure, an understanding of and solution to all of the novel's problems.

This principal temporal play is buttressed and further complicated by what we can call localized temporal inversions within individual sections, chapters, and chapter fragments. Moreover, a proliferation of flashbacks, fantasies, and prophetic statements reveals the intricate combination of structurally analeptic and proleptic movements generating the novel.[12] For example, in Chapter III a text from 1935 is placed after two from 1937; at the end of Chapter VII a letter dated 23 August 1937 is read after several from April of that same year, though it precedes texts in Chapters VII and VIII that are dated July and early August 1937; and in Chapter III (the narrative unit in which the August 1937 letter from Chapter VII "belongs") we read both a medical report dated 11 June 1937, whose "correct" place seems to be in Chapter VI, and a police document, written on 29 July of the same year, whose "proper" place is between two letters juxtaposed in Chapter VII. The temporal operation that spans at least two decades of the novel's story is complicated further and mirrored by the same kind of inversion within individual, and sometimes contiguous, chapters. All of these maneuvers signal the controlling and confusing presence of a textual subject whose movements, we shall see, are not unlike those of some of the subjects over whom his powers are apparently exercised.

The novel's temporal complexity is generated not only at the level of authorial activity. The work of the narrator and of the characters within the fiction compounds these complicated temporal structures. The authorial manipulation of the localized and intercalated inversions works with the temporal superimpositions that are effected within some of the characters' own discourse. For instance, although Nené's letters to Doña Leonor in Chapters I and II are dated 12 May through 12 August 1947, thus coinciding with, as well as following from, the date of Juan Carlos's death, her texts also represent a temporal regression to the 1930s. Nené in fact writes as much about that past decade—about how and where "Todo empezó" ["It all began"] (23)—as she does about the one in which she lives while she writes. Her epistolary activity, her graphic self-representation, manages both to mark and to efface the distance between her time of writing (1947) and the time about which she writes (the 1930s). Her writing returns (us) to another temporal and spatial frame into which she herself is also absorbed. But at the same time, as she comments upon the nostalgic gaps between the past and present eras, the differences and distances between them are stressed.[13] The analeptic movement within Nené's written discourse represents a proleptic movement within the discourse of the whole novel. Because of the novel's major temporal inversion, Nené's letters take us back to a time that is yet to come in the story but to which, paradoxically, we will continue to return throughout most of the novel's pages. Nené's retrospective leap is followed by a movement forward as she narrates to Doña Leonor her own life story up to the moment in which she writes. The movement backward and forward in these initial chapters is precisely the syntactic pattern to be articulated in all the novel's episodes.

From those first chapters onward the novel's narrative route is developed as an intricate path among texts that seem to jump ahead and back, texts that summarize and encapsulate the passing of time and texts that select and bracket specific, and apparently significant, temporal instances. For example, the narrator's "Recapitulación" (a technique typical of serial fiction) at the beginning of Chapter IX (127–28) provides a synoptic regression to events that immediately precede the opening of the second part of the novel, while the omniscient, camera-eye description of Juan Carlos's photo album in Chapter III (35–39) and the hidden dialogue that provides a fortune-teller's "reading" of Juan Carlos's future in Chapter VI (85–92) give us premature, proleptic summaries of events in the protagonist's life. In addition, the minutely detailed description of Mabel's bedroom in Chapter III ("*Dormitorio de señorita, año 1937*," 39–46) summarizes the present appearance of that scene; it is a scene that also reveals part of Mabel's own story through the objects seen by the omniscient spectator-narrator. The narrator's series of textually consecutive but anecdotally simultaneous descriptions of the main characters' activities on specific, and sometimes significant, dates—23 April 1937 (each character's situation as a desiring or designing subject is set up), 27 January 1938 (Raba's child is born), 18 April 1947 (Juan Carlos dies), 15 September 1968 (Nené dies)—at once freeze and repeat time in Chapters IV-V, IX, XIV, and XV, respectively.

The elision of information, especially nominal details, is as important as the temporal rearrangement of the events in the novel. The mysteries of *Boquitas pintadas* have as much to do with the difficulty of identifying all the participants in the story's episodes as with understanding the nature and order of the events themselves. Moreover, secrets are kept within the fiction, by and among the fictional characters, as well as around it, by the mediating subjects who seem to control the whole text and the readers who try to follow it. The disparity between the positions of reader and author is underscored, for example, in the shifts among and returns to narrative techniques such as hidden dialogue (85–92: gypsy fortuneteller and "Juan Carlos"; 201–6: Mabel and "priest") and immediate, direct dialogue (145–54: Nené and Raba; 154–58: Mabel and Pancho; 179–83: Celina and the widow DiCarlo; 223–30: Doña Leonor and Celina). In these sections the problem of identity is raised and resolved rather quickly. Although the identity of the interlocutors is kept from the reader's immediate view (as we recall, in hidden dialogue the discourse of one of the subjects is suppressed from the text, and the names of both speakers are left out of its margins; in immediate, direct dialogue only the names of the interlocutors are elided from the text), the represented discourse also contains the identity of its own subject and that of the addressee to which it responds. The subjects cannot but reveal themselves through references to facts already known to us; they cannot but identify, directly or indirectly, their interlocutors when they are addressed.

The duration of the mysteries themselves is often short lived because the discourse not only refers to the instance of production (the exchange between interlocutors seen either partially or entirely in the text), but also refers us back to other texts, other bits of information already revealed within the novel. It therefore allows, even demands, that we look everywhere for the solutions to these nominal puzzles. Nevertheless, such texts point up the gaps between the knowledge held by author and reader, and the inherently ignorant position of the latter. The reader must try to catch up with an authority who already knows what is strategically suppressed, however briefly, by the narrative text. The reader therefore is bound to the text and its author by tactics that both promise and postpone knowledge. To read the novel is to (have to) allow oneself to be led along—perhaps seduced and betrayed as well—by a text that plays with one's desire and by a strategist who seems to be aware of the possible relations between knowledge and power.[14] We can already see that the structure of this dialogue involves the kinds of positions and patterns, actions and attitudes, that inform the novel as a whole.

The reader is not the only subject who wants or needs to know all that goes on in Coronel Vallejos. The novel is propelled by interlocking anecdotal and textual secrets that deal as much with the question of "who" as with "what." In fact, the principal problems of nomination that face the reader are also the best-kept secrets within the fiction.

The question of the identity of Juan Carlos's 1930s secret lover (i.e., Mabel) circulates as a compelling and even criminal puzzle to be solved by those on both sides of the text. While this is not the only secret kept throughout much of the novel, and "Mabel" is by no means the only hidden name within its story, the identification of this "mystery woman" is an exemplary enigma. Its solution, in fact, would solve only some of the novel's problems. Mabel's identity, hidden from us as an absolute fact until she makes a confession of this "sin" (along with others) in the hidden dialogue with a priest in Chapter XIV (we have information to suggest but not to verify this fact earlier in the text; see, for example, 40–44, 65, 72), and hidden from the fictional characters who surround her and Juan Carlos in Coronel Vallejos (e.g., from Celina and Doña Leonor, who, believing that a woman is responsible for Juan Carlos's death, privately accuse the innocent Nené, who also expresses her own interest in finding the culprit; 33), is a central but not unique "truth" with which the text plays.

This information cannot be separated from the facts about the secret pacts and promises, the hidden pleasures and powers, that are at work throughout *Boquitas pintadas*. However, this case does reveal some of the strategies deployed both around the text and within the fiction. It underlines the temporal structure that informs their designs—the temporality of truth. In this novel it is not just the elision of a name that arouses curiosity and impels hermeneutical activity. It is also the apparent revelation of truth—the inscription of names or images— that serves to arouse our suspicion even while seeming to offer solutions.[15] Here, as in mystery fiction, the route to truth is linear and direct, as well as circular and oblique. Only "after the fact," through a process of retroactive determination, can something like a verifiable truth be established. Moreover, only "after the fact" are we able to see that the truth that seems to be hidden from view is actually already visible. The artful and strategic cutting and combining of narrative fragments, as well as the deletion and inclusion of significant names, serve to both elide and reveal such truths not only within the text, but also within the fiction.

For example, in Chapters IV and V, wherein the activities of the five main characters on 23 April 1937 are described, the identification of Mabel as (one of) Juan Carlos's lover(s) is suggested and yet put into question by the juxtaposition of their texts. The cutting devices that interrupt the flow of anecdotal information (e.g., the cutting off of Juan Carlos's section at the moment when he is to meet his midnight lover) also provide us with important pieces of a puzzle. When assembled, these pieces seem to fit into a neat and "correct" pattern, revealing the figure of Mabel (see esp. the end of Chapter IV and the beginning of Chapter V, 65 and 72). However, the "truth" at which we might arrive is also complicated and concealed by additional information. That information offers possibilities beyond, or even contrary to, what is already apparently certified by the text (for example, the juxtaposition of Mabel's and Pancho's sections, through which their entanglement is "predicted" by the text in Chapter V; see also 46, 65).

The provocative parallel between this kind of technical apparatus or structural machinery and the fiction of seduction supported by it is indeed significant. The text that is orchestrated to seduce and betray its readers, perhaps even to control and to please them, presents a story of romantic intrigue wherein strategic arts and artful strategies are also emphasized. This convergence of fictional and textual plots also discloses a convergence of similar patterns of desire and power. In *Boquitas pintadas* the reader who is lured on by, and thus agrees to submit to, the plays of romantic mystery is the reader whose desire to find out the truth is fundamentally the desire to learn all the details about the desires of others. The authority who apparently sets up the text, constructing its erotic and political fictions, is the authority who would seem to desire a certain control over (and at the same time agree to play with) the reader upon whom his own projected power, and perhaps even pleasure, must also depend. Their dialogue is, to say the least, provocative.

The coincidence of these patterns of textual and fictional desire, the play between readerly and authorial positions, as well as the tactics designed to satisfy or sustain them, should not susprise us. As we realize from the beginning of *Boquitas pintadas*, Puig's novel pretends to be an example of the very genre whose thematic designs are, by convention, likely to lead us to romance and mystery and through scenes of seduction and betrayal; the genre in which the author-reader dialogue, and thus its politics and pleasures, are put into relief—that is, the *folletín*. One of the most problematic aspects of Puig's version of the popular form is that it appears to do the impossible. Contrary to what the novel's subtitle and the word *entrega* in each chapter's heading would affirm, *Boquitas pintadas* lacks the apparent *sine qua non* of serial fiction. Given that the text's installments are not, in fact, installments—they are not separated by the regular temporal gaps that would help to produce the kind of indeterminacy typical of the genre—and, given that the reader's appropriation of the text is thus coincident with, but not determined (i.e., postponed or regulated) by, the temporality of publication, as is the custom of serial fiction, *Boquitas pintadas* also renders impossible the identity that its subtitle and chapter headings insist upon affirming.[16]

Yet this impossibility is obscured by that very same text. Through the complex defamiliarization of an originally complicated story, and through the spatialization of temporal and narrative gaps achieved by that same deformation, Puig's novel is able to (re)produce the problematic special effects of the very genre it names.[17] The gaps of indeterminacy created by the temporal inversions and elisions of significant details, the juxtaposition of dissimilar narrative techniques and texts, and the absence of a single, continously represented narratorial or authorial position within the novel all serve to place its readers in positions characteristic of their role in "real" serial fiction.[18] Although we know that the story must soon end because we are presented with a finite textual object (the book itself) in the first pages of which we are already told of the protagonist's own end, Puig's novel would appear to resist acknowledging that fact. It seems to be able to (make us) forget its own originally fatal text (i.e, the obituary notice—the sign of the protagonist's death and the text's future closure) and the limits of its own pages, as well as the clearly visible contiguity of all of its "installments."

To a certain extent, then, Puig's version of a *folletín* is grounded in and made possible by the way the novel works against closure, the way it seems to keep its fiction and text open and ongoing. This apparent lack of finality is also derived from and supported by its dialogues with other texts and traditions, dialogues through which the problem of defining endings, or closing off the novel, is raised in several ways at once. This intertextual web is analogous to that of the complex relations among the novel's narrative fragments and its fictional characters. The effects produced by the novel's temporal complexities, even within separate chapters, seem to be matched by the moves among the textual fragments whose connections to diverse thematic, discursive, and narrative models form those dialogues. The linear movement from one *entrega* to another calls into play a variety of shifts within individual chapters and across the whole novel, shifts that take us in several directions at the same time. In Puig's *folletín* the temporal gaps among installments are transformed into and disseminated within all kinds of ruptures within story and text alike. The novel breaks with and yet attaches itself to diverse models of language and narrative technique. It also produces breaks and bridges within its own progression toward a deceptive kind of closure. This progression develops as a multilayered fabric of dialogues that follow and unfold with one another.

The most significant dialogues through which *Boquitas pintadas* works involve the generic and thematic paradigms that seem to meet as the novel's "perfect match": the *folletín* and the Don Juan figure. The self-conscious reworkings of that form and figure are, in a way, analogous. Puig seems to keep alive both the subliterary model and the legendary character by deforming and yet perpetuating the basic relationship that defines each of them. Juan Carlos and Puig's serial novel deviate in similar ways from the models from which they seem to be generated. The powerful effects of these paradigms are produced by, and their provocative dialogue is created through, that same deviation. In fact, the recuperation of the *folletín* and the potential attack on the Don Juan figure are concurrent with and entirely dependent upon one another.[19] The genre from which Puig's novel is clearly distanced is also the one it succeeds in regenerating. The legendary figure killed off in the novel's first pages, wherein his ultimate demise is both prefigured and promised, is also the very figure that the text succeeds in resurrecting. Both models are at once suppressed, because also replaced, and revived by their new versions.

It is not only in the interplay of potentially recuperative and repressive operations that we can see Juan Carlos as a provocative match for the textual apparatus that carries him along, or Puig's *folletín* as a suggestive vehicle for the story of a provincial and popular Don Juan character. In addition, some original structural analogues between the life of a Don Juan and the *folletín*'s basic pattern, as well as parallel changes in those models, are displayed by Puig's novel. As we know, the backbone of the serial(ized) novel and the legendary figure's classic biography is, as the popular genre's name in English reminds us, the notion of a series. This pattern informs both the story told and the method of telling. The latter is crucial for and exaggerated in the popular text.

Puig works with a paradox inherent in the serial progression itself. The diachronic movement that underlies the notion of a series as we see it developed in the *folletín* and the Don Juan story is also a movement of repetition and return. Given the typicality of the scenes and relationships, as well as narrative devices, that make up popular serial fiction, and given how erotic relations of the Don Juan character are similar to, and thus potential repetitions of, one another, we can see that in these series (and serials) there is little or no fundamental progression. Puig has transformed into an essentially synchronic network of relations the typically successive and serial events, as well as the temporally spaced episodes, at the heart of the models with which he works. In so doing, he both differentiates his story and text from their apparent sources and highlights, by returning us all to, the very essence of the fictions and narrative patterns that originally determine those models.

While the novel's deviation from these models calls attention to the distances between "original" and "secondary" texts, and thereby uncovers the reflexive, critical treatment of the former by the latter, the reworking of those textual and cultural models remystifies them as well. The significance of *Boquitas pintadas*'s intertextual dialogues is disclosed precisely within this double operation and contradictory movement. The inherently ambivalent features of the novel—features produced by maneuvers that are apparently both parodic and stylizing in intent or effect—make questionable the possibility of closing off or entirely resolving either its text or its fiction.[20] Not unlike the turns and paradoxes that support *La traición de Rita Hayworth*, those in *Boquitas pintadas* reveal that the novel's position, as well as the image of authority behind it, are difficult if not impossible to pin down. In Puig's treatment of the serial novel and the Don Juan figure we see two connected and apparently disparate movements superimposed in a text that seems to produce, or call for, a redoubled set of contradictory readings of those models. We can read the novel as an homage to the serial form (that is, as a stylization) or as a critical analysis of the Don Juan figure (that is, as a parody).

In the end, each of these possibilities is also betrayed. *Boquitas pintadas* simultaneously turns what may be intended as a tribute to the serial novel into a critical evaluation and what may be plotted as a critique of the Don Juan syndrome into a remystification. The reflexive distance from the textual and cultural models effects a critical commentary on each of them. The involvement with and entrapment by them effaces that distance. Let us first consider the case of the popular genre. If we want to read the novel as a revaluation of the subliterary genre that Puig "rescues" from its "lowly" position, we must also take into account, and perhaps consider privileging, the parodic results of that enterprise. As theorized earlier, the effort to treat the model as an equal, so to speak, would raise it to a respectable position. However, the mechanisms through which that inversion of its status could be produced would also have the power to make that model so estranged—from both its "old" and "new" positions—that it could also be put "down" by them. On the other hand, if we feel it must be read as a parody—that the distance taken from the object is, in the first place, an essentially critical one; that it is indeed being kept "down" in its originally "low" position while also being raised "up" to a place from which it can be seen—then we must reconsider those effects as being both recuperative and critical. The distance taken from the "low" object would move it in another direction—"up," to where it could be rescued from the forces that otherwise would seem to suppress it.

In the case of the Don Juan figure at least two such contradictory readings are also possible. This case may be more complicated, since the original position of the model is based as much on popular opinion as on tradition. If the Don Juan is viewed as a figure still idolized by Western culture in his modern incarnation as the "macho" lover (as Puig believes), then Puig's novel would seem to want to bring him "down" by parodying his strategies and secrets. This parody would, as we know, carry with it a certain reinvestment of that figure's powers. (These are powers that a stylization would more directly seek to assert.) On the other hand, if this figure is taken as one who has, in fact, lost all his powers in his modern incarnations, then he would serve as yet another "low" model around which would circulate the same paradoxes, of either parody or stylization, as postulated for the serial novel.[21] The problem in Puig's novel is that the text (and we, in moving with and responding to it) seems to (have to) turn in all those directions at once. Stylization, or what can be read as such, seems to be more and less than stylization; parody, or what can be read as such, seems to be more and less than parody. The apparent unstable combinations of these forms of double-voiced discourse manage to superimpose and confuse the aims and effects of a text whose basic ambivalence and simultaneous turns in different directions are brought to light by their equalizing and inversionary, democratic and revolutionary, mechanisms.

. *Boquitas pintadas* is a particularly suggestive and problematic novel precisely because of its complex treatments of the *folletín* and the Don Juan figure—the "popular" models that are put into dialogue with each other throughout its pages. If, for the sake of argument, we consider the novel as an attempt at stylization of the serial form and the world of popular culture—that is, if we accept Puig's denial of any parodic intention regarding the genre, thereby acknowledging the text's successful and serious recuperation of the subliterary form through the development of its experimental narrative devices and strategies— then we can see that Puig's novel also betrays itself by rescuing not only the originals to be raised "up" but also those apparently to be put "down."[22] We must remember that the protagonist who seems so well suited for the popular serial form deemed worthy of its own "salvation" may be precisely the figure in whose critical evaluation the text also seems to be engaged. If *Boquitas pintadas* offers itself as a kind of "anatomy of donjuanism" and a critique of the privileged position of the macho male, it also manages to remystify that same object of its analysis and attack. We realize that, although Juan Carlos's strategies for deception are laid bare and thus a devaluation of the powerful and original model, the legendary figure and myth, is accomplished through the portrait of a small-time, small-town version, it is also his glorification—his powerful ascent—that the novel generates.[23]

This kind of paradox is inherent in any text that seems primarily parodic, as noted earlier. However, in *Boquitas pintadas* the superimposition of stylizing and parodic maneuvers, or the possibility of reading the novel as developing both at once, also turns each of those forms of double-directed speech back on itself, transforming each into a doubly dialectical and ambivalent process. Here the seductive powers of the Don Juan figure are seemingly dissected and judged by an authorial manipulator who also disseminates his own powers and spreads his practices among other fictional entities in the novel. They are figures who help to perpetuate his position of textual privilege and pleasure. But this is a position that seems to be as unstable as the text it would support. Let us turn to Juan Carlos himself, as well as to the story he helps to write, so as to examine how this mobile dialogue between popular legend and literary model develops and, in particular, how the novel turns around, while also connecting, these powerful traditions to which it refers.

That Juan Carlos is cast in the mold of a long line of Don Juan figures and that the novel displays that link in a number of ways is suggested by the following: early descriptions of Juan Carlos as "muy mujeriego" ["a real woman-chaser" (trans. mine)] (41); descriptions of his strategies for seduction and deception (e.g., 64, where the narrator tells of his consciously designed plan for seducing Nené and describes ". . . las maniobras que infaliblemente la seducirán como habían seducido a muchas otras" [". . . the tactics that would infallibly seduce her as they had seduced many others"]); mention of his own cliché version of himself (on 64 we are told that Juan Carlos ". . . pensó en el picaflor que deja una corola para ir a otra, y de todas liba el néctar . . ." [". . . thought of a hummingbird who leaves one blossom to go to another, sipping the nectar from all of them . . ."]); accounts of his relationships with his "sidekick" Pancho, who warns him of the dangers inherent in his amorous activities (on 76 we are told that ". . . Pancho le dijo que tuviera cuidado con ser descubierto en casa ajena . . ." [". . . Pancho told him to be careful not to get caught in somebody else's house . . ."]), and to whom, while openly plotting his adventures, he silently declares his willingness to sacrifice himself for passion to avoid a life of poverty (on 61–62 Juan Carlos secretly thinks, ". . . si tenía que renunciar a vivir como los sanos prefería morirse, pero que aunque no le quitasen las mujeres y los cigarrillos lo mismo prefería morirse, si era a cambio de trabajar como un animal todo el día por cuatro centavos para después volver a un rancho a lavarse bajo el chorro de agua fría de la bomba" [". . . if he had to give up living like healthy people he'd rather die, but that even if they didn't take his women and cigarettes away he'd rather die if it was in exchange for working like a dog the whole day for three pennies and then going home to a shack to wash up under the cold water of a pump"]; see the description of Pancho's daily life on 72–78); the representation of his defiance of authority, either religious (e.g., 48) or medical (e.g., 60); his dream of death and salvation by a woman destined to serve and save him (113); the explicit naming of the legendary figure in the title of the first tango ("Don Juan," 92) to be played at the 1937 town fair, around which several romantic plots develop, not only for Juan Carlos but also for the novel's other characters. Through these references in the text Juan Carlos and his story enter into dialogue with the popular legendary figure of Don Juan, as well as with the literary tradition through which that model has emerged and developed.[24]

Not unlike the narrative and anecdotal patterns followed in Juan Carlos's story itself, this dialogue is a kind of regressive progression that brings back to life, in a way, some traditional versions of the Don Juan figure and his legendary-literary story. *Boquitas pintadas* combines and superimposes those versions so that their final "positions" are left suspended. The question of just who or what is the subject or object of the text's recuperative and critical work seems to run throughout the novel. It comes to an emblematic—at once open and closed—finale in the novel's last pages. These final moments are significant in that they do, but also don't, close things off. They take us back into the text which, though seeming to resolve itself, remains, like them, suspended between one kind of end and another. In those final pages we see the apparent "salvation" of Juan Carlos and the Don Juan model. Yet, at the same time, both of these figures seem to be not only saved but also condemned.

Juan Carlos's final appearance is with Nené, the woman who sets out to recover him from her own past and his death. They are brought together in a scene that appears to both redeem and punish them. In that scene, moreover, each appears as a mobile actor in an ending not unlike those in which some important literary predecessors have become known to us (i.e., those that close Tirso de Molina's *El burlador de Sevilla* [1630] and José Zorrilla's *Don Juan Tenorio* [1844]). In the burning of Nené's and Juan Carlos's 1937 love letters by Nené's husband, Massa, in the fiction (per her instructions, Massa destroys the letters by throwing them into the incinerator after her death; 241) and in the revelation of pieces of Juan Carlos's letters by the omniscient narrator in the text (the novel's final page is composed of fragmentary sentences supposedly made visible only to this all-seeing eye) we witness the couple's final reunion. However, this reunion is at the same time another separation.

This last appearance by Juan Carlos and Nené is at once a romantic ascent and an infernal descent for each of them. It makes it impossible to place, or decide upon a final place for, not only Juan Carlos and Nené, but also the text of *Boquitas pintadas*. The novel works out a double inversion of the two most famous but opposing Hispanic endings to the life of a Don Juan. The one seems to cancel the other through their mutually parodic and stylizing meeting. In this final scene the figure of Juan Carlos cannot be separated from that of Nené, the woman whose writing sets in motion and whose death brings to a close the novel through which he is resurrected. She is the initial and final agent of his recovery, a recovery that is essentially textual. In fact, the immediate route to Juan Carlos's last appearance next to Nené is mainly described as a meeting of texts: "Las cartas atadas con la cinta rosa [those written by Nené to Juan Carlos in 1937 and returned to her by him that same year] cayeron al fuego y se quemaron sin desparramarse. En cambio el otro grupo de cartas, sin la cinta celeste que lo uniera [the letters written by Juan Carlos to Nené in 1937 and returned to him by her that same year, but sent back to her by his sister in 1947], se encrespaba al quemarse y se desparramaba por el horno incineratorio. Se soltaban las hojas y la llama que había de ennegrecerlas y destruirlas antes las iluminaba fugazmente. . . ." ["The letters tied in the pink ribbon fell into the fire and burned without scattering. But the other group of letters, without the blue ribbon to keep them together, curled as they burned and scattered down the incinerator oven. Pages broke loose and the flame that was to blacken and destroy them first illuminated them fleetingly. . . ."] (241).

The problematic nature of this ending lies in the contradictory movement of these letters and in the double value of the flames that unite, disperse, and destroy them. This last (re)union is at once passionate and punitive. The flames into which they are cast are, in a way, the flames of both salvation and perdition. Nené is the savior of Juan Carlos's letters and the agent of his (textual) recuperation through her own writing. But, given her own instructions to her husband, she is also responsible for Juan Carlos's final demise. This is an apparently infernal descent through which, interestingly enough, Juan Carlos also manages to pull Nené down into final destruction with him. As the object of the romantic recuperation by Nené, Juan Carlos is again brought back to life by the woman who, though pulled "down" by him, seems to remain intact until the end. (Her letters are not dispersed;

moreover, she remains "pure" in her desire for Juan Carlos—we remember that Nené not only refuses to be his lover as a young woman, but also "repents" for her desire at the time of her death by having her husband destroy the letters instead of having them lie with her in her grave, as she had previously wished and planned [see 236–37].) Juan Carlos is therefore allowed to defy death until—or, rather, at—the novel's end. There, literally at the end, he also raises himself "up" and closes off the whole text by having the last words in it.

But Juan Carlos, raised "up" by nostalgia and desire, is also pulled "down" by Nené's final repentant wish. Though he is saved by her, he nevertheless leads her along with him to her own "damnation." Nené, pulled "down" by Juan Carlos, also resists his seductive powers, rising "above" the dispersion and destruction that will bring his texts to an end. Done in by her own attachment to him, Nené is also "saved" by the texts in which Juan Carlos continues to address her, because they are texts that are raised "up" to be seen and heard again on that last page. The infernal descent that marks an ending not unlike that of Tirso's Don Juan (in *El burlador de Sevilla* Don Juan is pulled into the infernal flames by Don Gonzalo, the "convidado de piedra," who returns from the dead as the agent of divine justice [Act III, 2745–73]) seems to be superimposed on a scene of potential salvation-through-love akin to that which defines the end of Zorrilla's play (in *Don Juan Tenorio* Don Juan is saved by Doña Inés's love; together their souls ascend to heaven at the play's end [Part II, Act III, ii]). In Puig's novel these scenes, as well as the text's critical readings of scenes like them, contaminate and confound each other, pulling the couple, individually and together, along with the text, in disparate directions.[25] This apparent parody of classic scenes of final salvation and damnation would reduce to *folletín* size the figure of Don Juan, perhaps further popularizing the already popular figure. That figure keeps returning in Puig's novel as a figure who refuses to die. This legendary figure is empowered again both by the fictional Juan Carlos and by his authorial supporter.

A prior scene of death—that of Juan Carlos himself in 1947 (Chapter XIV)—playfully underscores that the notion of punitive death is inextricably linked with passion, and in *Boquitas pintadas* these notions are united in an apparently parodic embrace. The novel's final death scene can also be connected to the fatal scene that precedes it. The ending of Juan Carlos and Nené together calls up and continues to play upon another image of passionate death through which Juan Carlos's identity, and the novel's position, are further complicated. Juan Carlos's death in April 1947, during Holy Week, is described as follows: "El día sàbado 18 de abril de 1947, a las 15 horas, Juan Carlos Jacinto Eusebio Etchepare dejó de existir. Junto a él se encontraban su madre y su hermana, a quienes había venido a visitar en Semana Santa como todos los años. . . . A mediodía había comido con más apetito que de costumbre, pero un dolor agudo en el pecho lo despertó de su siesta, llamó a su madre a gritos y a los pocos instantes dejó de respirar, asfixiado por una hemorragia pulmonar" ["Saturday, April 18, 1947, at 3:00 P.M., Juan Carlos Jacinto Eusebio Etchepare ceased to exist. Beside him were his mother and his sister, whom he had come to visit for Easter as he did every year. . . . At noon he had eaten with more appetite than usual, but a sharp pain in his chest woke him from his siesta, he cried out loud for his mother and a few moments later he stopped breathing, asphyxiated by a pulmonary hemorrhage"] (206–7).

Given the locus of the mortal "wound," the image of the "sacrificed" son accompanied by his suffering mother, and the time of death during Holy Week, it is not at all difficult to read this death scene, as well as the "resurrection" at the novel's end, as a parodic *folletín* version of Christ's. (We might even note the coincidence of the initials of these two powerful figures.) In that reading, the "figures of passion" are juxtaposed in such a way that it is difficult to privilege the power of one image over that of the other. These images seem to move in a manner not unlike that of Juan Carlos and Nené in their final textual entanglement—turning back and forth, or up and down, along with and yet in opposition to one another.

If Juan Carlos were offered as a popular parody of Christ, then, through their irreverent meeting the figure of the latter could be devalued, while that of Juan Carlos could be elevated to take its place. Juan Carlos would thus be the promising figure of popular and revered resurrection who would be at once raised "up" to the level of his traditional and powerful predecessors and brought "down" by the inadequacy of, the distance from, the revered models referred to in his own vital, but also fatal, performance. His models are at once recuperated by his popular existence and debunked by his small-town performance. Although in each of these fatal scenes the dialectical turns of all of these images would disallow the ascent of any one figure to a place of absolute privilege, the figure of Juan Carlos nevertheless might seem in some way to win out. As noted above, the novel's last page (242) ends with fragments of the letters of Juan Carlos, who, in a rather neat and final move, returns to kill off the novel. His image, marked from the start for imminent destruction, is nevertheless empowered to linger on. It seems to rise "above" all efforts to bring or keep it "down." The apparently parodic enterprise would betray itself, then, since, not unlike an effort at stylization, it would also give a new place to a model otherwise deemed unworthy of redemption.

In these scenes, and especially in the paradoxical last performance by the texts of Juan Carlos and Nené, we are reminded of at least two things. First, we see that, even if we read Juan Carlos as a parody of the legendary figure recuperated in his small-time exploits, he is never really anything but a collection of texts, a set of fictions, that are read and reread by us all. Juan Carlos's legendary status is emphasized right from the beginning, in the obituary on the novel's initial page. There he is literally presented as nothing but part of a legend (i.e., a text to be read) even before he is elevated to the legendary, even mythic, position he occupies in the texts of Nené's letters and in the minds, the fantasies, of all his other admirers. Together they help to situate him in that powerful and seductive place. We come to know Juan Carlos most directly (as a subject who seems so powerfully present) through that obituary notice, then through Nené's letters, then through his own writing. (Chapter III includes part of his datebook or diary from 1935, and Chapters VII, VIII, and XI contain letters written while he is in Cosquín at the sanatorium.) Though those pieces of writing attest to Juan Carlos's absence, they also make him a powerful presence. An irrecuperable referent, he is nonetheless salvaged by the whole novel.[26]

Within both story and text Juan Carlos is but a fictional image created by the discursive subjects who name and describe him, and by the languages that he and they utilize. Like the objects of desire he pursues in his strategic quests, Juan Carlos is one and many. He is a composite of different yet similar versions of his own image authored throughout the novel. For example, through its exaggerated and sentimentally idealized version of Juan Carlos, the rhetoric of the obituary

103

presents us with only one of his images—that of the deceased "beloved son" ("Con este deceso desaparece de nuestro medio un elemento que, por las excelencias de su espíritu y carácter, destacóse como ponderable valor, poseedor de un cúmulo de atributos o dones—su símpatia—, lo cual distingue o diferencia a los seres poseedores de ese inestimable caudal, granjeándose la admiración de propios o extraños" ["This demise marks the loss of an element from our midst which, for his remarkable spirit and integrity, stood out among us as a human being of great worth, possessing as he did either vast attributes or gifts, such as his personal charm, which either distinguish or set apart those who possess this immeasurable wealth and who therefore earn the admiration, deference, or affection of either friends or strangers"] [9]). This version is very much opposed to his actions and thoughts as presented by the rest of the novel. This version of Juan Carlos reflects more about the formulaic discourse, the conventionalized setting and popular practice, through which he appears than it does about Juan Carlos himself. The obituary is only one among many versions of, and languages or conventions defining, the novel's protagonist: Juan Carlos is continually (re)invented, (re)authored, and (re)read by all who survive him. Through those consecutive but simultaneous rewritings, through those contradictory versions of Juan Carlos, we see a parallel rewriting of the legendary Don Juan, a replay of his dramatic lives and deaths, produced by Puig's novel.

Nené's and Juan Carlos's final textual performance also reminds us that, though Juan Carlos is the center of the novel's contradictory critique of the Don Juan paradigm, the novel's other characters are also scrutinized in a similar fashion. Though he is set apart, he is situated with them; though they are of course different from him, they are also exactly like him in the end. All of Puig's characters are accomplices in and protagonists of the same kinds of dramas in which Juan Carlos operates and orchestrates his strategic moves. They are all engaged and interlocked in relationships that are at once social, sexual, political, and textual. They operate together according to traditions and codes that their actions both reaffirm and challenge.[27] Clearly, Juan Carlos is not the only character who both breaks and respects a variety of laws in this novel. Moreover, all seem to "pay" for their "sins" in one way or another—even if, not unlike Juan Carlos, they are also saved and rewarded for their actions.

Juan Carlos is the expert strategist who consciously manipulates others in order to get what he wants. However, he also winds up paying for his transgressions. He is but the most successful of a group of calculating "operators" who vie for power in the name of passion.[28] The success of each is contingent upon the possibility of each for controlling, exercising power over, others. And that power is contingent upon each subject's ability to suppress information, to keep others from discovering the truth behind all the fictions they author, individually and together. To succeed with this chain of possibilities, each develops and displays an ability to formulate secret pacts, to engage in certain kinds of contractual agreements with other subjects (and, from another angle, other texts) upon which the position of each player also depends. As suggested earlier, the mechanisms utilized to author such agreements within the fiction are not so different from those that inform the dialogues supporting the novel as a whole.

The play between popular form and legendary story repeatedly returns us to questions of power and passion, pleasure and knowledge. These issues are connected with each other everywhere we turn, and especially through Juan Carlos's connections to everyone around him. He not only is modeled on other popular and classic versions of donjuanism, but also seems to become a model for other figures in his own story. They both benefit from and are forced to make payments on account of the example Juan Carlos reinvests with such privilege in Coronel Vallejos. When we read some of those other figures, then, we also automatically return to and reread Juan Carlos himself. And when we read him we also, of necessity, turn to the figures who stand behind him, supporting his every move. In keeping with his own seductive tradition, Juan Carlos reveals himself as a shifty manipulator who sets an example for those who would make promises only in order to break them.[29]

Pancho, his friend and "pupil," is an example of how (not) to read Juan Carlos's example. Following in the steps of his immediate and distant models, Pancho's actions are also a rereading and rewriting of some traditional versions of both of their predecessors' activities. Given the roles they play in relation to each other and the facts of their social, even economic, positions, it is not difficult to read the relationship between Juan Carlos and Pancho in terms of the classical Don Juan/squire-sidekick paradigm, as suggested above. The middle-class

Juan Carlos plays the role of master-adviser-teacher in relation to the working-class Pancho, to whom he narrates his exploits and with whom he plots his adventures. Pancho listens to and learns from his friend's narrative, venturing at times to advise his own adviser about how to succeed with his plots, and, moreover, daring to warn him about the dangers inherent in them (e.g., 62, 76).[30] In Puig's novel this traditional friendship is also turned into an erotic rivalry, a rivalry that upends some of the cultural codes respected by the same Don Juan stories it also recalls. However, the subversion of those laws is, in the end, also kept in check by (the author of) *Boquitas pintadas*, the same text that would appear to revolve around the pleasures inherent in transgressing them.

If in the classical tale the squire is allowed to imitate his master, who in that imitation becomes a model of external mediation of desire, in *Boquitas pintadas* this model of imitation is upended.[31] The social, cultural, and literary laws that differentiate the "proper" places of those figures, the codes that define the limits of their spheres of action, are also undermined.[32] Though in the classical tale the lower-class sidekick may imitate his master, that imitation is constituted through the actions in a subplot developed around the relationships of servant characters. He may act and speak in the name of his master and thus represent him in either name or deed, but his representations are restricted to certain types of action that the two stage, individually or together. His imitation is allowed to go only so far. The sidekick cannot really take center stage; he is not permitted to replace (in a more literal sense) his master. While the Don Juan subject may serve as mediator of desire, as the model the lower-class figure would attempt to imitate in some way, the object desired by him merely parallels the one desired by the figure who is "above." The object of the former is not permitted by social or textual codes to coincide with that of the latter.[33]

In Puig's novel, however, the external mediation that characterizes the classical Don Juan tale is transformed into a play of internal mediation. The limits of the laws defining their possible actions and desires are challenged, if not done in, by the actions allowed Pancho. The object (Mabel), clearly situated in the realm of and desired by the figure from "above" (middle-class Juan Carlos), is not only desired but also possessed for a time by the figure from "below" (lower-class Pancho), the object of whose desire should be, and in a way also already is, someone from his own social sphere. (It is to Raba, in fact, that a reminder about the laws of the social hierarchy is given. Her 1937 employer warns her of the dangers of mixing with "muchachos de otra clase social" ["boys from another social class"] and advises her to stick with ". . . cualquier muchacho bueno trabajador, palabras con las que designaba a los obreros de toda índole" [". . . any good hardworking boy, words which indicated any blue-collar worker"] [80].) This displacement of Juan Carlos by Pancho denies such a proper order, such a division among classes and desires. It challenges not only the stability but also the authority of those social laws.

This rebellious, perhaps carnivalesque, turn by the text, by Pancho, or by Mabel (we should remember that she is a willing participant in this erotic "crime") seems to elicit its own punishment. Pancho, who (along with his "accomplice," Mabel) would upend the codes of society and transgress the laws preserved by the texts in which his own predecessors have appeared, is caught in the act of breaking those laws. Pancho's mimetic impulse here propels, while also being propelled by, betrayal and transgression; and for this he is swiftly punished. He is murdered by Raba, the figure who rises "up" to restore and redefine the preexisting order.[34] In being faithful to, in taking too seriously perhaps, his chosen model (Juan Carlos), Pancho manages to betray him, and of course to betray himself, as well as both lines of predecessors. In acting according to his appropriated desire, his own desire is appropriated; it is literally denied and cut from him.

Pancho's death and Raba's murderous deed together constitute an economically criminal event. In his death we see the murder of a character who, not unlike Juan Carlos, can also be seen to sacrifice himself for passion. This passion is not supposed to belong to him, and for it he seems therefore to be punished. Raba's crime of passion is a crime against a certain kind of passion—a passion that defies and betrays social and literary boundaries, a passion that chooses an "improper" object of desire. The crime that is designed to punish seems to exempt itself from punishment. (Raba is "saved" by Mabel, who, in order to save herself from being discovered by everyone or from being attacked by Raba herself, authors a fiction, a story of self-defense, for her maid, whose actions are thereby justified [175–76].)

Pancho's death at the hands of Raba, the betrayed woman, marks a return to other popular paradigms as well. Her murderous actions are themselves, the text suggests, the acting out of the kinds of passion characteristic of the popular songs she hears on the day when she kills Pancho (see 159–67). Her violent intervention in Pancho's erotic designs puts an end to his treacherous challenge to traditional plots. It marks the beginning of her ascent to a better position at the novel's end. In repaying Pancho for his betrayal of her, Raba also punishes him for his trangression of the social laws according to which they are supposed to act. When he betrays her he also betrays his own class, while also defying the class to which he attempts to attach himself. Raba's punitive and passionate act cuts short Pancho's subversion of social authority and returns him to his "proper" place. His ascent to a place beside Mabel, the woman allowed but finally prohibited to him by the text, is turned on its head. His desire to move "up" is violently put "down." Pancho's relationship with Mabel (see, for example, their encoded erotic conversation on 154–58) seems to go beyond the limits set for him by a social order he initially respects in his affair with Raba. Curiously enough, Pancho succeeds and fails—or, rather, he fails because he succeeds—in his imitation of his adventurous teacher. He dares too much, forgetting to follow all the rules his model might have taught him. He forgets, or doesn't seem quite to understand in the first place, the nature of and distance between his own performance and that of his model.

(It is possible, however, that the distance between Pancho and Juan Carlos can't really be measured, and that the nature of the relationship between their performances can't quite be defined. Within the fiction, Pancho's "imitation" is not unlike a stylization; he does take rather seriously the model whose place he would also challenge. Yet, in that he would usurp that place and take it for his own, he would also deny that his is a stylization, for such a performance would recognize the distance between itself and its model. Pancho therefore might seem instead to parody his friend, inasmuch as he knows the difference between them, and it is precisely this difference that he would seek to mock and betray. But, since he apparently wishes to move closer, rather than to distance himself from his model's privileged position, his move bears a different kind of antagonism, an antagonism that signals the subject's quest for the privileges and powers of their "rightful" bearer. A question arises, then: How are we to read this relationship of performances? Perhaps it can be determined within the text, if

not within the fiction. It could be argued that, through Pancho's performance, that of Juan Carlos—or perhaps that of the Don Juan figure
itself—is parodied. Yet the text protects as much as parodies the Don
Juan's place through Pancho's punishment. If we read it as a stylization,
we have to account for the fatal end that befalls not only Pancho, but
also Juan Carlos and, with him, the traditional Don Juan figure. The
effect of Pancho's performance is to bring "down" not only the privileged figure it would seem to either parody or stylize, but also the
agent of either operation. Not only Juan Carlos, as a model, but also
Pancho, as his "commentator," is affected by this gap. It is a gap of
intention and effect to which a definitive name [i.e., "imitation," or
"stylization," or "parody"] cannot be given. For here we have one
model superimposed on another, one operation overlapping with another, so as to confound those performances and our readings of them.)

Pancho acts out the desires of and is finally put "down" for his attempt to act in the place of Juan Carlos, himself merely a follower of
the popular legendary predecessors who are, in turn, both put "down"
and raised "up" by his performance in Puig's novel. Pancho's version
of Juan Carlos's version of the rebellious lover rewrites the original
dramas so as to subvert the underlying order both of the traditional
and of the more modern small-time versions of the story. Through that
revision and rewriting Pancho's actions become more radical, more
subversive, in relation to the laws and structures intrinsic to the traditional stories. However, this successful attempt to subvert that order—it is an attempt upheld from both ends of the social scale because
of Mabel's complete agreement with its design—is also turned around
by the text in which it is first made possible. In the apparently final
return to order and tradition orchestrated in Pancho's death scene,
another figure from "below"—Raba, Pancho's original partner and victim—acquires a new authority, a new position through which that
same order is upheld. However, in another turn, it also is overcome.

To the extent that Pancho's murder can be read as poetically just,
Raba's innocence can be defended. Indeed, her actions are more than
excused by the text—they are legitimized. She appears to function as
the agent of justice for a set of laws that the novel turns to counteract
yet support. Raba is the agent who is empowered to return Pancho
and Mabel, partners in a kind of criminal act, to their "proper" places.
She restores a certain amount of order to a system that she herself also

seeks to defy, precisely through her own criminal action. It is not insignificant that justice, if only poetic, is meted out, not by an institutionalized figure of authority, but by a character who seems to have
little or no authority, no "high" position. As a working-class woman
who is, moreover, betrayed by those "above" her, Raba is an apparently powerless figure situated at the bottom of the social order. This
inversion puts Raba in a new place by the novel's end, supporting her
desire to move up within a social structure whose stability she also
supports. She is saved—or, rather, allowed to save herself—by a text
that seems designed to raise her "up" while putting others "down."

In this acting out from "below," while also crossing over to the realm
from "above," Pancho and Raba play out another version of a traditional
subplot from some classical stories. This version seems to supplant and
radicalize the originals it appears merely to emulate from afar. Here
in *Boquitas pintadas* the lines of action cross over in ways that keep
us turning from one level to another, from one radical, but also traditional, move to another. The democratic thrust of those turns is rein-
forced by the novel's ending, where all the characters are assigned
their final due regardless (perhaps, in some cases, precisely because)
of their social positions. This procedure, however, seems to allow certain figures to rise "up" while holding others "down."

As noted in the comments on the final appearance of Juan Carlos
and Nené, the positions of these characters, their text, and even their
author (whose image emerges again through those final appearances)
remain unfixed. The possibility of closing off the text's play, or interrupting its turns, is always cut short. The *folletín* that is also not a
folletín and the Don Juan who is also not a Don Juan are left suspended, like the models they renew and to which they refer but from
which they are also distanced. By the time we reach the final summaries of the "rewards and punishments" accorded each character, we
see that *Boquitas pintadas*'s somewhat traditional ending also seems
to break with tradition.[35] In the end all the main characters seem to
pay either for the success of their secret plots or for the betrayal of
their secret pacts. No one is entirely innocent in either Coronel Vallejos or Puig's novel. In fact, everyone seems to have been involved in
some kind of transgressive, even "criminal," act. In their attempts to
satisfy a variety of desires they design moves that frequently imply the

110

transgression of some social law or personal contract, some public or private obligation, as well as a textual tradition.

The serial review of the whereabouts of the principal figures takes off from the report of Nené's death in 1968 and follows up on the lives and deaths of the other characters. In the novel's final chapter each description of the means of survival or the demise of each character contains within itself a poetically just prize or punishment. As each character is assigned what seem to be his or her just desserts, an image of an authorial figure emerges as the apparent agent (as well as director) of poetic justice. The "crimes" for which the characters "pay" are at once social and familial, public and personal. They all seem to involve a betrayal of a promise or trust, a violation of a silent or spoken contract or law. Nené, for instance, reaps the rewards of her relative innocence. Her marriage and middle-class life seem to be everything to which she would aspire. Yet that marriage and the life it entails are targeted for retribution, perhaps because she can be seen as guilty of at least two betrayals of trust, one marital and the other familial. Her obsession with Juan Carlos and her dissatisfaction with married life are recorded in her letters to "Doña Leonor" (Celina, Juan Carlos's sister, we recall, corresponds with Nené disguised as her own mother; her true identity is revealed on 218–23). These letters, when sent by Celina to Massa, provoke Nené's separation from him in 1947 (see 223, 228). And Nené's apparently selfish refusal to send money to her family for her father's medical treatment in 1939 seems to be repaid to her, so to speak, in her own illness and death from cancer, the very disease that kills her father (see 146–47, 151).

If the possible payments made by Nené seem to exceed her debts, the imbalance in her account is later rectified. Her fantasy of final union with Juan Carlos (see 232–33) is transformed into a textual reality. Her desire is in a way rewarded by her passionate, though also punitive, final meeting with Juan Carlos, the desired object whose designs she resists in life but to whom she is once again attached in death. Nené is killed off at the opening of Chapter XVI, much as Juan Carlos is at the beginning of the novel. She is brought back to life, along with him, at the end of the same chapter where, amidst the flames whose final effects can't quite be determined, they again appear together. Nené's end, her final rewards and punishments, carry her "up" and yet bring her "down." Her innocence or guilt cannot be proven (or so the text's judgment of her would imply), and she remains on the move with Juan Carlos, the figure whom she is at last allowed to follow so closely.

This conclusion, or lack thereof, occurs also in the case of Juan Carlos, who appears next in the chapter after Nené. Even in death Juan Carlos is both rewarded and made to pay for his actions; the final decision on him is also left suspended. When the narrator provides a description not of Juan Carlos but of the memorial plaques that surround his funereal niche and commemorate the twentieth anniversary of his death (237; we recall that he dies in 1947, two decades before Nené), we are reminded of his absence from the scene. His status is that of a fiction, a text to be read, and his function is that of an invented, though passionately remembered, lost object. Those plaques bring back the familial version of Juan Carlos as a figure who suffers a tragic death and whose passing is never quite accepted by those who believe in his innocence, his distance from "crime" (i.e., Juan Carlos is seen as the innocent victim of a woman to whom he is believed to have sacrificed himself, a woman who must be made to pay for his death, according to Celina's vow of revenge at the time of his death, 215–16).

We are reminded that Juan Carlos has, in a sense, been made to pay before his time, since he dies a young man. His "sins" follow traditional patterns: his life is one series of lies and broken promises, seductions and betrayals, violations and transgressions, for which he seems to have to make an early payment. However, this return to the image of Juan Carlos as the dead idol is a return to the story of his life and the beginning of his final recovery at the end of the chapter. His resurrection overcomes his apparently tragic and premature death—a death chosen for him by tradition, we must remember, as well as by his own suicidal design. In this return to the image of Juan Carlos as the already dead, and then again living, subject at the end, the text seems both to keep killing him off and yet to keep letting him live. Though he is punished, or so it seems, for his many "crimes," he is also allowed to go on rising "above" the text that has put him "down." While this last chapter certifies his previous payment, it also allows him to continue his seductive moves. In the final, fatal performance of his letters on the novel's last pages, the question of whether he shall live or die remains open. His appearance as a powerful, vital figure remains intact, suspended within the last pages as an undefeated fiction.

The description of Pancho in this last chapter (238–39) offers a counterpoint to that of Juan Carlos. Pancho, murdered in 1939, is left by everyone, including the novel's author, to rot in a common grave in Coronel Vallejos. He is condemned to, at best, a cadaverous existence, while Juan Carlos, his model, returns and is venerated after his demise. It is as if Pancho's early death were insufficient payment for his actions. It is as if he had to be kept "down" at all costs, lest he rise again to challenge the authority and privilege of his master-teacher-rival. Pancho, who dies the death of an adventurous, rebellious lover—the death presumably intended for his friend Juan Carlos, who, in succumbing to and allowing himself to be consumed by tuberculosis, dies not the death of a robust hero but that of a romantic heroine—seems to be punished not only for his crimes against Raba, but perhaps even for his betrayal of Juan Carlos, whose place he does temporarily usurp.[36] (Moreover, that he is relegated to a place from which he cannot seem to rise "up" again would seem to please his friend, whose judgment of Pancho might seem to coincide with that of the textual authority who also plots his downfall. Cast as his rival by Pancho's relationship with Mabel, Juan Carlos is secretly, though guiltily, pleased to hear the news of his friend's death: "Piensa en el amigo muerto que tal vez lo esté mirando desde un lugar desconocido. Piensa en la posibilidad de que el amigo muerto note que la noticia del asesinato en vez de entristecerlo lo ha alegrado" ["He thinks of his dead friend who perhaps is looking at him from an unknown place. He thinks of the possibility that the dead friend realizes that instead of making him sad, the news of the murder has cheered him up"] [170].) Pancho's transgression against all kinds of traditions, even those the novel seems to challenge, also finds its punishment supported by the text, its protagonist, and its authorial strategist and judge.

While Pancho remains both literally and figuratively below, condemned without hope of renewal, Raba is allowed to prosper and rise. In the juxtaposition of the description of Raba and Mabel on the day of Nené's death, we see that, while she starts out as the bottom character (that is, her position is at the bottom of the socioeconomic scale and she appears destined to a place from which there is no escape), she manages to come out on top and, from a certain angle, in an even

113

better position than Mabel, the character who seems to have more than everyone else when their story begins (see the description of her bedroom, 39–46, as well as of her daily life, 66–72). Having paid, as it were, during her lifetime through poverty and hard work, having suffered betrayal as a matter of course, Raba is "saved" not only by Mabel at the time of Pancho's death (her plea of self-defense seems to work; 170, 205), but also by the authorial maneuver that allows her a life with which she is finally satisfied. The final description shows her preparing for her daughter's wedding, thinking about her son Panchito and her stepchildren by the husband who has now left her a widow. All of these offspring have prospered in one way or another (239–40). Raba rises not so much to a new social or economic position (although her lot is greatly improved from her days as a maid); rather, she ascends to the only position of contentment, instead of disillusionment, among all the characters in the novel (cf. Nené's view of her own life [23–30], and Mabel's and Nené's nostalgia for the past throughout Chapter XIII).

This ending for Raba is a kind of "happy ending" to the sequence of final summaries of the lives of the five main characters in 1968. It contrasts with that of Mabel, the figure whose description precedes Raba's. Mabel, the woman who starts out at the top, is brought down to a place not unlike the one first occupied by Raba. Mabel's description focuses on the literal as well as figurative payments she must make for "crimes" that have not been forgotten. Although she is ready for retirement, Mabel continues to work as a teacher and private tutor in order to help pay for her grandson's medical care (he suffers from polio; see 238). Her grandson is an innocent but apposite victim of retributive violence. He appears as the counterpart to Raba's son, the responsibility for whose education and welfare Mabel, in her prenuptial church confession, promises to assume as a way of atoning for her lies to the authorities when Pancho is murdered (206). (She never follows up on that pledge.)

Raba's relative prosperity and contentment are the flip side of Mabel's ending. It is as if one had to fall so that the other might rise; one had to be punished so that the other might finally receive some reward. Raba is, in a way, rescued by the authorial director whose distribution of justice entails the defense and support—the "salvation"— of the figure who has seemed most helpless of all, the person who has been the victim of harsh socioeconomic circumstances as well as of her lover's betrayal. Much like the "helpless" popular models whose positions are enhanced and whose value is renewed by Puig's writing, Raba is supported and protected in the end, it seems, by an apparently powerful controlling authority. The authorial subject would seem to take up the cause of some figures, as well as texts, over others, and ultimately to put them where they seem to belong. However, that figure seems unable to control everything completely in the end.

In *Boquitas pintadas* there is no totally innocent or guilty party, no absolutely authoritative or free agent. No maneuver or design, no matter how powerful it may appear is untouched, or in a way uncontaminated, by the seductive model followed and incarnated by Juan Carlos. Oddly enough, that model suspends the authority not only of its own protagonist but also of its author. Though judgments are made everywhere within text and fiction alike, the turns taken by all of the main characters—especially Juan Carlos—make what seem to be punishments look like prizes, and prizes like punishments. The discussion of the final appearance of Juan Carlos and Nené at the end of Chapter XVI has addressed that point. We have seen that even there, where the novel closes, we cannot finally determine the place, or perhaps the value, of those two characters. We cannot position Juan Carlos or his author. Each, through the turns taken by the other, resists being locked into one position. However, this is appropriate for a text in which a *folletín* and a Don Juan story meet. It is fitting for a text over which the words of popular songs (e.g., tangos) hover, and in which all of the fictional characters and textual figures are tied to one another by the variety of "contracts" that keep everything moving in Coronel Vallejos and Puig's novel.[37] These contracts push everyone to adhere to, and to disavow, the changing positions they share.

Within the fictional world of Coronel Vallejos a variety of secret pacts bind the characters. Each makes promises, seals secrets, negotiates personal "contracts" that overlap with one another. If we could review all the implicit and explicit agreements that construct that complex network, we would see that, although certain kinds of pacts seem to dominate the fiction (e.g., promises of secrecy), in fact no individual pact, no single pair of contractual players—or, to view the contract as a kind of dialogue, we might call them interlocutors—is more important than the others.[38] Each character is a partner in many different kinds of agreements that may or may not be causally related. Each is also external to, but nevertheless not entirely beyond the reach of, the many pacts formulated by other pairs of partners. In reading each contract as a kind of dialogic exchange (or even, to follow a metaphor suggested by some popular models referred to by the text, as a kind of dance, like a tango) we would see its participants shift among many positions, both in relation to others to whom they are directly attached and to those to whom they are tangentially connected.

For example, we would see Juan Carlos situate himself within certain pacts but outside others whose partners at the same time move in very much the same way. We could see him, or any other character, move from a position of contractual "person" to that of "non-person" as the text moves from one episode to another.[39] These pacts among the fictional characters seem to reflect the narrative and textual contracts of the other subjects who move around them. Because of its heterogeneous narrative techniques, discursive forms, and complex structure, the novel seems to turn its reader in much the same way that it turns its fictional characters. In both arenas different kinds of agreements are solidified, broken, and renewed by the various partners who make them possible.

While the complications within the fiction are developed by the shifts presumably orchestrated by the characters themselves, the narrative complexity is the work of an authorial subject who, along with the sporadically visible omniscient narrator, engages in a provocative dialogue with a reading subject who is bound to those moves. Just as the characters' grammatical and narrative, as well as thematic, positions seem to shift, so do the positions accorded the reader. The text's turns from one technique or discourse to another imply related shifts in the position of the reader. Though the figure of the reader can be posited in the stable position of the general receiver/perceiver of the entire text, there are other positions to which the reading subject also turns. The dialogue between author and reader has superimposed on it a shifting set of narrative situations through which everyone's position seems to change. Fictional and textual entities alike seem to alternate roles, to identify with and distinguish themselves from one another, because of the novel's narrative heterogeneity. The shifts from narration in first person to narration in third person, the mixture of letters, written documents, spoken dialogues, interior monologues, and stream-of-consciousness texts, and the intermittent reports of the omniscient narrator throw the reader into different positions through this difficult but seductive "choreography." And the novel's authorial figure thereby emerges as a playful though calculating presence whose partners are at once his adversaries and his accomplices.

As we know, different modes of narration both communicate information from different perspectives and establish different kinds of relations among narrators, characters, and narratees, between author and reader. The narrative variety of Puig's novel thus implies a variety of pacts between the various senders and receivers of the text. As the novel moves from one narrative technique to another, all the participants in its exchange are alternately cast as subjects and objects, as "persons" and "non-persons." Narration in third person, a narrative form excluded from *La traición de Rita Hayworth*, implies an apparently stable pact between (omniscient) narrator and narratee, author and reader, from which the characters within the fiction are excluded. While there might be a stable pronominal or discursive relation between textual interlocutors, the positions of the fictional characters, though stable in relation to the overall textual dialogue (they are the "hes" and "shes" not present to, but outside of, the exchange between virtual "I" and "you"), are at the same time constantly shifting their ground as the narrative techniques proliferate and put them in new positions. In a similar fashion, the text's readers can be viewed as repeatedly switching places in relation to the fictional and textual figures with whom they are confronted. The complexity and variety of these relationships are revealed throughout the novel, as the text turns among mediated and unmediated narrative fragments.

The reader's relation to the mediated sections is indeed complex. (See Chapter XIII, for example, wherein narration is handled by a single omniscient narrator but where, nevertheless, the text develops a complex relation among its fictional and textual participants because of the virtual disappearance of distinctions between narrative levels through the juxtaposition of mediated and unmediated discourse.) However, the proliferation of, and thus the diverse relationships implied by, the many examples of unmediated narration highlight the reader's shifting relation to the text. Those sections reveal, while also seeming to negate or obscure, the narrative hierarchies supporting the whole novel, the hierarchies within which the reader (along with everyone else here) seems to turn from and yet remain fixed in one place. If we were to review all the texts of both spoken and written discourse in *Boquitas pintadas*, we would see the multiple positions accorded the reader. Let us take Nené's letters to "Doña Leonor" in Chapters I and II as examples, since they will allow us to focus on this issue. They will also show us how Puig's novel returns us to a position from which we can see what happens in works of narrative fiction in general.

In Nené's letters the first-person pronoun, which, as we recall, automatically posits the other pole in the correlation of subjectivity ("you"), appears to address itself within the fiction to Juan Carlos's mother. Doña Leonor is the letter's intended reader and Nené's apparent interlocutor; her responses are suppressed from view. (Chapters I and II present only Nené's letters and are something like a scriptural hidden dialogue. The letters from "Doña Leonor" provided in Chapter XV are responses not to the letters we have read at the beginning of the novel but to others that, on the other end, have been kept from us by the authorial subject.) That primary correlation within the fiction initially posits everyone who is not Nené ("I") or "Doña Leonor" ("you") as exterior to the exchange and outside (as "he" or "she") the correlation of personality through which the two subjects specularly imply each other. Various fictional and textual entities seem to share and be identified through the position of "non-person" which, from the perspective of the author-reader dialogue, is also the position of all the fictional characters. (It is the linguistic position and role that betrays the absence, the fictional status, of what it names.)

Of those whose fictive nature and absence from the exchange is implied by these letters, the figure of Juan Carlos is the most emblematic. It is indeed significant that Juan Carlos, the story's apparent center, is excluded from the discursive situation—that is, from the virtual communication between writing and reading subjects to whom he, in his "non-personal" position, is opposed. Nené writes in order to get back in touch with, to make present, this lost, nonexistent material reality (i.e., Juan Carlos). But her letters demonstrate that, while her writing project may lead her, as well as us, to believe in the power of her efforts, it is, of course, but a fiction—a memory, a desire, a fantasy—that she and the novel as a whole offer. Even though she does indeed present Juan Carlos as a character in her own letters—a character who will later seem to assume the status of a "person" in the novel's fiction and text, as he moves from a "he" to an "I"—he is still, we realize, excluded from the present in which she writes her letters.

Juan Carlos's fictional status is blatantly emphasized in the novel's opening chapters, where we find Nené's letters following on, as they are generated by, the notice of his death. In the obituary we see that Juan Carlos is indeed a "non-person": he is dead. The pronoun Nené must use to refer to and represent him—the "he" that signifies a "non-person"—doubly marks his absence. It reminds us, and perhaps Nené, that the only space in which Juan Carlos can live, as it were, the only way he can become a "person" and subject, is in language. But he can only exist in the language of someone else, in the discourse of another subject whose status is as problematic as his own. In Nené's letters, as well as in the novel as a whole, Juan Carlos is "brought (back) to life" by a subject who writes, but who is also a cover for another writing subject. That other subject is the one who writes "somewhere else" and yet right here, in the text of this novel. Nené's relation to Juan Carlos is of course very much like the relation between the novel's other primary writing and/or narrating subjects and all the "non-persons" to which the novel as a whole refers.

The layering of fictions in *Boquitas pintadas* results in a superimposition of subjects that calls attention to the fictional "truth" that supports the novel, even as it conceals that same fiction through its elaborately plotted maneuvers. The interplay of narrative levels turns us from the fact of textuality to the fiction and back again. The display of one writing subject seems to have the power to temporarily blind us to the "real position" somewhere else (behind, above, between the lines, somewhere on the other "side" and yet "within" the text) of the other authority of whose maneuvers we are also all too aware. Just as this pursuit of a writing subject might lead us "inward" to a figure who is finally unlocateable, the pursuit of its textual partner—the reading subject whose place is also above and yet within the novel—would lead us to much the same place on the other "side" of the text. Nené's letters again serve as instructive examples, for they also turn around the question of the identity of their reader(s) in a surprising and significant fashion.

As we recall, although Nené explicitly addresses her correspondence to Doña Leonor in Chapters I and II, in Chapter XV it is revealed that the "you" to whom she and we think she has been writing is not the one who has actually read her letters. When we discover the identity of Nené's "real" reader, we are faced with an important textual fact. At the moment of that discovery—it is a discovery of another referent, another proper name (here within the fiction, it is the name "Celina"), in the place of or behind the pronoun that marks the place of the addressee—we are reminded of the essentially discursive value of the word "you." This term has the potential for covering up, while also directing itself to, anyone who happens to be (placed) in a position to receive it. Here, that means that any reader, anyone who reads Nené's letters (or, for that matter, any of the other spoken or written texts in the novel), in fact assumes the place of the one who is supposed to read (or, in other cases, "overhear") it. That reader becomes the one to whom it is addressed, while at the same time remaining outside that exchange.

When we discover that Celina and not Doña Leonor receives and reads Nené's letters, we also discover what we already know but have been led to forget. We are reminded that Nené's letters can be and are in fact received by "interlocutors" unknown to but already posited and marked by her in her writing. Oddly enough, all of those "unknown" readers of her letters are precisely the ones for whom her texts are already written. Nené's letters are of course Puig's letters; they are epistolary texts that have been written for us. They therefore reveal, as well as veil, the virtual dialogue in which not only the fiction's characters but also the text's readers are engaged. They return us to the fundamental nature of such dialogic, two-sided relationships and "contracts" upon which any text of narrative fiction is based and with which Puig's novel plays so powerfully. To be either, or both, reader or writer in this novel is to be located in, even defined by, an impossible position, the kind of position that supports narrative fiction itself. It means to be always in at least two places at once: on both "sides," as well as "within," the text; in one's own place, but also elsewhere, in what seems to be the place of another subject.

Boquitas pintadas's exaggerated play upon narrative technique and discursive material, its seductive juxtaposition of generic and thematic models known to popular traditions, are precisely what help to put us off balance. But they also instruct us about how texts of fiction work. By taking to such extremes both the techniques and traditions of narrative fiction, Puig seems to expose the basic properties and practices not only of his novel but also of the genre itself.[40] However, as emphasized at the outset here, what seems to be a controlled exercise of authorial powers to undermine certain traditions and systems also shows that it can't quite be what it seems to want to be when things begin. In this seductively modeled novel the figure of authority that seems to direct every move in order to manipulate and control its readers must, at the same time, become a partner and player in it. The novel that seems to disperse among its pages the place in which an authorial figure might be located cannot conceal some image of a judging but playful authority within it. The authorial figure that emerges from the pages of the novel as an apparent partisan of certain positions or characters, certain traditions or issues, also returns us to the problems inherent in attempting to play such a role. It is a role that actually creates a number of problems. The positions produced with that role resemble, curiously enough, those accorded and played not only by this novel's own protagonist but also by the famous movie star who hovers above another of Puig's texts.

Boquitas pintadas is a reflexive novel whose relation to its apparent models—indeed, whose whole enterprise—appears in the end to be more problematic than we might at first suppose. Not unlike Puig's first novel, this second one also seems to turn in different directions at once, leading not only its characters but also its apparently totally authoritative subject to a position from which not everything can be controlled. To attempt to stabilize that position and identify the novel's "voice," to try to reduce the text to a kind of monologue, is to confront the unstable ground upon which author and text seem to stand. Even when we think we have identified that novel's, or its author's, position with respect to a specific tradition, or language, or character, or social reality, for example, we discover that somehow the text can also reverse that position and our conclusion. We might return to the treatment of the generic model and legendary figure, upon which attention was focused earlier, in order to see how such a turn can be taken up again.

If we accept that Puig seems to draw attention to various forms of popular culture to which he would attach new value, and that he also examines the legendary model of male performance in a way that may be designed to contribute to its devaluation, we can see that this type of combined enterprise must also work against its own designs. Such designing authorial desires—read both within and from outside the text—must in a way clash, eroding the position of control in which we might have thought them to be grounded. That is, it could be argued that, in order to succeed in what seems to be one of his projects, Puig would have to sacrifice himself to another. In order to save, or defend, one model he would also have to undermine (unwittingly, of course) the attack on the other.

The development of the author-reader dialogue (or "dance") here discloses that the success of Puig's *folletín* is grounded in several ways in the successes of the Don Juan model. Indeed, that model operates according to a seductive, unstable, and ultimately problematic pattern that binds fictive and textual figures alike. To become the author of a *folletín*, to assume the apparently privileged, stable position of the one whose power, and perhaps also pleasure, are determined by the ability to manipulate and deceive, to laugh at while also playing with one's accomplices and victims is, of course, to follow in another way and to keep alive the performance of someone like a Don Juan. This kind of performance has the power to seduce even the subject who appears to attempt to diffuse its attraction. In *Boquitas pintadas*, then, it never becomes clear who or what is in or out of control. It is not possible to know whose "voice" is finally heard, since opposing voices are heard in turn and, therefore, also at the same time. The text repeatedly discloses its ambivalent positions and moves around a variety of figures and traditions. In so doing, it not only resists our readerly mastery until and beyond the end; it also seems to control the author(ity), the master-manipulator-seducer who seems to hover above and lurk behind it. This authority, this apparent master of seduction is, of course, nothing more than one of the suspended, mobile fictions produced by that very same text.

NOTES

1. Manuel Puig, *Boquitas pintadas: Folletín* (Buenos Aires: Sudamericana, 1969) 9; hereafter page references appear parenthetically within the text. Another edition of the novel has been published by Seix Barral (Barcelona, 1972). The version in English is *Heartbreak Tango: A Serial*, trans. Suzanne Jill

Levine (New York: E.P. Dutton, 1973). Quotations in English are from this edition, unless otherwise noted.

2. Cf. the remarks related to the notion of control in another of Puig's novels (*El beso de la mujer araña*) by Alicia Borinsky in *Ver/ser visto: Notas para una analítica poética* (Barcelona: Bosch, 1978); hereafter cited as *Ver*.

3. The novel is composed of sixteen chapters, divided equally into two parts of eight chapters each. There are no titles other than the successive ordinal numbers and the word *entrega* at the head of each chapter. However, lines from well-known songs of the 1930s and 1940s serve as subtitles for the two parts of the novel (Part I: "Boquitas pintadas de rojo carmesí" [7]; Part II: "Boquitas azules, violáceas, negras" [125]) and as epigraphs for each episode. See Margery A. Safir, "Mitología: otro nivel de metalenguaje en *Boquitas pintadas*," *Revista iberoamericana* 41 (1975): 47–58, regarding how the novel progresses from the image of the lyrics heading Part I to those introducing Part II. See the following for Puig's comments on some of the problems entailed in translating these lyrics from Spanish to English: Sosnowski, "Entrevista" 79–80; Rodríguez Monegal, "Folletín" 27; and Suzanne Jill Levine and Manuel Puig, "Author and Translator: A Discussion of *Heartbreak Tango*," *Translation* 2.1–2 (1974): 32–41 (esp. 33–34). In the last discussion, Levine, Puig's translator, notes how Puig betrays his reader by betraying the tango in the Spanish title of the novel (the English version presumably rectifies this): "The Spanish title is from a song of the thirties, sung by Carlos Gardel, a famous tango singer, and the words in the original are *Boquitas pintadas*. . . . the song these lyrics come from ('Rubias de New York' or 'Blondes from New York') is not a tango but a fox trot, and it's from a movie Carlos Gardel starred in called *The Tango on Broadway*. This is a relevant and ironic point, since Manuel is already being 'unfaithful' to the tango, by using the words of a fox trot as the title. But I guess Carlos Gardel was 'unfaithful' before him by singing a fox trot on Broadway" (33). In several places Puig has asserted not his desire to betray but, rather, his desire to "seduce" his (real or imagined) reader, whose participation in his text is demanded by the narrative methods he uses. See his two talks with Ronald Christ: "Interview" 54, and "Interview with Manuel Puig," *Christopher Street* April 1979: 25–31 (esp. 30; hereafter cited as "Puig"). For comments on the erotic implications of the term *entrega* in the novel, see Sarduy's "Notas" 556.

4. This view of *Boquitas pintadas* as a network of texts "grafted" together is suggested by Severo Sarduy, first in "*Boquitas pintadas*: parodia e injerto," *Sur* 321 (1969): 71–77, and then in the expanded version of that essay, "Notas" 555–57.

5. See Wolfgang Iser, "Indeterminacy and the Reader's Response in Prose

Fiction," in *Aspects of Narrative* 1–45 (hereafter cited as "Indeterminacy"), for a discussion of the correlation between the degree of indeterminacy in a text and the reader's interaction with it.

6. See, for example, Christ, "Interview" 54, 61, and Rodríguez Monegal, "Folletín" 26–30, for Puig's views on the relation between his novel and the extra-literary reality upon which it seems to comment. In our personal interview Puig emphasized his desire to call into question the Don Juan/macho figure through this novel. See also Torres Fierro, "Conversación" 511.

7. This order is drawn from the novel itself. In Chapters IV and V, for example, the activities of each character during a single day (23 April 1937) are narrated successively in precisely this order; see also Chapters IX (27 January 1938) and XVI (15 September 1968) for identically ordered descriptions. A departure from this ordering occurs in Chapter XIV, where Nené and Juan Carlos switch places, Juan Carlos preceding Nené precisely because it is in his death (18 April 1947) that the sequence originates and it is on him that the text makes a point of focusing.

8. See, for example, Michel Butor, "Research on the Technique of the Novel," *Inventory: Essays by Michel Butor*, ed. Richard Howard (New York: Simon and Schuster, 1968) 15–25 (hereafter cited as "Research"), for comments on how even "classic" novels prove difficult to transform into perfectly linear narratives. See Gérard Genette, *Narrative Discourse: An Essay in Method* (1972), trans. Jane E. Lewin (Ithaca: Cornell UP, 1980) 33–85, for discussion of the basically "anachronistic" nature of modern fiction.

9. See Butor, "Research" 18–20, and Iser, *The Act of Reading*, on the dynamic and multi-directional process that is a reader's encounter with a literary text. See also Eric S. Rabkin, "Spatial Form and Plot" (1977), in *Spatial Form in Narrative*, ed. Jeffrey R. Smitten and Ann Daghistany (Ithaca: Cornell UP, 1981) 79–99, for related comments on the simultaneously diachronic and synchronic nature of reading narrative texts.

10. See also Carlos Raúl Yujnovsky, "*Boquitas pintadas* ¿folletín?" *Nuevos aires* 8 (1972): 49–58 (esp. 53–56).

11. The links between *Boquitas pintadas*'s narrative structure and that of detective fiction have also been noted by Rodríguez Monegal, "Folletín" 27. For discussions of the temporal deformation characteristic of detective fiction, as well as the narrative procedures of mystery texts in general, see, for example, Shklovsky, "The Mystery Novel," and Tzvetan Todorov, "The Typology of Detective Fiction" (1966), in *The Poetics of Prose* 42–52 (hereafter cited as "Detective Fiction").

12. The observations made about the narrative prolepses and analepses in Puig's novel draw on Genette's *Narrative Discourse*.

13. On the temporality of epistolary texts, see Altman, *Epistolarity*, and Ronald C. Rosbottom, "Motifs in Epistolary Fiction: Analysis of a Narrative Sub-genre," *L'Esprit Createur* 17 (1977): 279–301. Aspects of the temporal structure of *Boquitas pintadas* have been discussed by Angelo Morino, "Tanghi e pellicole hollywoodiane nei romanzi di Manuel Puig," *Belfagor* 32 (1977): 395–408 (hereafter cited as "Tanghi e pellicole"), as well as by Mac Adam, "Things."

14. On the relation between power and knowledge, see Michel Foucault's *Discipline and Punish: The Birth of the Prison* (1975), trans. Alan Sheridan (New York: Pantheon, 1977) and *The History of Sexuality*, Vol. 1: *An Introduction* (1976), trans. Robert Hurley (New York: Pantheon, 1978).

15. See Frank Kermode, *Novel and Narrative* (Glasgow: U of Glasgow Publications, 1972) esp. 9–10, for a discussion of reading as an inherently "interpretive or hermeneutic activity." See also Roland Barthes's analysis of the "hermeneutic code" in Balzac's *Sarrasine*, in *S/Z* (1970), trans. Richard Miller (New York: Hill and Wang, 1974).

16. See also Borinsky, "Castration: Artifices" 106; Mac Adam, "Chronicles" 61–62; and Yujnovsky, "*Boquitas pintadas* ¿folletín?" 53–56. Iser uses the serial novel as the main illustration of the types of narrative technique that create indeterminacy (gaps of indeterminacy, etc.) in a text, forcing the reader's participation in it; see his "Indeterminacy" 14–17. On the serial novel's history and characteristic features, see, for example: A[ngela] Bianchini, *Il romanzo d'appendice* (Turin: ERI, 1969); Umberto Eco, "The Myth of Superman" and "Rhetoric and Ideology in Sue's *Les Mystères de Paris*," in *The Role of the Reader: Explorations in the Semiotics of Texts* (Bloomington: Indiana UP, 1979) 109–24, 125–43; Juan Ignacio Ferreras, *La novela por entregas, 1840–1900* (Madrid: Taurus, 1972); Antonio Gramsci, "Letteratura populare," in *Letteratura e vita nazionale*, Vol. 4 of *Opere di Antonio Gramsci*, 4th ed. (Turin: Einaudi, 1954) 103–42; and Jorge B. Rivera, *El folletín y la novela popular* (Buenos Aires: Centro Editor de América Latina, 1960).

17. In addition to Shklovsky's fundamental statements concerning the term "defamiliarization" ("making strange") in "Art as Technique" (1917), in *Russian Formalist Criticism* 5–24, see also R. H. Stacy, *Defamiliarization in Language and Literature* (Syracuse: Syracuse UP, 1977), for a recent discussion of the concept. Partly because of the variety of its defamiliarizing techniques, Puig's novel can be read as a special case of "spatial form" in modern fiction. It is not only in the various disjunctions between story and plot, but also in its peculiar relation to its generic model, whose characteristic temporality is spatially manipulated, that *Boquitas pintadas* could represent this phenomenon. See the essays in *Spatial Form in Narrative* for recent attempts to expand and clarify

Joseph Frank's original essay, "Spatial Form in Modern Literature" (1945), in *The Widening Gyre: Crisis and Mastery in Modern Literature* (New Brunswick: Rutgers UP, 1963).

18. See also the following on *Boquitas pintadas* and the *folletín*: Alicia G. Andreu, "El folletín: de Galdós a Manuel Puig," *Revista iberoamericana* 49 (1983): 541–46; Bella Josef, "Manuel Puig: reflexión al nivel de la enunciación," *Nueva narrativa hispanoamericana* 4 (1974): 111–15; Julio Rodríguez-Luis, "*Boquitas pintadas* ¿Folletín unanimista?" *Sin nombre* 5.1 (1974): 50–56 (hereafter cited as "Folletín unanimista"); Gilberto Triviños, "La destrucción del verosímil folletinesco en *Boquitas pintadas*," *Texto crítico* 9 (1978): 117–30 (hereafter cited as "Destrucción"); Yujnovsky, "*Boquitas pintadas* ¿folletín?"

19. See "Folletín" for Rodríguez Monegal's and Puig's comments on the recuperation of this and other popular models; see also Sosnowski, "Entrevista" 73.

20. See Christ, "Interview" 54, and Rodríguez Monegal, "Folletín" 32–34, for discussions of the author's ambivalence (i.e., his ambivalent attitude toward the cultural reality in which he himself was formed and toward the people he claims to have taken as models for his characters in this novel).

21. See Otto Rank, *The Don Juan Legend* (1924), trans. and ed. David G. Winter (Princeton: Princeton UP, 1975), for a view of the history of the Don Juan legend as a gradual degeneration and corruption of the character's originally elevated stature. See also J. Saint-Paulien, *Don Juan: Mythe et réalité* (Paris: Plon, 1967).

22. See Christ, "Interview" 58, Torres Fierro, "Conversación" 508–11, Rodríguez Monegal, "Folletín" 20–29, 33–34, and Sosnowski, "Entrevista" 73, for Puig's statements regarding parody in his novels and his declaration of "serious," "artistic" treatment of forms of popular art (e.g., the serial novel). The novel abounds with representations of popular discourse and culture. For example, besides the tango lyrics that serve as epigraphs to each chapter, there are lyrics "heard" or remembered within the fiction (words from tangos in whose reality Raba believes run throughout her interior monologue, 160–66). There are excerpts from a women's magazine (see the "correo del corazón" columns that are "shown" to us by the omniscient narrator in Mabel's 1937 bedroom, on 41–45) and from a local magazine (see the social item entitled Lúcida Celebración del Día de la Primavera" from 1936, which Nené encloses in a letter to Doña Leonor in 1947 on 20–21, as well as the obituary notice for Juan Carlos on 9). There are examples of legal, medical, and government documents and discourse (see the medical report dealing with Raba's pregnancy in 1937, on 119; the police report naming Pancho among a group of trainees, on 119–20; extracts from the police investigation of Pancho's mur-

der, on 171–79; the document dealing with a suit brought by Mabel's father against her fiancé, on 120). There are diary excerpts (see Juan Carlos's *"Agenda 1935"* 46–49), and a verbal translation of a photo album typical of the era (see the description of Juan Carlos's photos and inscriptions, 35–39). There are transcriptions of parts of dialogues by a gypsy fortuneteller (see the hidden dialogue, which reveals only the gypsy's discourse with Juan Carlos in 1937, on 85–92) and by a confessor in church (see Mabel's confessional discourse with a priest in 1941, on 201–6). And there is a transcription of an entire episode of a radio soap opera program, heard by the characters while read by the reader (see Chapter XIII, where a conversation between Mabel and Nené in 1941 is interspersed with the discourse of the program announcer and the soap opera characters).

23. The term "devaluation" is used by Rank in *The Don Juan Legend*. See esp. Chs. 9 and 10, where he explains the psychoanalytic function and meaning of this process within both the history of art and the development of the work of an individual artist.

24. The links between Juan Carlos, or his story, and the Don Juan tradition as it is developed over the centuries in legendary and artistic versions revolves around not only his characteristic "donjuanism" (e.g., he seduces and betrays women; he seems to live only for erotic adventure, sacrificing everything else, even his life, to his desires), but also the pattern of his relationships with, or the lines of action connecting him to, other key figures (e.g., his friendship with Pancho, whose admiration he accepts but whose advise he refuses to heed; his rebellion against institutions and figures of authority, for which he seems also eventually punished). See, among others, the following for information about the legend's development (its sources, its many versions, its interpretations) in several forms of art: Georges Gendarme de Bévotte, *La légende de Don Juan: son evolution dans la littérature des origines au romantisme* (Paris: Hachette, 1906); Dorothy Epplen MacKay, *The Double Invitation in the Legend of Don Juan* (Stanford: Stanford UP, 1943); Oscar Mandel, ed., *The Theatre of Don Juan: A Collection of Plays and Views, 1630–1963* (Lincoln: U of Nebraska P, 1963); Otto Rank, *The Don Juan Legend*; Mercedes Saenz-Alonso, *Don Juan y el donjuanismo* (Madrid: Guadarrama, 1969); J. Saint-Paulien, *Don Juan: Mythe et réalité*; H. G. Tan, *La matière de Don Juan et les genres littéraires* (Leiden: Presse Universitaire de Leyde, 1976); and Leo Weinstein, *The Metamorphoses of Don Juan* (Stanford: Stanford UP, 1969). For an extensive bibliography of literary and critical texts dealing with the Don Juan legend, see Armand E. Singer, *The Don Juan Theme, Versions and Criticism: A Bibliography*, rev. ed. (Morgantown: West Virginia UP, 1965).

25. See Gustavo Pérez Firmat's "Carnival in *Don Juan Tenorio*," *Hispanic*

Review 51 (1983): 269–81, wherein the notions of contamination and carnival meet in one of *Boquitas pintadas*'s possible "interlocutors."

26. See also Marta Morello Frosch, "La sexualidad opresiva en las obras de Manuel Puig," *Nueva narrativa hispanoamericana* 5 (1975): 151–57 (esp. 152–53; hereafter cited as "La sexualidad opresiva"); Borinsky, "Castration: Artifices" 106–9; and Mac Adam, "Chronicles" 62–63.

27. See Rodríguez-Luis, "Folletín unanimista," for comments on the characters as part of a social group whose relationships offer material for sociological analysis.

28. In Christ, "Interview" 54, Puig discusses his attempt to present the characters in terms of the contradiction between their "belief in the rhetoric of passion" and their "real attitude [which is] a scheming one." See also Levine and Puig, "Author and Translator" 34–35; Safir, "Mitología" 54; and Douglas C. Thompson, "Manuel Puig's *Boquitas pintadas*: 'True Romance' for Our Time," *Critique: Studies in Modern Fiction* 23.1 (1981): 37–44.

29. The verb "prometer" is used extensively by a number of characters as they form their secret pacts; see, e.g., 100, 111, 118, 136, 177, 205–6, 216, 221, 237, 241. On the Don Juan figure's involvement with the verb "to promise" and the idea of promising as a whole, see Shoshana Felman, *The Literary Speech Act: Don Juan with J. L. Austin, or Seduction in Two Languages* (1980), trans. Catherine Porter (Ithaca: Cornell UP, 1983).

30. Pancho's own models could very well be both Catalinón, from Tirso's *El burlador de Sevilla*, and Sganarelle, from Molière's *Don Juan ou le festin de pierre* (1665). Even though he differs greatly from those characters, his role as a loyal friend, confidant, and accomplice, as well as his socially and economically subordinate position, establish a number of points of contact (see esp. Catalinón's warnings and his master's famous replies in *El burlador de Sevilla*). See Rank, *The Don Juan Legend*, Chs. 3–4, on the servant figure's crucial role as conscience.

31. The differences between external and internal mediation of desire have to do with the distance that separates the desiring subject and the mediator from one another, according to Girard's theory in his *Deceit, Desire and the Novel*. The term "external mediation" is used "when the distance is sufficient to eliminate any contact between the two spheres of *possibilities* of which the mediator and the subject occupy the respective centers," but the term "internal mediation" is used "when this same distance is sufficiently reduced to allow these spheres to penetrate each other more or less profoundly" (9).

32. See also Rank, *The Don Juan Legend*, 49–52.

33. We might note that the restriction seems to hold only for the desires of lower-class male figures and not for those of upper-class males (i.e., the Don Juan character seduces women of all classes). Moreover, while the classical

Don Juan is a rebellious character who goes about defying figures and systems of authority, his stories and texts seem to uphold traditional social hierarchies in the separation of and opposition between the desires and actions permitted entities from both ends of the social scale.

34. See Bakhtin's discussion on carnival in *Rabelais and His World*.

35. See also Yujnovsky, "*Boquitas pintadas* ¿folletín?" 53, and Triviños, "Destrucción" 120–21. See Alurista, "*Boquitas pintadas*: Producción folletinesca bajo el militarismo," *Maize* 4.1–2 (1981): 21–26, for comments on how the "rewards" and "punishments" support and condemn certain characters, following the line of thought developed here.

36. In presenting Juan Carlos, a consumptive, as the protagonist of a serial novel, Puig's novel renders literal a characteristic feature, as well as paradox, of his identity. As a small-town Don Juan, Juan Carlos is a character whose mythic quality and elevated status in Coronel Vallejos, in this text, and in literary tradition would seem to attest to his position as an invulnerable and "inconsumable" entity. But as a Don Juan whose serial story is told by a serial novel, Juan Carlos is in fact also destined to consume himself in erotic adventures that must, according to tradition, bring about his early death—perhaps, as we have seen, his consumption by infernal flames. However, this is a death which, according to the literary genre through which he is generated or resurrected, might never seem ready to consume him, given its potentially uncontrollable, open ended, turns. See Eco, "The Myth of Superman," for pertinent observations about another popular serial superhero who "must remain 'inconsumable' and at the same time be 'consumed'" (111). See Safir, "Mitología" 51, on Juan Carlos's illness.

37. Given the apparent privilege granted to the tango, whose lyrics may deal with sentimental, melodramatic, or tragic stories of struggles for love and life, and whose choreography develops a pattern of movements that are not without their erotic and political qualities, it would be possible to read both textual and fictional pacts and performances in terms of that model. On the tango tradition, see, for example, Jorge Luis Borges, "Historia del tango," in *Evaristo Carriego* (1930), Vol. 4 of *Obras Completas* (Buenos Aires: Emecé, 1955); Arturo Horacio Ferrer, *El tango: su historia y evolución* (Buenos Aires: A. Peña Lillo, 1960); Francisco García Jiménez, *El tango: historia de medio siglo, 1880–1930* (Buenos Aires: Ed. Universitaria, 1964); Julio Mafud, *Sociología del tango* (Buenos Aires: Américalee, 1966); Tomás de Lara and Inés Leonilda Roncetti de Panti, *El tema del tango en la literatura argentina* (Buenos Aires: Ediciones Culturales Argentinas, 1961); Ernesto Sábato, *Tango, canción de Buenos Aires* (Buenos Aires: Ediciones Centro de Arte, 1964); and Daniel D. Vidart, *Teoría del tango* (Montevideo: Ediciones de la Banda Oriental, 1964).

38. For instance, the following sequence of consecutive and simultaneous relationships, whose success is predicated upon pacts of secrecy, provides a sample of the intricate and secret interconnections among the main characters: Nené has a secret affair with a town doctor in 1935, but refuses to do the same with Juan Carlos, whose strategies for seduction she resists and who, while seeing her from 1936 to 1937, at the same time becomes secretly involved simultaneously with both the widow DiCarlo, with whom he maintains a relationship until his death, and Nené's friend Mabel, who also becomes engaged to another man while seeing Juan Carlos, and who, later in 1939, has a clandestine affair with Pancho, Juan Carlos's friend who, in 1937, is previously involved secretly with Raba, whose child he fathers but whose paternity he wishes to keep secret.

39. The possibility of reading the characters as "persons" or "non-persons" within specific contracts or pacts assumes a similarity between the situation of discourse, with its interlocutors, etc., and that of the other types of dyadic exchanges, such as the characters' two-way "deals." See Benveniste, *Linguistics*, for a clarification of these terms and situations.

40. In this sense, *Boquitas pintadas* might be read as a "typical" novel, as the term is used by Shklovsky in "Sterne's *Tristram Shandy*" 57.

A Case of Criminal Repetition:
The Buenos Aires Affair

It would be difficult to talk about Puig's third novel, *The Buenos Aires Affair*, without taking up the question of its generic form.[1] Like *Boquitas pintadas*, this text has a subtitle ("Novela policial") that identifies from the outset the form of popular literature with which it works. The detective novel is the genre of "low" origin whose laws seem to govern *The Buenos Aires Affair*. In Puig's version, though, we see those laws at once upheld and violated. The novel's text moves in opposing directions, now seeming to parody, now seeming to reproduce and renew the popular model. *The Buenos Affair* makes this "low" genre both strange and familiar; it recognizes and yet redefines the status of that popular model through its turns in narrative structure and thematic material. Because of its experimental narrative techniques and its playful yet serious commentary on cultural models, Puig's *novela policial* situates itself well within the realm of "high" art, the category to which Spanish American "new" narrative and modern experimental fiction in general belong. Since Puig's novel also pertains to that "higher" category (a category presumably closed to forms such as the detective novel) its identity as a form of popular, "low" art is questioned as much as it is affirmed by his writing.

The Buenos Aires Affair is a rather strange yet familiar kind of text. It is familiar because we know the popular model it presumes to perpetuate and represent. It is strange because it "defamiliarizes" or estranges that popular form through the deployment of techniques clearly identified with texts of "high" origin. This *novela policial* is also

131

unfamiliar because it is linked as much with texts of "high" art as with the familiar, popular traditions situated somewhere "below" them. Or, to put it another way, it is familiar because of its adherence to the unconventional conventions of modern fiction, yet strange because of its recourse to a popular, formulaic model apparently well removed from the realm of "artistic" experimentation.[2] Whether we look at this novel from the perspective of the "high" or the "low," we see that it doesn't quite fit either category; its place is at once outside and within the limits of each. Yet those disparate and seemingly opposing categories meet, much like the novel's protagonists, in a seductive, although transgressive and criminal, embrace. *The Buenos Aires Affair* brings together traditions that are legitimized and also challenged by one another. It questions the boundaries and rewrites the possible relations between those traditions without, however, resolving the problematic nature of their encounter.

The Buenos Aires Affair follows up on, expands, and takes to another extreme some of the structural and narrative elements, as well as the thematic concerns, of *La traición de Rita Hayworth* and *Boquitas pintadas*. Like both of those novels, its text is composed of sixteen chapters, divided into two equal parts. Like the second novel, it bears not only a subtitle that identifies its model as a form of popular literature but also epigraphs drawn from the world of popular culture. (They appear to be fragments of 1930s and 1940s Hollywood filmscripts that focus on a situation or relationship not unlike that which is presented in the chapter each heads or follows.[3]) The heterogeneity of its narrative techniques and discursive forms resembles most that of *Boquitas pintadas*. The text includes medico-legal discourse, the language of psychiatry and psychoanalysis, women's magazine topics and talk, vocabulary and motifs from the art world, and the language of popular journalism, as well as the epigraphs' melodramatic movie dialogues. The story is told through third-person narration, interior monologue and stream-of-consciousness texts, direct dialogue, hidden dialogue, and the presentation of official documents and forms (e.g., police and coroner's reports, a *curriculum vitae* outline, newspaper clippings). Within this proliferation of discourses and narrative techniques, however, the figure of an omniscient narrator, whose authoritative but also variegated discourse surfaces through the many instances of third-person narration, emerges as an apparently knowledgeable, controlling subject who works as a counterpart—or, more appropriately here, as an accomplice—to the authorial figure who engages the reader in a text designed to seduce and betray.

The Buenos Aires Affair brings together, rendering more literal, more thematically explicit, much that is only implied by the narrative techniques and anecdotal relations of Puig's other work. In the first two novels we begin to see the possibility of talking about not only the resemblance between their narrative structures or strategies and those of mystery fiction, but also the importance of the repeated returns to matters at once criminal and sexual, to scenes at once punitive and passionate, to relationships at once political and erotic. In *The Buenos Aires Affair* these structural and thematic patterns dominate the text entirely, and it is precisely those kinds of seductive and transgressive repetitions and resemblances that we are made to confront directly. Moreover, *The Buenos Aires Affair* presents what looks like another set of "perfect matches" between fictional characters and generic model, between authorial subject and readerly figure. These partners meet in a set of "perfect crimes"—crimes that are legitimized by the textual laws the novel upholds, curiously enough, through its plotting of their apparent violation.

The fictional characters who are involved in these criminal situations are Gladys Hebe D'Onofrio, an artist, and Leo Druscovich, an art critic. Theirs is a story of crimes at once real and fantasized, artistic and artificial, that each helps to develop primarily in and around Buenos Aires, the city where they are born in the 1930s and have their criminal encounter in 1969. The text provides what seems to be the necessary information about these characters and the criminal activity around which it, as a supposed *novela policial*, revolves. It focuses first on the situation and apparent scene of the crime. It then moves back in time, only to move forward again, so as to provide all the information leading up to the initial criminal scene, to which we return at the novel's end, where its enigmatic appearance is resolved.[4] Puig's novel adheres to the genre's formulaic temporal inversion, taking us on a textual detour in order to postpone our arrival at and full disclosure of the truth until the end. The apparently criminal scene, which takes place on 21 May 1969, is presented in Chapter II; information about the characters involved in and the events leading up to that scene are provided in Chapters III-XII, which take us from the 1930s to 1968; Chapter XIII returns to and reveals the solution to that criminal act and is followed by three chapters that focus on the two days following the events in Chapter XIII, during which time a criminal is punished and a lone victim is left on the scene. However, it also deforms further this originally, and "properly," deformed temporality.[5]

Part I of the novel—that is, Chapters I-VIII—works against pure chronology through a series of moves that retard the story's progress. Besides the characteristic analepsis that takes us from a criminal scene to the history behind it (the text takes us from the scene in Chapter II back to a summary of the life of Gladys, the scene's apparent victim, in Chapter III), there are other moves that take us back just when it looks as if we are about to move forward. While the move from Chapter III to IV, which takes us from May to June 1968, slowly begins to carry the narrative forward in time, some of the moves that follow interrupt that progression, taking us back and forth, impeding instead of promoting the temporal flow. As we advance in the text from Chapter IV to V, we move back in the fiction to the month preceding the temporal frame of the previous chapter (from June back to May 1968). And as we read Chapter VI, the text takes us back even further in time, before returning us to the 1968 time frame that is only briefly left behind. (Chapter VI is, like Chapter III, a summary biography of one of the protagonists: Leo's life is described in terms that parallel, in both technique and thematic focus, the story of Gladys's life.) However, this forward movement dominates the last two chapters of Part I (Chapters VII and VIII), both of which focus on events that occur in April 1969.

The moves back and forth over time keep us from making significant progress yet assure that progress will eventually be made. Puig's novel plays with, exaggerating by proliferating, the genre's typical problems of temporality, revealing through that process precisely how its model operates. Only by moving back is there any possibility of moving forward. *The Buenos Aires Affair* stresses that closure in the detective text implies, in a way, going nowhere, for we always return to where we have already been and to what we have already seen.[6] Part II works with and exaggerates in a different way this paradox of the genre to which it supposedly belongs. After moving forward, first to a summary text that bridges the gap between the novel's two major divisions by following upon the last actions of Leo described at the end of Chapter

VIII (Part II opens with a "Recapitulación" [158], a popular technique used also in *Boquitas pintadas*), the narrative text jumps back briefly to a time three days prior to the last date mentioned in Part I (that is, from 24 April to 22 April 1969). Thereafter it unfolds in a strictly chronological fashion, moving from late April to late May 1969.[7] But in the last eight chapters the temporal flow is retarded as much as it is advanced, for time moves so slowly—the narrative covers events of only one month in these eight chapters—that adherence to chronology seems to mean also the deformation of temporal progress.[8] In the first eight chapters progress is postponed since, even if we move relatively quickly, often that movement is in the "wrong" direction. In the second part a similar effect is created since, even if we move steadily forward, the pace is so slow that it is as if time itself prevents us from getting anywhere.

This manipulation of time is aided by the deployment of diverse narrative techniques throughout the novel, especially in the second part. The effects of the temporal inversions in the earlier chapters are intensified by that technical diversity. The turns from one narrative method and form of discourse to others undermine the possibility of acquiring information from a single perspective (a single "eye") or subject (an "I") so as to proceed uniformly toward the level of knowledge we expect to reach and which those same narrative ruptures lead us to desire. Likewise, in the last eight chapters the narrative heterogeneity has a significant effect. It appears to undermine the chronological progress, however minimal, made by the text and seems to produce another deformation of a time already seemingly deformed by its (lack of) velocity. The proliferation of narrative forms in individual chapters as well as throughout all of Part II produces a series of ruptures. Yet those apparently discontinuous, because heterogeneous, chapters are also propelled by the continuous chronological movement toward the novel's closure. As we move from one chapter to another through the whole text, we move from one temporal framework, and thus one kind of temporality, to another.

It is indeed the question of time that figures so importantly in the reader-author dialogue in *The Buenos Aires Affair*. This is a novel (much like *Boquitas pintadas*) where a crucial factor is not only how but also when the reader acquires knowledge, when the authorial manipulator allows certain details to be seen and when he obscures them.

135

The experimental features of the novel's technical apparatus and temporal structure play an important part in constructing that dialogue between the figure of the author and that of the reader. Those features help to control our access to knowledge and to regulate the time and place in which the novel's "truth" might appear. We discover that, in Puig's detective novel, truth is more often than not only an appearance, a fiction designed to be read according to the conventions that same text upends.

It is not suprising that Puig's novel takes up and plays with the question of truth, since the detective genre revolves around that very notion. Indeed, a detective novel assumes and always seems to assure the possibility of arriving at a solution to a criminal problem by means of the rational, logical, stable procedures that conventionally constitute an investigation. The genre asserts not only the law of truth but also that of justice, each being bound to the other and having an inevitably teleological status in the text.[9] In *The Buenos Aires Affair* the manner in which truth is both uncovered and questioned is itself a surprise. It is a surprise upon which the text's power (over the reader) is generated, just as it ought to be. Somewhat like *Boquitas pintadas*, perhaps, the manner in which this novel breaks with convention might also be read as a conventional turn, a turn in a direction that we could be expected to anticipate but that, precisely because it also follows convention in a curious manner, blinds us to its manipulative, though artful, operations.

In the story of Gladys and Leo, and in the dialogue between authorial and readerly figures, the novel also turns around issues of pleasure and power. The erotic and political natures of those relationships come into view as transgressive and yet conventional elements. These two partnerships are not unlike one another. Each is, in its own way, a conventional contract between willing participants in some type of crime—that is, some kind of apparently transgressive, but nonetheless perfectly fitting, activity. In Puig's novel the author-reader dialogue is a relation between a subject who seems to know everything, to know the truth of the mysteries that generate the text, and another who is made to desire what the other knows, to seek out the truth that appears merely to be hidden from immediate view.

While Puig's *novela policial* leads its reader into a familiar trap, a trap agreed upon in a way by both these accomplices in textual crime, it does so without the aid of an authorized investigator—that is, a detective—whose steps we could follow to find solutions and closure. *The Buenos Aires Affair* renders literal the not uncommon figurative connection between the detective and the reader (that is, the detective as a kind of reader or the reader as a kind of detective) as the functions of the one are superimposed on the activities of the other. Although here there is no fictional character who, according to convention, could properly be charged with examining the evidence of the cases at hand and who is set up to both track down the truth and mete out punishment, these functions have not been eliminated from either story or text. While the author seems to "kill off" the character whose presence would seem to be a generic *sine qua non*, that figure's functions do not disappear from the novel. They are instead dispersed among and displaced onto the reader for whom the text is set up, and the fictional characters around whom the narrative charts its seductive and criminal path.

The truth that all the novel's investigators seek is not a singular, univocal truth. It is therefore difficult, if not impossible, to locate. A number of problems circulate in the novel, just as different roles or functions are played out by disparate and otherwise opposing subjects. The truth of the text we read is as much a fictional as a textual construct, and the truth of the story the text manipulates is as much a sexual as a criminal fiction. That is, the story is as much two "perfectly matched" stories of frustrated and seemingly criminal desire as it is the story of a genre in which those kinds of desire are, as a matter of course, to be frustrated. Curiously enough, Puig's characters are as much the protagonists of a play on a psychoanalytic or psychiatric case (Leo's and Gladys's biographies in Chapters VI and III are organized around the details of their psychological and sexual development, and each comes to look like a "classic case": Leo the sadist and Gladys the masochist are designed for each other) as they are the main actors in a criminal one (Leo appears as the criminal and Gladys as the victim).[10] And the novel's readers are as much the investigators of a crime of desire as they are the conventional subjects of a desire for crime.

In both fictional story and narrative text, those who appear to be victims are also accomplices in crime. Those who are cast as the novel's criminals are also its accomplished authors. And those who function as witnesses and readers are at the same time important actors in the crimes they merely appear to investigate. The play between these theoretically opposing roles and disparate functions is an important feature of the intertextual dialogue created by *The Buenos Aires Affair*. It regenerates, while also rewriting the relationships and recasting the identities that usually structure, the detective story. In the crucial chapters and scenes where those relationships and identities are established, one discerns the unstable relation between Puig's novel and the genre with which it works. To be sure, Puig's novel deforms that model in an apparently parodic reworking of its conventions. Yet, as with his other novels, the inventive operations through which that "deformation" is effected also regenerate and raise "up" the form.

One of the main problems here, then, has to do with reading: how to read this text "properly" (that is, both on its own terms and from a critical distance), not only to see how it operates as a form of narrative fiction, but also to determine its position in relation to a "low" tradition and a popular genre to which it displays its "high" connections. We must of course return to the novel itself, in order to read it as it is designed to be read, and to see how that question is played out from beginnning to end. In fact, throughout the novel the question of how to interpret things correctly is presented for us to read and work with simultaneously in several ways.[11]

From its opening chapters to its final pages *The Buenos Aires Affair* moves along as a play between the possibilities of reading and mis-reading, which are, in turn, connected to the question of seeing and not seeing things as they ought to be seen.[12] . As we turn to those first chapters and move along the path that has been charted for our interpretive activity, we can begin to understand how that play develops the criminal potential of the whole novel. The first two chapters reveal the beginnings of these problems of reading and seeing in a particularly suggestive way. Chapter I opens with the disappearance of Gladys and with her mother's investigation/interpretation of that mystery; Chapter II presents the "criminal scene" in which Gladys and her perfect partner, Leo, make their first appearance. In these chapters we are led to read Gladys's disappearance as the result of an abduction, while later, in Chapter XIII, where the reality of the criminal fiction is revealed, we are turned instead to the vision of a seduction.

Gladys's disappearance from one site (her bedroom in the house she shares with her mother in Playa Blanca) appears to lead logically, and even conventionally, to her appeareance at another (the "scene of the crime" in Leo's apartment bedroom in Buenos Aires, described in detail in Chapter II). The criminal scene is in a way just what it should be. It is to be read by those for whom it is designed; it has been set up so as to resist a correct, while promoting an incorrect, reading of things. This scene demonstrates that being able to read a scene or a text "correctly" depends on a number of things, not the least of which is the expectation held about what should or could be seen, as well as the kinds of details presented for view. A paradox characterizes the outcome of this first reading of Chapter II's important scene: the more we see, the less we are able to see things properly—that is, as they will be seen later on. Here so many details dazzle the eye that virtually nothing can be seen. All the details that look like facts turn out to be fictions that hide the truth which, by convention, will not be revealed until we arrive at its proper place—the end of the novel.

The novel's first two chapters are thus readable, but readable in a "wrong" way. We are literally able to read the text, to see clearly every detail presented. But the manner in which those details are presented, the manner in which the "lies have been framed," leads us to interpret them so as to miss the truth that they actually veil.[13] The details take us in the "wrong" direction, away from truth and toward a fiction. But, as we know, the wrong reading is also the right one in the detective genre. To read things correctly is to read them as we are meant to read them, to follow the role established for us by the novel's author and the genre's conventions. This is a role for which the text's reader is, and in a way agrees to be, set up. But in Puig's novel the reader is not the only subject who is being set up. Everyone here plays some kind of conventional role in what turns out to be a rather dramatic, even spectacular, reminder of the fundamentally theatrical nature of the criminal scenario in its conventional, as well as experimental, narrative forms.

In Chapters I and II we are given a set of details by an omniscient narrator who continually limits our view of things. (The view of some of its fictional characters seems to be limited as well.) Each detail presents us with a mystery whose solution is suggested by a series of cover-ups that hide the fact either that there is no solution at all or that the solutions suggested are nothing but suspended, seductive fictions. At the end of the first chapter we know little more than that Gladys has disappeared and that there may or may not be reason to suspect "foul play." Nevertheless, the text of that chapter repeatedly suggests that there is more than meets the eye of either the reader or Gladys's mother, Clara Evelia, who first investigates the situation. The facts of this first mystery are revealed simultaneously to Puig's reader and to Gladys's mother by a narrator who seems to allow the reader to see more than Clara Evelia, as she begins her investigation when she discovers Gladys missing from her bedroom.

Clara Evelia's investigation is a combination of efforts to put together evidence grounded in what is observed directly on the scene of the disappearance and, most significantly, in what is imagined and recalled while conducting the search. Her moves are registered by an omniscient "I"/"eye" from whose perspective we are also allowed to see what Clara Evelia seems to be missing from her restricted point of view. Consider the following: "Durante breves instantes sobre una de las ventanas se proyectó una sombra, tal vez los árboles del jardín se habían movido con el viento, pero Clara Evelia no prestó atención . . ." ["For a few seconds a shadow fell across one of the windows, perhaps the trees in the garden had moved with the wind, but Clara Evelia didn't pay attention . . . "] (10); or "La madre se puso de pie, no miró hacia la derecha—donde habría percibido una presencia inesperada—y corrió a buscar en el baño el canasto. . . . Volvió a la sala repitiendo el mismo recorrido en sentido inverso, por causas fortuitas no miró esta vez a su izquierda" ["The mother stood up, did not look to her right—where she might have noticed an unexpected presence—and ran to the bathroom to look for the basket. . . . She returned to the living room repeating the same course in the opposite direction, for fortuitous reasons this time she didn't look to her left"] (14).

There is a seductive but treacherous play between seeing and telling, between appearances and truths. We are apparently shown what the hidden, all-seeing narrator says Clara Evelia does not herself see. However, we do not know and cannot determine whether or not there is really anything to be seen, whether Gladys's mother has in fact missed anything of significance, and thus whether there is any truth in what the narrator appears to be telling us. The mention of "una presencia inesperada" or "una sombra," among other suspicious details (these are, we know, the types of details from which the clichés of mystery fiction are made), renders almost visible a "presence" whose reality is implied but unverified. This kind of description, with its emphasis on terms of incertitude, its use of rhetorical questions, verbs in the conditional and the subjunctive (see esp. 13–15), creates a setting that is just right for making us interpret the scene in a way that is also "wrong." The interpretation the text seems designed to elicit from the reader, if not also from Gladys's mother, is of course a criminal one. We are led to believe that Gladys has been abducted and that she might even be dead. We are likely to come to this conclusion even in the face of, or precisely because we see a potential denial of, a final, fatal appearance—the appearance of a dead body—at the chapter's end.

Significantly enough, Clara Evelia's procedures, her process of reasoning, finally lead her away from a criminal conclusion. At the end of the chapter, after having headed for the police station to report her daughter's apparently criminal disappearance, Clara Evelia turns from the police and that solution, concluding instead that her daughter may be in no danger at all, that she may have returned to the familiar place that Clara Evelia herself has just left. This final moment of the chapter is significant because it hinges on a set of contradictory turns. When Clara Evelia turns from one hypothesis to another—that is, from an image of Gladys in danger to an image of her safe at home—she also turns from the place where crime is all too familiar, the place where it can and should be addressed (i.e., the police station) to the place where crime seems at once familiar and strange, the place where she seems to want both to see and to hide it (i.e., her home).[14] In these parallel moves she would appear to turn from a vision that certifies death to one that promises life, from an interpretation of the facts at hand as criminal to a reading of them as innocent. However, that same turn away from a deadly crime coincides with another kind of return to it. There is a criminal displacement of death at the chapter's end. The disappearence of a live body from one potentially criminal scene makes possible the appearance of a corpse in another.

This turn toward death is a turn toward a text of fiction—a poem— whose fatal thematics permeate the thoughts of Gladys's mother and the text of the whole chapter. Interspersed with the narration of what she does and the description of what she thinks while she tries to locate

Gladys are the verses of a poem that Clara Evelia tries to remember and recite. Those verses interrupt the narrative, erupting into the text and the fiction at regular intervals. Gladys's mother is just as concerned with her effort to recall correctly all the verses of the poem and, therefore, to solve a "poetic" problem as she is with trying to read correctly the scene from which her daughter has disappeared. Although the poem might appear to be a distraction for the reader of Puig's novel (as it interrupts, it also postpones the advancement of the narrative action and defers the presentation of the "real" problem and investigation) and a flight into fantasy for the fictional character, its "irrelevant" poetic appearance turns out to be relevant after all.

Precisely at the moment of Clara Evelia's turn home, she finally succeeds in remembering all the words to the poem that centers on and also ends with an appearance of death. The poem, by Bécquer, is in fact a Romantic meditation about death. It focuses on the figure of a dead girl, whose burial place its verses also describe.[15] This image of death is present even before Gladys's mother discovers that her daughter is missing. Clara Evelia is in fact already thinking about death, and especially about the relationship between the dead and the living (e.g., 10), from the beginning of the chapter. The text of the chapter thus presents us with a vision of impending death, even the figure of death itself, before anyone can identify its victim.

Clara Evelia terminates not one but two searches on the morning of 21 May 1969 (the text supplies the date and place on its first page; see 9). She arrives at two parallel solutions: she opts for a noncriminal view of Gladys's disappearance, and she finally locates the missing words to the poem. Yet this coincidence of solutions brings with it the reappearance of a criminal question in the form of a dead body. This body (re)appears at the very moment when Clara Evelia also acknowledges that she doesn't know where Gladys might be. Clara Evelia's investigations come to an end as follows: "' . . . cuando las maderas / crujir hace el viento / y azota los vidrios / el fuerte aguacero, / de la pobre niña / a solas me acuerdo. / Del húmedo muro / tendida en un . . . / tendida en un . . .' ¿cómo seguía? consultó su reloj-pulsera, eran las nueve y media de la mañana ¡qué no hubiese dado por saber dónde estaba su hija en ese preciso momento! '. . . allí cae la lluvia / con un son eterno; / allí combate / el soplo del cierzo. / Del húmedo muro / tendida en un . . . en un ¡*hueco*! / acaso de frío / se hielan sus huesos

. . . ', logró por fin recordar, con satisfacción" ["' . . . when the wind makes / the rafter creak, / when the violent rain / lashes the windows, / lonely I remember / that poor girl. / Stretched in the . . . in the . . .' what came next? she looked at her wristwatch, it was nine-thirty A.M., what wouldn't she have given to know where her daughter was at that very moment! 'there falls the rain / with its noise eternal, / there the northwind / fights with the rain. / Stretched in the . . . in the *hollow*! / of the damp bricks, / perhaps her bones freeze with the cold . . .' finally she remembered, to her satisfaction"] (17–18; italics mine).[16] Clara Evelia here recuperates the lost and last word of the poem, and with that word recovers the entire text. This vision made whole, along with the poem reconstituted as a complete, finished vision of death, produces in Gladys's mother a certain kind of pleasure. The pleasure of solving this poetic problem is, ironically enough, also the pleasure of seeing a dead body in its place. This pleasure seems to put an end to (or perhaps it only covers up) Clara Evelia's worries, her fantasies of death, as well as the uncertainty intrinsic to an investigatory process that actually remains suspended, without a solution.

The word that first eludes Clara Evelia and that she finally recalls, capturing and returning it to its proper place, is significant. When "hueco" ("hollow" or "hole") is put back where it belongs, it manages to fill in the spaces that its prior absence creates in her recitation and in the narrative text. Nevertheless, it doesn't really put back anything at all. The space left empty before the word's return is finally filled by a sign of emptiness, by a word that asserts that what is in its place is virtually nothing, literally a hole, a void. This relationship between an image of something that proclaims itself to be nothing—a kind of fiction—and the textual space into which it is inserted, where it occupies a powerful, if also puzzling, place, is like the relation between the poem and the chapter in which it appears. The poem, a fiction that fills in much of Clara Evelia's thoughts while she conducts her search for her daughter, whose body is nowhere to be found, fills not only part of the chapter's text and Clara Evelia's mental ramblings, but also the criminal space created by the whole chapter. In that poem it is a female corpse that fills a funereal niche—a place designed for a body that is and isn't there, a body that in a way no longer exists except to mark the place of death. Clara Evelia's recitation of the poem therefore speeds up, at the same time that it postpones, the appearance of death and our arrival at an apparently fatal scene. It supplies the text with a body, a potentially criminal figure, that seems to fit perfectly into and fill the empty space created by Gladys's disappearance.

When we read the poem together with the events of Clara Evelia's investigation, we are forced to transpose the corpse from one fiction (the poem) into another (the narrative surrounding it). The disappearance seems to make possible this transposition and the moves that generate it. The chapter turns around a void and yet fills it both with theories about its origins and with images of its ends. In fact, that disappearance and the empty places it leaves behind—an empty bed, an empty room, an empty house—set everything in motion at the beginning and keep things moving until the end. The whole novel turns around a mystery, the absence of a solution that, as it turns out, will later be revealed for what it is—a criminal fiction. Not unlike the deadly image of Gladys's mother's poem, this fiction fills in as one kind of truth while hiding another.

The move from the first chapter to the second also charts a path very much like the one we are made to follow through Clara Evelia's poem and the narrative that surrounds it. The reading we undertake in moving between the first two chapters is, moreover, not unlike the reading we are made to give the whole novel. The process by which both Clara Evelia and the novel's reader are led to accept and discard different answers to the problem of Gladys's disappearance is a process that turns us all from one criminal fiction to another, from one image of death to another. The text fills its perplexing voids with a dominant fiction: the image of death solidified in the corpse of the young girl seen in the poem of Chapter I and in the body of Gladys found in Chapter II. Though this fatal image seems to be a possibility too horrible for Clara Evelia's imagination, it is, we must remember, the very fiction toward which she is drawn and with whose complete representation she is finally so satisfied.[17]

The image of Gladys as the victim of some apparently violent crime, possibly as a corpse, is but another fiction, another fatal image designed to obscure the facts of this case. Chapter I's image of possible crime appears to be transformed in the second chapter into an image of crime made possible. It is a powerful image that seems to grow more real, more verifiable as we move along with the narrative text, which appears to fulfill our expectations along with Clara Evelia's fantasies.

What might seem to have been too horrible to be imagined directly in the first chapter is really what we are all waiting for and convinced we see in the second. The satisfaction of Chapter II is (not unlike the satisfaction figured at the end of Chapter I) the fulfillment of a desire to see something that is also too horrible to be seen.[18] The criminal scene that at first could only be imagined is here presented for full view. The body missed at the beginning of the text reappears for our careful examination. The apparent scene of one crime (an abduction) gives way to what looks like the scene of another (a murder).

The scene of the crime in Chapter II is both a set and a set-up. It is a kind of theatrical scene, a spectacle, designed for a specific audience. It is a trap in which that audience is meant to be caught. The set includes a man and a woman whose appearance is described at exactly 9:30 A.M. on 21 May 1969 (22; this is meant to coincide with the events and report of the time at the end of Chapter I, as the end of Clara Evelia's search, cited above, also indicates). It also contains a set of potentially criminal objects to be found in the apartment where the man stands, wearing only a towel while listening to the sounds of someone who approaches his door, and where the woman lies gagged, bound, and apparently unconscious on a bed. These characters and objects are described in such a way that it would be hard to avoid seeing them as protagonists and props of some kind of criminal scene.

That the objects (they include a cleaver, a pair of scissors, a Smith .38 [*sic*] revolver, a pair of acupuncture needles, a piece of cotton saturated with chloroform, two injection vials, and a metal sterilization box; see 21–23) are potentially criminal is suggested not only by their apparently violent functions but also by their conventionally criminal nature (as recognizable clichés of detective fiction). That the characters are the protagonists of some crime is suggested by the powerful but ambiguous description of the apparent victim: "La piel de la mujer inmóvil es muy blanca, la mordaza de la boca ha sido improvisada con un pañuelo de hombre de seda multicolor pero sobria, las manos están atadas por detrás con una corbata de luto. El color de los ojos de la mujer no se alcanza a percibir porque están cerrados, además, debajo del párpado izquierdo falta el globo ocular correspondiente. En el resto del cuerpo no se vislumbran huellas de violencia, tales como hematomas violáceos o heridas con sangre coagulada roja oscura. Tampoco hay rastro alguno de violencia sexual" ["The woman's skin is very white, the gag in her mouth has been improvised out of a man's silk handkerchief, multi-colored but sober, her hands fastened behind her with a mourning tie. The color of the woman's eyes cannot be seen because they are closed, besides, under her left eyelid the corresponding eyeball is missing. On the rest of the body there are no signs of violence, such as purple bruises or wounds clotted with dark blood. Neither is there any sign of sexual violence"] (20–21).

Although the description of the apartment and its multitude of "criminal" objects never tells us, even in some way denies, that there is a crime to be seen, the manner in which it does so—the manner in which the all-knowing but unidentified "I" tells what the all-seeing but hidden "eye" sees—makes it impossible not to imagine the violent acts toward which it also lures us. For example, in the description of the "victim" above, the narrative dares the eye to see what it also tells us is not there. Although the woman looks like a victim of violence, there is in fact no evidence of violence on her. However, by stating graphically what is not to be detected, what is indeed not "written" on her body ("hematomas violáceos o heridas con sangre coagulada roja oscura"), the narrator also makes us see the very signs of crime that are supposedly absent. The narrator's words inscribe a fiction of violence on the body of this woman, making it difficult to erase those violent marks or to see her as other than a victim. If the traces of violence are refused a place within the scene itself, they are granted a special, powerful place within the narrative discourse that presents it, within the language that is used to construct the fiction and through which that scene is contaminated and circumscribed in a criminal fashion.

We read this scene not only as a self-enclosed fiction but also as a narrative unit within a textual sequence. What we are led to believe in the chapter that precedes it has as great an effect on our interpretation of it as what it presents by itself. If in the first chapter a woman's body is missing (a woman described in a certain incriminating way: she has no left eye; she is presumed to be wearing only a nightgown covered by a fur coat [15–16]), in the second that body seems to be found and, moreover, identified as Gladys, the daughter of Clara Evelia (the woman in this scene is missing her left eye; there is "un camisón de tela sintética arrumbado en un rincón" ["a synthetic nightgown thrown in a corner"] [23]). Just as the first chapter suggests that there may be something horribly criminal to be seen, the second seems to reveal it in all its gory detail. Our reading, though, goes in two directions. What we read in Chapter I turns us toward a certain reading of Chapter II. What we read in Chapter II pushes us retroactively to read Chapter I in a criminal way, to certify the criminal implications (the image from the poem) and to negate the claim of innocence (Clara Evelia's conclusion). Of course, we also await and are ready to read (here that also means being ready to help author) this scene of crime because the novel's subtitle tells us that it has to be there, somewhere.

We discover in Chapter XIII that this scene is made to look like what it is not but nonetheless might yet become. This chapter is set up so that on a first reading we can't quite see it or place it correctly because of both the temporal play that surrounds it (the temporal inversion that structures the novel's narrative development) and the temporal play within it. Narration in this chapter is essentially description—a mechanical, meticulously detailed presentation of what an omniscient photographic eye sees at one specific moment ("un reloj eléctrico de madera y bronce . . . marca las 9.30" ["a bronze and wooden clock . . . says 9:30"] [22]).[19] This description removes the scene from the flow of time, fixing its contents in both time and space. The characters and objects appear "frozen" in a criminal tableau or set.

Consider, for example, the opening of the chapter, which describes Leo, the apparent criminal, and a later passage, which both describes objects just as they are and suggests a criminal way of seeing things: "Está de pie en medio de la habitación, el cuerpo alerta. Como única vestimenta lleva una toalla arrollada a la cintura que muestra los músculos en tensión de las pantorrillas velludas, en tanto los brazos fuertes extendidos hacia adelante presentan las manos crispadas, con los dedos enarcados. La boca entreabierta denota sorpresa" ["He stands in the middle of the room, his body alert. His only garment is a towel, wrapped around his waist, which doesn't cover the tensed muscles of his hairy calves, while his strong arms, thrust forward, display contracted hands with arched fingers. His half-opened mouth shows surprise"] (19); "En el cajón más alto están guardados los cubiertos, abrelatas y sacacorchos. Pero el borde más filoso corresponde a la cuchilla, habitualmente guardada, por su tamaño mayor, en el segundo cajón, más espacioso, junto a servilletas y manteles de uso diario. No se encuentra allí en este momento, y además sería difícil determinar si dicha cuchilla no es menos filosa que la tijera de acero inoxidable traída como

147

regalo de Toledo, y colocada sobre el escritorio de la habitación principal junto a una pila de revistas y diarios con artículos marcados para recortar, a pocos centímetros de un cortapapel de borde casi romo" ["The silverware, can openers, and corkscrews are kept in the highest drawer. But the sharpest edge belongs to the kitchen-knife, usually kept, because of its size, in the more spacious second drawer next to the everyday napkins and tablecloths. It is not there at this moment, and besides it would be hard to determine whether or not that knife is sharper than the rustproof steel scissors brought as a gift from Toledo, and placed on the desk in the main room beside a pile of magazines and newspapers with articles marked for clipping, a few inches from an almost blunt-edged paper cutter"] (22).[20] This manipulation of time—this freezing of objects and entities—makes it impossible to situate the presumed criminal action within it. It is impossible to tell, for example, whether certain objects have already been or will be used in a criminal act. It is impossible to tell whether the narrative catches the characters prior to, in the middle of, or after some criminal scene.

Even though we cannot see exactly what is going on here, the technique used to present the scene makes it seem as if everything is entirely visible and thus interpretable in a correct way. There seems to be nothing to impede our view or our reading of the scene, because everything seems to be protected from the changes that the passage of time can bring. As we follow the record left by the omniscient narrator who registers every detail, catching and revealing what might be missed if time were allowed to flow on, the scene takes on a truthful appearance. Yet, precisely because the temporal flow is tampered with, the truth that appears here is nothing more than a fiction—a fiction grounded in a view that seems decidedly omniscient. Though this fiction would appear to close off further investigation, it actually leaves things open for examination. Here where things seem not to move at all, or at best to move slowly, it is as if they were moving too fast. Even as we imagine or believe ourselves to be "with" the narrator, and perhaps even "ahead" of the scene itself, we later discover that we are still somewhere "behind," trying to catch up with the mystery in which we are also getting caught.[21]

Puig's novel catches us getting caught up in catching the two main characters getting caught. As they are frozen in this scene, Leo and Gladys appear to have been "caught in the act." This act is at once criminal and sexual; it is, in either reading, rather theatrical as well. The chapter and the scene it presents are analogues of one another. They are perfectly staged "crimes" authored and directed for their respective audiences by the manipulative authorial figure that seems to move above the text and by the artistically criminal character who moves within it. Just as the text's author has set up the novel's scene for its reader, one of its protagonists (Leo) has arranged it for a particular witness in the fiction. The text of Chapter XIII reveals that the crime of Chapter II is not in fact a crime, even though it has been staged to look like one. When we finish the novel, we see our expectation of a solution frustrated. However, it is not that there is no solution to the text, even though there is no solution to the "crime," for the absence of a solution to that crime is itself the solution to the text.[22]

Leo's crime is a "perfect crime" because it is a perfect fiction: its players are perfectly matched and its audience perfectly chosen. Leo stages this criminal scene in order to hide a previous one—a criminal scene in which he actually identifies himself as a murderer. Having virtually confessed that crime to an artist named María Esther Vila, whose anonymous reports to the police (see esp. 83–85 and 175–80) bring Leo under brief investigation (197–200), Leo fashions a scene designed to convince his interlocutor that what she has been told is a lie and that what she sees is the truth. The scene in Chapter II is a cover-up for that other criminal scene that follows it in the text but precedes it in the story. The original crime in the text is therefore not the original crime in the fiction. It is, rather, a substitute, an artifice which nonetheless also tells the truth.[23]

The "real" crime, described in Chapter VI, is displaced in the novel, its place having been usurped by Leo's fiction. His staged scene comes out into the open to distract its viewers from what has already happened but is not yet available for us to see. (The original crime takes place in 1949, twenty years prior to Chapter II's scene; we "see" it in Chapter VI.) That crime is virtually hidden within the novel, along with others that match it in significant ways, as we shall see. Yet from that position (its undercover place) it motivates and supports the many artificial scenes that structure Puig's *novela policial*. Leo's exercise in criminal art has as its goal a mimetic (re)production so convincing, an artificial scene so verisimilar and powerful, that readers might suspend their disbelief and take it for the truth, the very truth that it is meant to obscure.[24] However, this scene is based on a prior criminal truth from which it derives its own structure. This structure is at once textual and fictional; through it both of its authors work to imitate a conventional truth in order to impede the appearance of a criminal reality.

The reality to which Leo's scene refers is itself not an entirely substantiated or verifiable truth, for the crime for which Leo regards himself as guilty is never totally established by the text. Two kinds of truth, two sorts of reality, are at play here—one material, the other psychical. In *The Buenos Aires Affair*, where psychoanalytic models seem to be both parodied and stylized, the psychical rather than the historical reality seems to carry the most weight for the principal characters.[25] Whether Leo is in fact a murderer matters less than that he believes himself to be one. The chain of associations and actions that derive from that 1949 scene and that are determined by Leo's perception of himself as a guilty subject involve a series of crimes, both real and fictional, both historically related yet unconnected, that finally converge upon him. In the end this subject plays the role of both criminal and victim and functions as both guilty actor and prosecuting witness in a violent scene of punishment whose details we see only on the body it leaves behind—Leo's own body (234–37)—near the novel's end.[26]

The descripton of Leo's 1949 crime is given in the section entitled *"Juventud de Leo"* [*"Leo's youth"*] (103–8). We are told that, while out on a walk one Sunday (the date is 4 October 1949), Leo is approached by "un sujeto rubio de caminar delicado" ["a slight blond person of the masculine gender and with a delicate gait"] (106), whose proposition for a homosexual encounter he accepts. What is intended as a sexual meeting turns into a violent confrontation. (This turn, by the way, is not surprising if we consider Leo's "case history" as a sadist for whom sex and violence are never far apart.) Leo's sexual accomplice becomes his criminal victim. His partner's resistance to his desire to inflict pain for his own pleasure provokes a more violent response (Leo strikes him with a brick) through which the unidentified "sujeto rubio" is turned into a compliant victim (107). The scene of this *crimen del baldío* is where the meeting between sex and violence, already linked in Leo's psychical biography, is taken to its limits in his material reality. Moreover, this criminal scene is at the same time so overdetermined that it leads Leo himself to read it incorrectly.[27]

Leo assumes that the outcome of his violent act is indeed fatal, and his exaggerated sense of guilt later pushes him to confess, while also compelling him to cover up, his actions. The murder, however, is never really verified by the novel's text. The morning after Leo himself anonymously reports the crime to the police (107), the narrator declares that " . . . entre las noticias policiales del diario figuraba el caso de un amoral encontrado en fin de vida en un baldío, por aparentes motivos de hurto. Nunca apareció crónica referente a la captura del culpable. Tampoco se publicó la noticia de la muerte de la víctima" [". . . among the police chronicles there was a notice about a pervert found near death in a vacant lot, the apparent motive robbery. A report referring to the capture of the guilty party never appeared. Neither did the notice of the victim's death"] (108). While this wording certainly suggests that Leo's victim dies, it never actually certifies that fatal end. As it is written, the newspaper report (or the narrator's account of that report) can be read to mean either that the victim dies but that no report of his death is ever printed, or that the news of the man's death never appears because he does not in fact die. This textual ambiguity, however, informs only the representation of historical reality within the novel. In Leo's psychical reality there is no question of interpretation. This psychical reality dominates Leo's world and the novel's text; it authorizes the construction of the criminal scene of Chapter II/XIII; it is the view of things that leads Leo on a path to both penitence and punishment.

Immediately following the description of the *crimen del baldío*, for example, we see how this criminal version of Leo's actions—the image of Leo as a murderer still undiscovered and unpunished, but already pursued—begins to inform his interpretations of material reality as well. In the section entitled "*Actividades políticas*" ["*Political activities*"] (108–9), Leo's experience in prison is transformed into a painful punishment and pleasurable purgation.[28] Having been tortured, Leo confesses the political secrets he is "guilty" of possessing but is finally unable to keep. He not only suffers but also analyzes that suffering so as to make himself pay (through both pain and pleasure, it seems) for his various, and now superimposed, crimes. In his mind these crimes become inextricably bound to one another as they meet in scenes imagined by him, their guilty subject: "Cuando vio que uno de los agentes volvía a enrollar el cable, Leo pensó si el sujeto del baldío antes de morir habría sufrido tanto como él. Se preguntó si con la tortura recién infligida habría ya pagado en parte por el crimen cometido, y se respondió a sí mismo que ahora además de asesino era delator, las lágrimas fluyéndole gruesas como gotas de glicerina. Fue sintiendo un alivio creciente, pensó en la satisfacción que los mártires cristianos habrían experimentado en medio de sus peores sufrimientos" ["When he saw that one of the policemen was rewinding the wire, Leo wondered if the person in the lot had suffered as much before dying. He wondered if, through the torture he had just undergone, he had already paid in part for the crime committed, and he answered himself that now besides being a murderer he was an informer, tears flowing from him as thick as glycerine drops. He then felt a growing relief, he thought of the satisfaction the Christian martyrs must have felt in the midst of their worst suffering"] (109). In this play between pain and pleasure, between suffering and satisfaction, Leo turns from the position of criminal to that of (his own) victim through an internal process by which he both punishes and pardons himself. Moreover, his experience as both victim and victimizer is turned into a type of (erotic parody of) religious experience. It is precisely this combination of criminal positions that proliferates and is repeated throughout both Leo's and Gladys's stories. Those stories become stories of that same repetition, as well as repetitions of the same story.

That Leo's crime is not forgotten and that, even after twenty years, it still remains to be paid for is duly emphasized by the events that immediately precede his staging of the criminal scene that sets the novel in motion. Appropriately enough, it is around and, finally, toward the question of justice that Leo's actions seem to move in the month or so preceding that staged scene and in the several chapters that lead up to its reenactment. Leo's obsession with the question of justice manifests itself in relation to two other "criminal" cases through which he tries to pay for his crime and to right a wrong for which he is, or imagines himself to be, responsible. The case in which he is most directly involved is a case that has to do with artistic judgment and justice. An art critic by profession, Leo participates in the selection of Gladys, an artist "discovered" by him, as Argentina's representative in the 1969 "Muestra de San Pablo." This selection is complicated by the fact that Gladys and Leo become lovers while he is choosing her as his candidate for the show.

To an extent, their meeting represents a perfect encounter between partners who seem to be designed for each other both by "fate" and by the text's author. This match is considered by Gladys, moreover, to represent the transformation of romantic desire and fantasy into certifiable reality. The meeting is described in precisely these terms in Chapter VII, where we read an imaginary magazine interview that Gladys authors. Gladys, who is actually lying next to Leo in a hotel room, plays the interviewed "star" who, in response to the questions typical of the popular format, relates her meeting and first sexual encounter with Leo, whose seduction of (or, rather, sexual assault on) Gladys seems to represent the fulfillment of her romantic fantasies. The interview's title is identical with the title of Puig's novel and is supposedly chosen as much for the readership of *Harper's Bazaar*, the magazine for which the interview is granted (" . . . a sus lectores dirijámonos en un lenguaje chic e internacional, 'The Buenos Aires Affair' será el título" [" . . . for your readers let's use a glamorous international language, 'The Buenos Aires Affair' will be the title" (trans. mine)] [123]), as it is for the readers of the novel, since its intriguing, melodramatic quality situates its "story" and "characters" in the same realm as those of the novel's filmscript epigraphs.

This meeting is, however, not so perfect for Leo. He interprets Gladys's desire and their "match" as an artificial reality, because he reads them as part of a plan to manipulate and deceive him into doing precisely what he first desires and decides to do (i.e., to choose Gladys as the Argentine representative). Convinced that his own judgment is somehow in error and that the selection is unjust, he decides that another selection must be made, that a more deserving and properly chosen artist must be substituted for Gladys. On 22 April Leo begins to make that substitution. He decides to withdraw his support of Gladys and to put in her place María Esther Vila, a sixty-year-old artist who, given her views on art and artistic creation, is a decidedly different type of representative. (María Esther believes her art to be an expression or translation of an idea and previous plan that she formulates before undertaking to work on a piece; she does not believe that the unconscious plays a major role in the artist's work [159]. Gladys seems to have no intellectual or theoretical understanding of her work or any such basis for creating it; her work is a kind of unconscious "dialogue" with natural objects transformed into art by her "conversations" with them [126–27, 131].) Simultaneous with this seemingly artistic decision and displacement is another concerning a crime that Leo reads as an uncanny repetition, even duplication, of the crime he committed in 1949. By trying to take restitutive action for the one through the other, Leo is determined to pay for his criminal acts. The artistic and criminal cases are obviously linked, as the narrator emphasizes, because through each " . . . procuraba reparar una injusticia" [" . . . he was attempting to make amends for an injustice"] (158).

These two cases are also, in a sense, two potent criminal fictions invented by Leo. They are fictions generated by his sense of guilt; they are grounded in the previous, apparently original crime. If in one he imagines a plot from which he wants to extricate himself, in the other he fabricates a situation into which he desires to be inserted. In deciding to offer financial aid to the family of the victim of the 1969 *crimen del baldío* from under the cover of his position as a member of the press, Leo identifies himself with all its significant parties and virtually reveals his criminal identity, or at least his guilty conscience, in the process. At once reader of and author/actor in the scenario, Leo offers financial aid to the family in what seems to be an effort to pay for his own crime. In making such a payment he would atone and yet be punished for the effects of the crime, which, by virtue of that payment, would in a way also be erased. The payment would allow him to fill the position left vacant by the missing head of the family. He seems to want to support that family because he casts himself as the criminal responsible for the disappearance of its father-provider. He would substitute himself for the figure who has been vacated from his proper place. (Leo's identification with that victim is also suggested by the description of the dead man as a political activist who has suffered physical torture [154; cf. 106–7].) Yet, in that the widow at first refuses to accept his offer (158) and later changes her mind when it is too late to pursue the offer further (165, 247), Leo is prevented from carrying out his plan to work in the name of justice. By the end of the novel, however, he is given another chance to see that justice is done and that his final payment can be made.

Leo's actions in both of these cases are at once restitutive and confessional. He is at once the upholder and violator of laws from which he is unable to escape. His effort to conceal his own guilt brings with it the revelation of his criminal identity. This is a revelation over which he seems to have less and less control as time passes, both in the fiction in which he operates and in the text that presents all his fictions. His ultimate plan for covering up that criminal truth is, like the cases in which he involves himself before Chapter XIII, a design through which that truth is also revealed. However, repeating as he does the "criminal" strategies of the textual authority also responsible for all of his crimes, it is precisely through his artistic unveiling of the truth that he is also able to cover up the criminal facts. In each case it seems that Leo shows himself for what he is, but to those who cannot see it. This is especially true for the scene of the crime he sets up for María Esther to see. This scene doesn't allow itself to be seen or interpreted "correctly" when it first appears. Its secret is kept from view of the witness within the fiction (María Esther) and the reader of the text, each of whom is set up to see it in a certain way. The techniques used to set up María Esther for the scene are orchestrated by Leo. Like the authorial figure implied in the text, Leo first predicts and then produces a scene his reader is afraid to see but into which she is nevertheless lured as an interested, if not also active, party.

In the course of a series of talks (hidden dialogues) with María Esther in Chapter IX—talks that result from his decision to replace Gladys with her for the San Pablo show—Leo confesses his "unjust" action. After declaring himself repentant for that action, he tries to enlist his interlocutor in a plan to "fix things," to somehow get rid of Gladys (160–61). His discourse moves from the theme of repentance to a declaration of his desire to kill Gladys and to a confession, elicited by his interlocutor, of a past crime, and back again to those points in the sequence of their conversations. The crime to which he seems finally to confess is the murder of a young woman, and it is around that image that he builds his scene for María Esther. She takes him seriously and anonymously reports him to the police (Chapter V), who, in order to investigate a scene to which they have no direct access, call in Leo for an interview (Chapter XII). However, his encounter with the police allows him to establish his innocence by remaining under the cover of the fictions he has authored.

Leo, pursued now not only by his own sense of guilt but also, apparently, by the authorized representatives of justice (the police), authors a scene for the very subject who, through his confession to her, virtually has become a witness to his crime. It is precisely around her role as witness that Leo works. He consciously decides to fashion a scene, to author a criminal scenario, just for María Esther's "incorrect" reading. Chapter XII describes his "criminal" logic, ending with the omniscient narrator's formulaic presentation (the summary statement is repeated throughout this section; see 202–5) of his final plan: "Por entonces sus razonamientos, en términos resumidos, eran los siguientes: si María Esther Vila llegaba al lugar en que el crimen estaba por cometerse—era él quien iba a matar a una mujer—y lo desbarataba—aparentemente—con su presencia imprevista, ella no dudaría más de la intención que él tenía de matar a una mujer; impidiendo de ese modo el asesinato de una mujer a manos de él, María Esther Vila terminaría por convencerse de que el crimen del baldío había sido de la misma índole" ["By then his reasoning, in summary, was as follows: if María Esther Vila came to the place where the crime was about to be committed—it was he who was going to kill a woman—and she prevented it—apparently—with her unexpected presence, she would no longer doubt his intention to kill a woman; thus preventing the murder of a woman at his hands, María Esther Vila would be convinced that the crime in the vacant lot had been of the same sort"] (205).

Leo lures María Esther to the scene with the promise of a crime to be seen. However, her status as mere witness is upgraded, so to speak, to that of an accomplice. In the surprising, but in a way not unexpected, set of turns taken by the scene, she becomes one of the actors in it. María Esther is set up by Leo to enter the scene when, after telling her that Gladys is unconscious in his apartment and that " . . . ya no respondía de sus actos" [" . . . he was no longer responsible for his actions"], he insists that " . . . solo María Esther podía impedir una desgracia, debía acudir a su lado" [" . . . only María Esther could prevent a tragedy, she must rush to his side"] (208). Leo here puts the responsibility for his apparently imminent crime on someone who would seem to have nothing at all to do with it, someone who is an innocent outsider. Yet the question of crime and guilt does indeed also rest with María Esther. She is the subject in whom the question of Leo's criminality has come to rest; she is the "mother confessor" onto whom he has transferred knowledge of his criminal desires, if not also his criminal actions. Although the police no longer suspect him of a crime (indeed, they believe him to have been falsely accused), he would still look guilty in the eyes of María Esther. And that is what seems to matter most to him. Leo stages a fictional scene that, if it works, will obliterate the real one from the mind and eye of María Esther. In fact, by authoring a fiction designed to appear as a reality, Leo manages to transform a reality into a fiction. Yet the fiction performed and staged by Leo also tells a truth—the very truth that he attempts so "artistically" to hide. The role in which he casts himself is precisely the one he wishes to erase from the mind of his audience. The scene he sets up is precisely the kind of scene he wants to deny. The scene he constructs with Gladys is a scene apparently both sexual and criminal, a scene in which a sexual act appears to have been turned into a murderous one. Leo's guilty role, as well as the nature of the scene in which his criminal identity is first (1949) established, are here displayed for everyone to see.

Not unlike the authorial strategist under whose eyes Leo the fictional character would seem to take shape, Leo the criminal artist deploys a tactic we have already seen. In this criminal scene staged by Leo for María Esther, the only way the facts can be hidden is if there are too many other facts to be seen. The only way Leo can hide his crime is to veil it with another criminal fiction, a fiction that also tells the truth. Here the possibility of obscuring the truth or impeding its perception is grounded in the manipulation of the scene's temporality. Leo's design involves stopping time, in a way, as well as convincing María Esther that she is the one who has stopped it. Leo stages the scene in a present that, masquerading as the future, seems also to erase the past. Just as the interruptive strategies of the text impede the development of that scene, María Esther's entrance stops the scene from moving on as it seems to have been planned by Leo. (We recall that between Chapters II and XII time virtually stands still for this scene. The scene in Chapter II is frozen at the moment when María Esther is about to enter it; the rest of the novel slowly brings us back to that scene, reinserting it into the temporal flow whose velocity gradually decreases as we again approach it. We move toward it, into it, and beyond it with the novel's text.)

This scene takes another turn as we and María Esther enter it. It moves in surprising and yet predictable directions. This turn, moreover, is also a return to the original scene of the crime (that is, the crime committed by Leo in 1949): the scene that is set up to look like a prelude to death turns out to be an introduction to sex. This scene moves in the opposite direction from the one in Leo's youth (the latter moves from sex to apparent death, the former from apparent death to sex) and thereby seems to undo or rewrite it. However, the scene in 1969 goes beyond the bounds of its criminal predecessor in other ways as well, for the seduction scene into which it is transformed involves a seduction of those who are presumably beyond as well as within its borders. María Esther, originally cast as the witness to crime, is seduced not only by the fiction set up for her but also by the actors engaged in its provocative activity. When she enters the scene, it is as an accomplice in sexual activity: although Leo begins by pretending that he will kill Gladys with the revolver he holds in his hand, he ends by having intercourse with her and, at the same time, caressing María Esther, who all the while also watches everything that goes on.

Not unlike the reader of Puig's novel, perhaps, María Esther is seduced by and into a fiction of criminal seduction.[29] She acts just as she is meant to act. She sees what she is supposed to see, what has been arranged and authored with her in mind. But she is so caught by the characters who seem to be caught by her that she is unable to keep her distance from the situation. She is unable to stay outside the scenario to which she is being led as both witness-reader for and accomplice to its author. María Esther's presence is necessary for the scene itself to (appear to) take place. She is involved in it from the start, even as she appears to remain outside it. This witness turned accomplice is in fact already an accomplice from the moment she becomes a witness. She nevertheless resists and rejects the positions that she holds; she refuses to play further the roles she has initially agreed to fill.

When María Esther leaves the "scene of the crime," she does so apparently in order to work against the spectacle to which she is initially so attracted. She seems to become aware of the fact that she has been caught, that she has been manipulated, that she has been "had" by Leo and perhaps even by Gladys. Her statement, reported by another witness (the *portero* of Leo's building, whose potential account of what he sees when he arrives on the scene appears in Chapter XIV, 226–30), clearly marks her exit from the drama: " . . . dijo que a esa casa no venía más, y que ella no se quería meter más en el asunto . . ." [" . . . [she] said that she wasn't coming to that house anymore, and that she didn't want to have anything further to do with the matter

. . . "] (228). To reach María Esther's exit from the scene is not, in the end, to leave the scene itself behind. Its principal actors remind us in several ways that no crime has really been solved, that the truth remains to be seen and justice to be done in this *novela policial*. Moreover, even after it seems that the criminal is finally punished and, therefore, that some of the laws of the genre are upheld, much remains to be read in the text, much that can't quite be read within the bounds of that textual form.

Of particular interest here at the end of the novel is the way the text moves around the question of truth, the way it goes about carrying out justice, so as to work against and yet with the generic model to which it so openly refers. Puig's novel questions the possibility of ever establishing anything like the truth, even while it would seem to put truth on display. It fashions some form of justice as the inevitable end to the story and at the same time leaves the question of justice suspended. These issues are raised partly because, as noted earlier, the traditional seeker of truth and agent of justice (i.e., the detective) is not present— he is, in a sense, "done in" by the authorial figure who, from above it all, shares only with the omniscient narrator the knowledge that is sought by a variety of subjects in the novel. Yet that figure's functions—that is, his essentially investigative and judicial roles—are not at all denied their place in Puig's novel. As noted earlier, not only the reader of the novel but also several character-readers in the fiction take on the duties and positions generally assumed by that generically significant and central figure. Since there is no single investigator-interpreter, there seems to be no single truth to be sought and found in the novel. Since there is not just one crime in the text, there is no univocal solution to be represented. In fact, the investigations of Gladys's mother, the police, and Leo's psychiatrist reveal that the question of truth is here a question of interpretation. In the end, we see that the idea of truth is determined by how things can be seen—or made to be seen—in any situation.

The case of the "investigation" undertaken by Leo's psychiatrist is an apposite example of these interrelated questions because of the techniques and setting it involves and because of the material it examines. Leo's session with his psychiatrist on 24 April 1969 is presented in the form of a hidden dialogue from which the doctor's discourse has been suppressed (143–54). This reader-investigator is, nonetheless, implied by, because his comments are inscribed within, the discourse of Leo, his interlocutor.[30] The psychiatrist is a special kind of detective who, according to the practices (that is, the conventions) of his profession, remains essentially impassive as he presses for details and responds to the responses of his patient. In his apparent silence and invisibility, Leo's psychiatrist is a reader who, though reflected by his interlocutor's performance, remains outside but also bound to the discourse of the "text" with which he works. What Leo's psychiatrist appears to examine in their session together is not unlike what a variety of other readers—those within the fiction, as well as the reader inscribed within the text—have to read. Leo's ramblings take him toward a criminal scene whose details keep changing and whose truth remains open to question. The psychiatrist pushes, perhaps forces, Leo to reveal the facts of an apparently criminal scene that circulates insistently in his discourse. That scene and its authorial subject resist being seen, even though the doctor almost suceeds in uncovering (that is, getting Leo to uncover and thus to disclose) the truth, the material facts of the criminal act around which they both move. The course of his investigation, appropriately enough, follows a temporally inverted route. The effort to locate this truth is an effort to reconstruct events, to reveal the relationship among different details of both historical and psychical reality, so as to bring everything out into the open (i.e., into language) where it might be examined and resolved. However, what develops from this investigatory dialogue is a sequence of scenes, a set of variations on an ostensibly original scene that cannot, in the end, be revealed or known.

Leo, the author of the crime that refuses to be seen, resists and yet complies with his interlocutor's strategy. The session and the chapter in which this particular specialized reader seems to come so close to the truth are cut off, however, abruptly ended before any solution appears. In this exchange the psychiatrist can only work with the material Leo gives him. From that material he begins to move toward a "correct" interpretation of things. But, we recall, the truth for which he searches is as much psychical as material. The arrival at that truth would mean not the end but the beginning of another investigation, a search for the explanations of its origins, and so on. Regardless of how far the psychiatrist or the other readers in the novel proceed in their investigations, truth turns out to be something that cannot be seen in its fullness. It turns out to be something they have to construct, "correctly" or not, for themselves. That the truth is, after all, only an interpretation, a particular version of things, is a notion that Puig's text readily develops. However, it is an idea that the classical detective text would seem to deny, since it upholds the belief in solutions, answers, and truth through its conventional endings. As suggested above, even when we reach the end of *The Buenos Aires Affair*, we still do not possess a final solution for everything we have seen. While the case of Leo is in its own way solved, that of Gladys, the figure with whom the novel begins, remains open, even as the text turns back to her, apparently to close things off. On the other hand, Leo's case is closed in a manner that seems particularly appropriate for him. The ending to his story finally seems to give him what he appears to want all along and what the text itself, according to convention, seems to need: a sense of justice.

Leo, the author of at least one criminal scene in which everything seems to be placed so perfectly, is the figure chosen again to ensure that everything appears in its proper place. After the criminal-sexual scene of Chapter XIII in which he winds up rewriting, from a different angle, the scene he first works so hard to erase, Leo orchestrates a dramatic ending to his own criminal narrative. That narrative ends with its author playing all the major roles in another "perfect crime." Having failed to fashion an adequate cover for his guilt, having failed to find or create the witness-judge who would at once punish him for and absolve him of his guilt, Leo is left to close his case by himself. On the day after the scene in Leo's apartment, Leo continues to be pursued by the vision of crime that, although concealed from the (real or imagined) witnesses who surround him, remains all too visible to his mind's eye. While out on a drive—a drive upon which he embarks precisely because he feels himself to be pursued—he imagines that his guilt is seen by those who, appropriately enough, derive their positions from, because they are trained to work with, crime: the police. Although he alone knows the truth of his criminal identity, he believes it to be perceived by the world at large. His vision of that truth finally revealed is, of course, but an interpretation that appears to originate in his own desire to be seen. When the two policemen come after him for speeding, he reads the pursuit as proof of the discovery of the truth and the arrival of justice: "Lo atribuyó a que el crimen del baldío había sido finalmente descubierto por la policía, en complicidad esta última con su médico y María Esther Vila" ["He attributed this to the fact that the police had finally discovered the crime in the vacant lot, in complicity with his doctor and María Esther Vila"] (233–34). However, what appears to be just punishment is meted out not by the police but by Leo himself, not by those who are authorized to uphold the law but by the criminal who has violated it. Leo loses control of his car and is killed in an auto accident.

The economy of this end for Leo is rather neat and, oddly enough, somewhat conventional. On the person of this protagonist there converge a number of familiar roles and identities. As both victim and victimizer, "detective" and criminal, Leo manages to solve his own crime economically. By virtually acting in the name of justice, he punishes himself as the criminal. He thereby "solves" the crime that he himself has committed and closes his own case. This final death is itself a kind of final crime, a murder, to be precise, which only a criminal or, more conventionally, a detective can fashion. This final crime is a necessary crime, necessary for the character upon whom it makes its mark and for the text that is designed to compose it. The text turns out to be a circuitous and conventional return to death and crime which, in the end, allows some of its conventions to survive.[31]

Leo, the guilty subject, seems to search for and finally to author a crime that would be great enough to equal and merit his guilt. His death, moreover, puts an appropriate end to the criminal scenes that he authors and acts in throughout the novel. As we recall, Leo is the subject of a sexual biography in which victims and victimizers proliferate. His lived and fantasized realities all seem to revolve around relationships involving dramatic scenes that play out those roles (see esp. 104–5, 113–15, 118–19, for his sado-masochistic fantasies). His own death represents an uncanny and satisfying end to his problematic desires. Through that death he finds in himself the perfect partner for whom he seems to search throughout his life. As we remember, while Gladys, his "perfectly matched" opposite, would seem to fulfill what his fantasies of a victim describe, she does not in fact fill that fantasy. She is not, after all, the partner-victim for whom Leo searches. Leo, the sadist, seems to desire power over another whose pain appears to give him pleasure. Yet, even when he actually meets what he seems to have desired, that desire seems destined to be satisfied by no one but himself. His fantasies can only be equaled, or matched, by a reality filled with death—not the death of another subject, but the death of his overriding desire; that is, by his own suicide. Leo's death turns out to be a perfect meeting of desires, a moment in which fantasy and reality seem to coincide. His death appears as the ultimate and perfectly executed act of desire from which nothing remains. This suicide, this final death of desire, becomes a kind of "perfect death," another "perfect crime" through whose self-contained and reflexive moves the desires to stifle and yet satisfy desire meet.

This death of desire in Leo is, however, not the death of desire in the novel. As final as it may seem and as neatly as it may appear to close off this *novela policial*, this last murder does not solve everything. Something—actually someone—left over takes on the appearance of a criminal residue. That is, something remains from a set of crimes which is itself the sign of a crime that still remains to be resolved. The novel continues after Leo dies. Its final chapters return to Gladys, the protagonist of the first two chapters, as well as to the scene of the novel's original crime (i.e., Leo's apartment). These last two chapters focus on Gladys. She is the victim whose body is never removed, who remains as the sign of a crime that still needs to be solved. Her remaining image returns us to the network of criminal substitutions and repetitions that structure the whole novel.

The mystery of Gladys is mostly the mystery of an unsolved crime in which she initially plays the role of victim. There is another crime (a "real," as opposed to fantasized, crime; see 62–80) that parallels Leo's 1949 scene. In fact, both of these crimes are hidden within the middle of the text, where they first leave their marks on their central players: Leo, the criminal, emerges with a guilty conscience and Gladys, the victim, loses an eye. (There is an uncanny symmetry to the outcome of each criminal scene: the eye lost by Gladys in Chapter IV is in a way picked up by Leo, who imagines himself to be seen by the eyes of witnesses around him.) The mark left on Gladys is a mark that repeats itself, even before it appears as a result of the scene in which she is physically violated. Gladys is marked as a victim, even as a masochist, throughout the biographical account offered in Chapter III, as well as in the two preceding chapters. Gladys's biography focuses both on her development as an artist and (as for Leo) on the details of the family structure and relationships in which we are sup-

163

posed to see the origins of her problems. It repeatedly returns, either in fact or in fantasy, to the details of her sexual activities. As this biography focuses on those details at every stage of her life, it sets her up as a prospective victim of (sexual) violence. This victim's role is determined as much by her own desires as by the desires and designs of others. And, as we come to expect in *The Buenos Aires Affair*, the crime in which she is involved is a crime that unites sex and violence.

This crime appears to be another version of the crime we later see Leo perpetrate, even though some of the facts don't quite match. On 29 November 1962 Gladys is attacked while out walking one night; her assailant is a stranger who overtakes her; though his original intent to rape her is short circuited, she is nonetheless violently assaulted; her attacker runs off before he can be caught, leaving his identity and his fate a mystery. This scene is significant not only because it prefigures the future of Gladys's sexual fantasies and experiences, but also because it is structured as a symbolic scene that makes possible all of the repetitions that follow it. Like the crime in which Leo is involved, the scene of Gladys's attack turns in a direction different from the one that seems inevitable when it begins. Although one violent act is substituted for another and for a moment Gladys is empowered to work against her role as a victim, in the end she is forced to keep her place— the place where, we recall, she is actually fixed from the beginning of the text.

When approached and threatened by the unidentified assailant, Gladys begins to submit out of fear (" . . . la amenazó con una cachiporra recubierta de pinchos: no debía gritar" [" . . . [he] threatened her with a bludgeon covered with prickles: she must not scream"] [50]); but through a shift in her perspective (a shift that moves her from fantasy to reality, from an imagined fiction to a visible fact) she is also enabled to act in her own defense. This defense, which is also a kind of resistance to her assigned role, precipitates its own punishment, a punishment that she will later seem to use to her own advantage. She faces the reality of the situation and the corporal presence of her attacker—a reality at once less and more threatening than she had imagined, a reality whose power might also be undercut by parody (" . . . estaba embozado, de pie se bajó los pantalones y le mostró el miembro. Gladys notó que era mucho más pequeño de lo que había imaginado como tamaño común a todos los hombres, y al descubrirse el hombre el rostro ella vio que la boca era desdentada y la mirada perdida y demencial" ["His face was masked, standing up he lowered his pants and showed her his member. Gladys noticed that it was much smaller than what she had imagined as the common size in all men, and when he uncovered his face she saw that his mouth was toothless and the look in his eyes lost and insane"] [50]). She then becomes her own defender as she screams and drives off her assailant. However, this stranger quits the scene only after marking Gladys with a sign of their violent encounter, after precipitating the substitution of one kind of loss (her eye) for another (her virginity).[32]

Gladys seems to take the consequences of this event into her own hands, turning to her own advantage her image as a victim marked by violence. This criminal scene becomes for Gladys a crucial moment, a turning point in the sexual biography that she continues to author and act in. It is as if the attack constituted a kind of deflowering/castration through which Gladys is given, or perhaps gives herself, permission to begin to act out what up to that moment is only her fantasy. She first decides to lose her virginity and then embarks on a series of sexual relationships through which she gradually establishes her role as victim. In a way, she begins to prepare herself for her potentially perfect meeting with Leo. This image is bound up with the image of the criminal attacker whose identity remains undisclosed. However, his physical presence and performance are inscribed in all the similar scenes in which he lurks, under the names of the men who appear in Gladys's erotic fantasies, as the lover who repeatedly assaults her according to her own design (e.g., Bob, Frank, Lon, Leo; see Chapter IV).

The missing eye is likewise camouflaged and kept from view by two different but related strategies chosen by Gladys, the student of both "high" and "low" art and artifice.[33] She displays the various covers for the eye from the time she loses it in this first (also the second, according to its appearance in the text, as opposed to the story) unexpected criminal scene through the time of the other one that is meant to surprise us (first in the text, but second in the story). Immediately after the attack, we are told that she " . . . decidió llevar permanentemente anteojos muy grandes" [" . . . decided to wear dark glasses permanently"] (51). At the time of the crime that opens the novel, Gladys seems to have either substituted for or added to this covering device another that focuses on what is (as opposed to what is not) an eye to be seen, as her mother's mental description of her points out: " . . . Gladys antes nunca se maquillaba, pero con parte del rostro tapado por un mechón—no por una venda, ni por un parche de pirata, sólo la coquetería de un mechón—, el ojo resultó tan hermoso al pintarlo por primera vez" ["Before, Gladys had never put on make-up, but with part of her face covered by a lock of hair—not by a bandage, nor by a pirate patch, only the frivolity of a lock—, the eye looked so beautiful when made up for the first time"] (16; cf. 32). Gladys effects an appearance of mystery to which she herself is attracted. (She has a vision of herself as potentially "misteriosa y atractiva" ["mysterious and attractive"] before leaving for the United States, where "como extranjera" ["as a foreigner"] she would be viewed in this way, or so she imagines [43].) This image may even attract others to her (e.g., one of her lovers, in fact, finds her "interesante detrás de sus enormes gafas negras" ["interesting behind her enormous dark glasses"] [54]).

Gladys becomes the image of the "mysterious woman" and thus the woman she has fantasized about becoming, the woman about whose life others are curious to know. (Her "interview" in Chapter VII epitomizes some of the popular methods for getting at such a mystery, as well as perpetuating it; cf. Choli's discourse in Puig's first novel.) As the woman of mystery, moreover, Gladys points to the fact that her case has not been, perhaps cannot be, solved in the novel. The crime in which her mysterious loss and cover-up originate is a criminal mystery that remains, along with her, as part of a question suspended at the novel's end. What remains is a gap as well as a cover-up, for through Gladys we see that the meeting between fact and fiction, between reality and fantasy, is a difficult, if not impossible, scenario to orchestrate, even though the novel's strategies would lead us to see things otherwise.

These strategic turns lead us back to, by also taking us away from, the generic model named in the novel's subtitle. Let us return to that model for a moment to consider some of those relationships. As noted already, Puig's novel fulfills and yet does not perfectly match our image of a *novela policial*. It works with and around the genre's conventions, rewriting, revising, and regenerating its structure and strategies so as both to give us what we expect and to take from us what we want to read. For example, the displacement of the "real" criminal scenes in which Gladys and Leo are cast in 1949 and 1962, respectively, from the text's edges to a kind of hidden place somewhere in the middle (therefore close to but decidedly further from their "proper" places at beginning and end of the text) also signals the usurpation of their place by the "fictional" scene that opens the novel and later starts to close it. This displacement both hides and reveals the gap between what we are led to imagine and what we desire to see because of the genre's conventions and the text's own techniques—that is, what is presented by Puig's, as well as Leo's, fictional designs. This displacement turns the novel, as well as its readers, at once away from and toward the model it names. It both makes present and denies a place to some of the structures and strategies that originally empower the popular form.

What could be read as a parodically deforming play upon the genre's conventions also reaffirms that form's traditional development by turning around and to its own advantage some of its characteristic logic— that is, the logic of verisimilitude. Although the detective story can be read as an essentially formulaic, and thus "low," form of literature because it precludes the possibility of breaking with set structures and techniques the way "great" works of literature do, Puig's novel shows that there may be ways in which the popular form can be turned into the type of text to which it would be initially placed in opposition. If one of the conventions of the genre is the inversion of verisimilitude through which appearance and truth coincide only at the end of the text—that is, the inversion through which the guilty appear innocent and the innocent appear guilty, and through which the truth comes to look like a lie and a lie like the truth—then Puig's novel breaks with such conventions, paradoxically, by giving them another turn. It raises the text to a new and "higher" position while binding it to its original form. That is, here the guilty look guilty and the innocent look innocent right from the start. However, what they are guilty or innocent of remains to be seen. By inverting the conventionally inverted verisimilitude of the genre, *The Buenos Aires Affair* at once undercuts and upholds generic verisimilitude.[34] The genre survives and is renewed because of the simultaneously innovative and yet formulaic inversions that, in Puig's novel, keep it "low" and at the same time allow it to become an experiment of "high" literature. The problem with trying to situate Puig's novel in relation to that model and its tradition, then, is that we can't quite fix its ways of turning (and turning around) a model that itself needs to keep turning (that is, inverting itself) in order to stay alive.

These are the kinds of moves which, along with the narrative techniques and discursive forms already identified with Puig's writing, keep our eyes focused on the novel's text. As is the case in reflexive fiction generally, the novel turns us toward its textuality as well as toward its fictional story. These turns within the novel work with, even serve to reveal some significant realities of, the fiction it presents through the lives of the characters whose "cases" it develops. And, as noted earlier, the cases dealt with here are not just detective cases. While the lives of Gladys and Leo do indeed appear to be based on and illustrative of certain psycho-sexual models, models that also seem to participate in popular culture because of our knowledge of them (that is, our common knowledge of such "textbook cases" as they might originate in the text of Freud), they also emerge as the lives of subjects whose frustrated desires and failed designs, though decidedly conventional, are also particularized enough to be taken "seriously" and not merely as popular formulas.[35] Yet through their stories certain facts about desire in particular and the relationship between fact and fiction, fantasy and reality, in general are also revealed.

As we turn back to the novel's end, we can see how some of these features of its text and fiction reflect and support one another. When Gladys remains alone at the end of the novel, she figures as the emblem of a crime that is still unsolved and a desire that has yet to be satisfied. While Leo seems to find a fatal end to his criminal search, Gladys is left behind to continue hers. Yet, as part of the novel already reveals, the effort to match the desires of fantasy with the facts of reality cannot, by definition, succeed.[36] That gap, the distance between these realms, is precisely what the text highlights in scenes at once critically parodic and sympathetically stylized. For example, in Chapter XIII, where the criminal scene in Leo's apartment is played out as a scene for a sexual encounter, the graphic description of the actions and thoughts of the players reveals that Leo's and Gladys's fantasies find no place to coincide in the text. This chapter is structured as an alternating move among paragraphs that juxtapose brief formulaic italicized headings describing what is actually happening with paragraph-length representations of the characters' fantasies paralleling that action.

While Leo, Gladys, and María Esther become physically entangled in a triangular scene into which they pull one another, each is also pulled along by his or her private fantasy. Gladys's romantically bucolic and then criminally threatening visions later turn into a "symbolic" agricultural fantasy, ending the chapter with its cliché, discursively "dramatic" references to a farmer plowing the earth, as the scene reaches its parodic, theatrical, and sexual climax (201–12, 224–25). María Esther's fantasies are partly of a fatal auto accident (this, of course, prefigures Leo's death in the following chapter) and partly of a scenario involving a scientific conference at which the figure of a mature woman (María Esther is sixty) emerges triumphant among her younger colleagues (213, 222–24). Leo is affected first by his childhood visions, then by a fantasy related to figures from the Sistine Chapel's final Judgment, and finally by his lengthy mental staging of a Wagnerian opera that his Siegfried (i.e., Leo himself) directs and stars in, according to his own sexually violent and theatrical designs (214–22).[37]

While each of these discourses has some relation to the actions of the scene among the three characters and, moreover, interconnects with other details of their lives already revealed to us, they never coincide with each other or with the facts of the scene itself. The distance between the fantasy authored and the facts experienced by each subject is graphically demonstrated. Though the proximity of the two spheres of action within the text brings into close proximity the facts of the physical scene and the characters' fantasies, the difference in typeface and the move from heading to body in each fragment where those disparate scenes meet winds up emphasizing the limits of those realms, the distances among these entangled but isolated subjects. The scene that might have been imagined by each as the criminally exciting and perfect scene cannot be represented here, not only because their individual fantasies of that scene cannot coincide, but also because, as the text shows, no reality could ever match them. As close as we (or even they) might imagine the scene to come to that perfect meeting of desire and action, the proliferation of disparate fantasies and the graphic marks that separate one realm from the other remind us that that kind of meeting is repeatedly denied in Puig's novel. The only way to satisfy desire here is to do away with it, much as Leo does at the end and, for a moment, as Gladys contemplates in the novel's final chapters (e.g., 250). This perfect scene is, in the end, turned into

169

a scene of imperfection, a scene that both critically and sympathetically reveals the isolation of its participants and the impossibility of a satisfying meeting between its two main subjects.

Leo and Gladys are figures for whom what happens in Leo's apartment is in a way either too little or too much. What they do does not match what they desire. Their actions need to be covered or accompanied by some type of fiction. This kind of relation between fiction and fact—that is, the need for one as either a cover or an underlying cause for the other—and the gap that separates them, especially in a scene of desire, is also displayed much earlier in the novel. We see this in Chapter IV, where the omniscient narrator takes great care to provide a detailed description of Gladys's masturbatory practices. Here the body of the chapters contains her erotic fantasies. These fantasies consist of scenes in which Gladys plays victim to a male victimizer, whose attack on her is repeatedly interrupted by her own "staging" of things. Within the text of that chapter a series of asterisks appears in strategic points. They lead us to the foot of the page, where notes describing the mechanical facts of the scene are situated.

Much as in the conventional relationship between footnote and text, this set of notes shows that what goes on in the text is at once excessive and insufficient. There is much more to be seen or said than meets the eye or ear; at the same time, what is said or seen is too much. The reality of the printed page would remind us of what we can also see going on in the fiction—there is an irreducible difference that marks the relation between each kind of text, each type of fiction, which no real design can match. In an analogous fashion, Chapters V and XIII seem to present satisfying criminal scenes. But they are also scenes whose repetition and proliferation point to their excessive yet limited nature. When Leo and Gladys are brought together in a place that appears to be perfect for them (both in the scene in Leo's apartment and in the novel as a whole), they are forced to repeat a scene that has already been played. That scene will also be repeated over and over again either in fact or in fantasy until, perhaps even beyond, what looks like their story's end.

That criminal repetition, evidenced as it is in Leo's death scene, is a repetition that seems to give pleasure in this text, from beginning to end. Even though Leo solves the central crime, Gladys remains as the subject of another critical and criminal repetition. The scene in which we see her at the end of the novel continues to construct criminal scenes that seem incapable of finishing things off. (These scenes are, like those of the footnotes in Chapter IV, another kind of ending—a footnote of sorts—to the conventional narrative schemes of the detective genre.) What we see at the end is Gladys, who remains alone to consider suicide in Leo's apartment. She is in search of something she never names and we never see. That final search, moreover, certifies that the investigation of an originally criminal-sexual scene is not yet concluded. Gladys reopens it and returns to the form of activity that first sets the novel in motion. What she is looking for remains unclear, though it also seems that she might be searching for something she has already lost or cannot ever have. Gladys remains as the reader-investigator-voyeur whose job and pleasure it is to read the kind of scenes that she herself has repeatedly created and acted in, or has been forced or seduced into playing, throughout the novel. Although the scene she "reads" (i.e., the bedroom of the apartment next door to Leo's, the place where she winds up asleep at the end of the text, after talking with the young woman who lives there and whose place she would like to take) is not really her own, she manages to appropriate it as if she were originally meant to be there.[38]

This image of the last reader-investigator (a reader who does indeed derive pleasure from watching, listening to, and entering into the scenes inhabited by the other figures of her investigation) also returns us to its counterpart in and around the novel. The image of Gladys as the subject who depends upon the pleasures and pains of others is an image that suggests not only the text's own reader but also, in a specular fashion, the authorial figure who remains bound to, from "above" also dependent on, the performances of others whose positions and postures that subject would seem to create. That is, the ending that takes us to the figure of another reader also brings to the surface the figure of a subject supporting it. In *The Buenos Aires Affair*, though, the image of that figure is never really out of sight. The playful yet "criminal" turns taken by the text keep directing us toward that image. Moreover, to read the novel as its subtitle instructs us to do is to read it as a text that promises to present not just a problem but also its solution. It is a text that is supposed to lead us to the truth. To read it as such is to read it as the work of a figure who will, and must, as the generic model dictates, reveal himself at the end, implied as that figure would be by the appearance of such a final truth.

When we search for the solution, when we look for the end, we are led to an image of authority that comes from behind and supports such a judicial, reasonable, and stable ending. But here the authority who turns toward the idea of such an ending is also the authority who turns away from it. The authorial figure that emerges from this text is the figure of a subject who supports crime not by seeming to resolve or eliminate it through the revelation of truth, but by multiplying its appearances and effects, by making crime proliferate in an apparently uncontrollable fashion. The search for such a solution always leads to new (and, of course, really old) crimes with every textual turn, as well as in the many criminal scenes that are author(iz)ed by that same figure. In *The Buenos Aires Affair* this is, of course, what we should expect. It is the fiction we would also survive, along with that same authorial figure who, not unlike the novel's other partners in crime, may very well get and give us what we all want—a *novela policial*.

NOTES

1. Manuel Puig, *The Buenos Aires Affair: Novela policial* (Buenos Aires: Sudamericana, 1973). All quotations are from this edition; hereafter page references appear parenthetically in the text. Another edition has been published by Joaquín Mortiz (Mexico City, 1973); however, the subtitle has been omitted from it. The novel has appeared in English as *The Buenos Aires Affair: A Detective Novel*, trans. Suzanne Jill Levine (New York: E. P. Dutton, 1976); quotations in English are from this edition, unless otherwise noted. See also Juan Armando Epple, "'The Buenos Aires Affair' y la estructura de la novela policíaca," *Estudios filológicos* 10 (1974–75): 43–65 (hereafter cited as "Novela policíaca"); and Morino, "Tanghi e pellicole" 403–6.

2. For observations on the formulaic patterns and popular status of detective fiction, see Todorov, "Detective Fiction," and Cawelti, *Adventure, Mystery and Romance*, 51–105. See Michael Holquist, "Whodunit and Other Questions: Metaphysical Detective Stories in Post-War Fiction," *New Literary History* 3 (1971–72): 135–56 (hereafter cited as "Whodunit"), for observations on the familiarity and strangeness of postmodern detective fiction and on its relation to both kitsch and avant-garde writing.

3. See Emir Rodríguez Monegal, "Los sueños de Evita (a propósito de la

última novela de Manuel Puig)," *Plural* 22 (1973): 34–36 (hereafter cited as "Sueños"), and Epple, "Novela policíaca" 49–56, for comments on the epigraphs and their relation to the novel's body.

4. Although the detective genre has indeed changed since Poe's Dupin stories ("The Murders in the Rue Morgue" [1842–43], "The Purloined Letter" [1845]), the model of the "classical" tale seems to prevail in some fundamental way. The detective story involves the presentation of a problem (the mystery or "case") that needs to be solved. We expect that mystery to originate in a crime—preferably a murder. From the scene of that crime, in the course of the investigation that follows its discovery, the case is eventually solved. The stock set of characters implicated in that model and whose relationships form the skeleton of the case include the victim (that is, the corpse), the criminal, and the detective. Once the crime is discovered and its traces, in the form of the criminal scene itself, are examined in or near the text's opening pages, the rest of the text usually involves the representation of the investigation. The text moves forwad in time with the investigation while it also moves back to reconstruct the story leading up to the crime. The route is at once linear and circular, for the solution to the crime involves a return to the criminal scene, which can only be read correctly at the end of the text. See Todorov's discussion of the detective form's fundamental narrative and temporal duality in "Detective Fiction." In addition, the following provide a variety of discussions of the genre and its history: Howard Haycraft, ed., *The Art of the Mystery Story: A Collection of Critical Essays* (New York: Simon and Schuster, 1946); Howard Haycraft, *Murder for Pleasure: The Life and Times of the Detective Story* (New York: Appleton, 1941); A. E. Murch, *The Development of the Detective Novel* (London: Peter Owen, 1958); César E. Díaz, *La novela policíaca: síntesis histórica a través de sus autores, sus personajes y sus obras* (Barcelona: Acervo, 1973); [Pierre] Boileau-[Thomas] Narcejac, *Le Roman policier* (Paris: Payot, 1964); David I. Grossvogel, *Mystery and Its Fictions: From Oedipus to Agatha Christie* (Baltimore: Johns Hopkins UP, 1979); and Stephen Knight, *Form and Ideology in Crime Fiction* (Bloomington: Indiana UP, 1980).

5. As Todorov emphasizes in "Detective Fiction," the question of temporality is prominent in this genre, for the detective text is organized around two temporal sequences or stories. The first story ends when the investigation (the second story) begins; it precedes and makes that second story necessary. The first story is the story of the criminal events, the events that lead up to and include the crime, told in chronological order. The second story is a temporally reordered account of the first one. It begins at the end, so to speak, and reveals how the first comes to be known. The second story is identical with the text itself; its "normal" temporality is a "deformed" temporal move-

ment that must take us back in time in order to move things forward. The first story is contained within the second but can only be seen, recognized, or understood after the inverted temporal route is followed to its conclusion. Todorov points out that the distinction between the first and second stories corresponds to that between plot and story as defined by the Russian formalists (58). For observations on how mystery is created through the manipulation and rearrangement of cause and effect (this is essentially what the relation between the two stories is about as well), see, for example, Shklovsky, "The Mystery Novel." For related comments on narrative plots, as well as time and desire, see Peter Brooks, "Freud's Masterplot," *Yale French Studies* 55/56: *Literature and Psychoanalysis; The Question of Reading: Otherwise* (1977): 280–300. In Latin America, Borges seems to have been the first to take up the crucial relationship between these textual categories in "El arte narrativo y la magia" (1932); see Emir Rodríguez Monegal's discussion of this, as well as other aspects of Borges's poetics, in "Borges: una teoría de la literatura fantástica," *Revista iberoamericana* 42 (1976): 177–89. Through a fictional character (George Burton, alias J. C. Hamilton, writer of detective novels and author of *Meurtre de Bleston*) Michel Butor offers an analysis of the superimposition of the detective text's constituent temporal sequences. It is suggested, however, that the temporal play (that is, the positioning of the effect before the cause) of a detective text can be viewed as a natural (as opposed to unnatural or "deformed") ordering of things. See his *L'Emploi du temps* (Paris: Minuit, 1957) 171.

6. Closure in the detective text usually involves a neat solution, an answer to a problem of identity—the identity of the criminal. This is the goal of the interpretive or hermeneutic activity assigned the reader. The neat ending of this type of narrative puts all the puzzling pieces of the problem in their proper places by revealing what has already been seen but in a different sort of way, by bringing us to the point where the identity of the criminal is revealed, or even recognized, once it is seen at the end of the text. Seen in these terms, the detective text might be read as an exemplary Aristotelian work, as suggested by Dorothy Sayers in "Aristotle on Detective Fiction," *Unpopular Opinions* (New York: Harcourt, Brace, 1947) 222–36 (hereafter cited as "Aristotle"). See also Geoffrey H. Hartman, "Literature High and Low: The Case of the Mystery Story," in *The Fate of Reading and Other Essays* (Chicago: U of Chicago P, 1975) 203–22, 333–34. According to Hartman, Aristotelian recognition and reversal constitute some of the essential features of detective fiction.

7. The text's temporal development can be summarized as follows: Part I: Chapters I and II, 21 May 1969; III, 1934-June 1968; IV, June 1968; V, 8 May 1968; VI, 1930–1968; VII, April 1969; VIII, 24 April 1969. Part II: Chapter

IX, 22 April–14 May 1969; X, 15 May 1969; XI, 19–20 May 1969; XII, 20 May 1969; XIII, 20–21 May 1969; XIV, 21–22 May 1969; XV, 22 May 1969; XVI, 23 May 1969.

8. See Genette, *Narrative Discourse* 86–112, for discussion of duration in narrative texts.

9. A detective text would seem to be a text that functions in terms of its truth-bearing endpoint. It would seem to be a movement whose *telos* is truth itself, truth in the form of a solution to a criminal mystery. That final solution would be the true solution, as opposed to one of the false solutions manipulated by the author. (See Sayers, "Aristotle" 23–32, for directives regarding false solutions or "paralogism—the art of false syllogism.") This true solution is one that rights a wrong and certifies that Justice is indeed just. It assures us that the Answer can be found, that Truth is in fact accessible. It merely awaits being discovered and recognized through the operations of reason. Nonetheless, even the classic detective story also works against the central position of that solution and the idea of a supremely powerful and privileged truth for the text. If the solution, or the truth, were all that really mattered, if it were actually all that we were looking for in a detective novel, then the body of the text that should lead us to it would have little reason for existing. The major portion of the text would be rendered superfluous; the reader could simply move from the beginning of the narrative, where the problem and scene of the crime are uncovered, directly to the end of the text, where the crime is once again seen and the problem solved. But, of course, this kind of text has as much to do with the deferral of the truth—and thus the process of moving toward, rather than arriving at, a solution—as with the apparent realization of that final moment. See also Holquist, "Whodunit" 153.

10. The theories of psychoanalysis that might be seen to underlie the novel are considered to be a definitive subtext by Roberto Echavarren, who, in "La superficie de lectura en *The Buenos Aires Affair*," in *La casa de ficción* (Madrid: Fundamentos, 1977) 147–74 (hereafter cited as "Lectura"), reads the novel as if it were subtitled "novela psicoanalítica" instead of "novela policial" (147).

11. In detective fiction the question of how we read is paramount, since the effects of the text are predicated upon our reading, perceiving, and interpreting things exactly as they are set up to be read. In *The Fantastic: A Structural Approach to a Literary Genre* (1970), trans. Richard Howard (Cleveland: P of Case Western U, 1973) 89–90, Tzvetan Todorov discusses this feature of both texts of the fantastic and detective fiction; he emphasizes that the "irreversibility of reading time"—that is, the reading of a series of events or facts in the order in which they are narrated—has a crucial function for the success of this type of narrative. It determines the detective story's power to

175

surprise and satisfy with its solution ("[s]urprise is only a particular case of irreversible temporality"). To this feature is linked the common practice of reading such texts only once: "Since there is a truth to be discovered, we shall be confronted with a strict chain or series, no one link of which can be shifted; for this very reason, and not because of a possible weakness in the writing, we do not reread detective novels" (90). The reading undertaken here is, of course, a "meta-reading" (a second reading, a reading of the first reading) that focuses on both the "what" and the "how" of the text.

12. See also Borinsky, *Ver*

13. See Sayers, "Aristotle" 231–32.

14. Puig claims to have arranged the text so as to reveal the mother's "unconscious desire" for her daughter's disappearance, even her death, along with her other wish to find her and see her alive; see his statements on 602–3 of Jorgelina Corbatta, "Encuentros con Manuel Puig," *Revista iberoamericana* 49 (1983): 591–620 (hereafter cited as "Encuentros").

15. See poem LXXIII in Gustavo Adolfo Bécquer, *Rimas del "Libro de los Gorriones," Obras Completas*, ed. Joaquín and Serafín Alvarez Quintero (Madrid: Aguilar, 1973) 449–52. The poem, well known to Argentine students, is a text typically required for memorization and recitation, perhaps by teachers not unlike Clara Evelia. This is, in fact, the sort of poem that Clara Evelia, would-be poetess and teacher of declamation, would have made her daughter learn to recite as a child (see 30–31). In this description of her "poetic" endeavor in this first chapter, as well as the presentation of her "artistic" ambitions in the third, Gladys's mother also seems to function as Puig's parody of the profession.

16. The translation of lines from the Bécquer poem is by John Masefield, in *Anthology of World Poetry*, ed. Mark Van Doren, rev. and enl. ed. (New York: Halcyon House, 1939) 650. The remainder of the quotation is from the Dutton edition of Puig's novel.

17. Clara Evelia becomes the emblem of the curious reader, the reader who is enticed by a potentially criminal spectacle whose enigma she would relish as much as work to resolve, much like the detective whose place she first fills in the novel's opening investigation. The pleasurable curiosity represented by Clara Evelia—that is, the curiosity generated by the criminal scene, especially one that looks like a scene of death—has been viewed in terms of psychoanalytical categories by Geraldine Pederson-Krag, "Detective Stories and the Primal Scene," *Psychoanalytical Quarterly* 18 (1949): 207–14 (hereafter cited as "Primal Scene"), and Charles Rycroft, "The Analysis of a Detective Story" (1957), in *Imagination and Reality* (New York: International UP, 1968) 114–28. (Both of these references are suggested by Hartman, "Lit-

erature High and Low" 331–32.) According to Pederson-Krag, the relationship between reader and text is analogous to that between child and primal scene. The reader's addiction to the formula, his repeatedly aroused curiosity and the possibility of gratification from reading through identification, mostly with the detective figure, are likened to the child's relation to that scene. Rycroft views the disavowal of identification with the criminal as a less than satisfactory feature of such texts: "In the ideal detective story the detective or hero would discover that he himself is the criminal for whom he has been searching" (115). Of course, Rycroft here invokes the Oedipus myth as a model of his preferred story, one with which, for example, Alain Robbe-Grillet's *Les Gommes* works. Puig's novel also follows this model, but from a different direction, as we shall see. Cf. Echavarren, "Lectura."

18. The scene of the crime is, for Hartman, like the "scene of suffering" (i.e., Aristotelian pathos) and is the scene to which especially the North American genre, with its investment in things visual, is drawn: "the horror of the visible is clearly preferred to what is unknown or invisible" ("Literature High and Low" 216). In its play upon what can be seen or not in its criminal scenes, as well as in the connection between what is criminal (i.e., apparently murderous) and what is sexual, Puig's novel would seem to offer a model—perhaps both parodic and stylizing in effect—for a reading of detective fiction in relation to the notion of voyeurism. See Pederson-Krag, "Primal Scene" 210–13.

19. On the relationship between narration and description, see Gérard Genette, "Boundaries of Narrative" (1969), trans. Ann Levonas, *New Literary History* 8 (1976–77): 1–13 (esp. 5–8). On some relevant aspects of this narrative technique, see Alan Spiegel, *Fiction and the Camera Eye: Visual Consciousness in Film and the Modern Novel* (Charlottesville: UP of Virginia, 1976).

20. In our personal interview, Puig claimed that the narrative techniques of Chapter II, aptly illustrated by these passages with their exaggeratedly detailed, "frozen" examination of objects, are intended as a parody of the French *nouveau roman*.

21. In "Literature High and Low" 207, Hartman asserts that "'mystery' means that something is happening too fast to be spotted" and that in the detective novel "we are made to experience a consciousness . . . always behind and running; vulnerable, perhaps imposed on." In Puig's novel, moreover, what is set up to look like a "whodunit" can also be read as a "who-doingit." However, both kinds of appearances turn out to signal, to use Hartman's words, a "whodonut, a story with a hole in it" (206).

22. To a certain extent, this "non-teleological" aspect of the text becomes another kind of teleology governing it. Cf. Holquist, "Whodunit" 153.

23. For a reading of the novel in terms of the system of substitutions and play of artifices grounded in a theory of castration, see Borinsky, "Castration; Artifices" 109–14.

24. Crime has indeed been viewed as the object of artistic undertakings and, moreover, as a form of art itself. The titles of at least two discussions of murder remind us of the artistic elements and possibilities of the subject: Raymond Chandler, "The Simple Art of Murder," in Haycraft, ed. *The Art of the Mystery Story* 222–37, and Thomas De Quincey, "On Murder Considered as One of the Fine Arts" (1827), in *Selected Writings of Thomas De Quincey*, ed. Philip Van Doren Stern (New York: Random House, 1937) 982–1089. See also Epple, "Novela policíaca" 61–65.

25. Rodríguez Monegal locates one of the radical differences between Puig's novel and a *novela policial* in the emphasis that is placed on what we are here calling psychical reality: "el foco emocional de la novela no está en la investigación sino en las fantasías, los sueños, los delirios, de los dos protagonistas" ["the emotional focus of the novel is not on the investigation but on the fantasies, the dreams, the deliriums of the two protagonists"] ("Sueños" 36). While this holds, it seems, for the fiction, it doesn't quite suffice for the text, for it is difficult to separate the idea of the investigation from that of the elements mentioned as distinct from it. The investigation is an investigation of the psychical realities of the characters; it is also an investigation of the text's manipulation of them in a manner that connects everything to the popular model.

26. The appearance of Leo's dead body at the end of the novel signals yet another play upon what can be seen (or not) in either story or text, for those pages present both an *"Autopsia Médico-Legal"* [*"Medicolegal Autopsy"*] (234–35) and *"Referencias omitidas en la autopsia médico-legal"* [*"References omitted in the medicolegal autopsy"*] (235–37). Here the reader becomes a privileged viewer of the disappearance (we read, in fact, a record of a disintregation) of Leo's body from the text. It is a prolonged, detailed view shared by the narrator, who supplies us the information denied everyone else in the fiction.

27. The scene is also a rewritten version, and thus a displacement, of an immediately prior scene betwen Leo and a prostitute (105). Leo's walk that Sunday follows on a rejection by a prostitute who refuses his brutal treatment of her. It would seem that he takes revenge on her through his violent attack on his homosexual partner, the "feminized" accomplice upon whom he succeeds in inflicting pain for his own pleasure. This "successful" scene is at the same time but another version of Leo's characteristically violent encounters in both his lived reality and his erotic fantasies (e.g., 101–3, 104–5, 187–96). The origins of this pattern are ostensibly to be found somewhere in his early

life, described in Chapter VI (94–99). However, the text does not identify, cannot in fact present, any single scene or event that might be designated as the real beginning from which all his subsequent behavior (his criminal actions) can be derived. Here the "primal scene" exists as a fantasy to be authored, not only by Leo but perhaps also by his reader.

28. In this section of Leo's biography and in a section of Gladys's called *"Conciencia política"* [*"Political awareness"*] (42), the novel appears to take some kind of political position. In these passages each character is presented as anti-Peronist. Gladys's delight at the news of the downfall of Perón's "régimen fascista" in December 1955 is described openly, along with her hope for the development of the country's cultural atmosphere and for the improvement of its economic situation. Leo's opposition takes the form of political action. He joins the Communist party in 1950, but when caught by the secret police and tortured (in the scene referred to here) he betrays some of its members. There seems to be something of a critique of the Argentine left in the lack of understanding shown by his comrades for his treacherous action and in his departure from the party itself shortly thereafter. However, no final position is taken for any specific political model, and the novel leaves behind its concern with such issues as the story of Leo's and Gladys's lives advance. Each turns away from formal political concerns to participate in the world of art and culture, seemingly far removed from that of politics. *The Buenos Aires Affair* therefore continues briefly the critique of the Peronist regime apparently begun in a more oblique fashion in *La traición de Rita Hayworth* (see Chapter 2, note 30), and appears to begin to develop also a critique of the left, which will be taken up from different, though similarly shifting, angles in *El beso de la mujer araña* (see Chapter V). See also Rodríguez Monegal, "Sueños," for possible connections between Puig's characters and Eva Perón.

29. That María Esther is lured on by and then seduced into this scene is not inappropriate. The scene of the crime in any detective text is also a scene of seduction, a scene that must seduce the witness-reader. In order to succeed it seems that the detective text must be written as a text of seduction. It must lure its readers into its fabric—tease them, keep them guessing—and convince them that everything will work out in the end. In its representation of a reader's (double) seduction, Puig's novel plays with two models in which one seduction or another figures as a key event; one model is detective, the other psychoanalytical, and in each some kind of primal scene unites sex and death in either fact or fantasy. They seem to be models that this text examines critically but also supports sympathetically. See also Puig's explanation of his seductive strategies in Christ, "Interview" 31.

30. On "hidden dialogicality," a type of "double-directed discourse," see Bakhtin, *Dostoevsky's Poetics* 163–64.

31. This superimposition of roles on Leo—that is, Leo as criminal and Leo as "detective"—returns us to the fundamentally interdependent relationship between those figures in any detective story and the criminal repetition that actually informs the text apparently designed to do away with crime. Leo's suicide and self-sacrifice remind us that the goal of the detective's investigation in the conventional text is to catch the criminal by repeating his crime. The text repeats, by representing, the scene of the crime at the moment when its details can finally be understood. The reappearance of that original scene signals its solution. But this textual, as well as criminal, repetition of the (scene of the) crime also represents another crime that implicitly closes off the text. In Puig's novel this crime is rendered explicit. The discovery of the identity of the criminal, who must be "murdered" in the name of Justice, is what we await as the outcome of the investigation. In a way, the detective story is constructed around at least two murders: the criminal of the first murder must become the victim of the second, for which, of course, the detective takes his place as the "executioner" authorized to "kill" in the name of Justice, "par l'explosion de la vérité" (Butor, *L'Emploi du temps* 146–47). In general, however, the power of the detective resides in language, not in physical action. His "murder" is the work of the law, not of lawlessness. But he is empowered not only by the law but also by the criminal, the unauthorized murderer, after whom he patterns his own steps. He is a kind of Oedipus, powerful because of the criminal's ability to give him the power to solve the crime (that is, the murder) for which he is fundamentally destined (Butor, *L'Emploi du temps* 148). The detective literally would not exist were it not for the criminal who makes his work necessary. *The Buenos Aires Affair* underscores that the detective structure involves not the erasure or elimination but the necessary proliferation of crime. The figures whose identities on the surface seem so distinguishable are also interlocked as they criminally duplicate one another. Cf. Jorge Luis Borges's well-known play on this model, "La muerte y la brújula," in *Ficciones* (1944), Vol. 5 of *Obras completas* (Buenos Aires: Emecé, 1956).

32. See Borinsky, "Castration: Artifices," regarding the conventional signs of castration used here.

33. Gladys's connections with, even her origins in, the tradition we call "low" are suggested, if not underlined, by her biography in Chapter IV. First, we recall that the portrait of Clara Evelia, whose "principios estéticos" and operatically "poetic" ambitions (26–27) are revealed early in that chapter, show us that Gladys is the offshoot of a model that sees herself as linked with the "high" but whose apparently parodic appearance in the text resituates her below that tradition. Gladys's earliest attempts at art consist of copying the faces and figures she finds in the "Chicas" section of a men's magazine, *Rico*

Tipo. These female images are her models not only for her early artistic endeavors but also for her personal fantasies of female perfection: "Eran invariablemente altísimas muchachas bronceadas de breve cintura, talle mínino, flotante busto esférico y largas piernas carnosas. El rostro era siempre pequeño, de nariz muy respingada, largos cabellos lacios con las puntas levantadas y gran mechón, casi tapándole uno de los ojos verdes, grandes y almendrados que ocupaban la mayor parte del rostro. . . . Gladys . . . sentía una gran alegría al comenzar cada copia minuciosa si bien hacia la mitad de cada trabajo se sentía algo avergonzada de dibujar siempre lo mismo" ["They were invariably very tall with tans, narrow waists, floating round bosoms, and long fleshy legs. The face was always small, with a very turned-up nose, long straight hair with curled-up tips, and a big lock of hair almost covering one of the large, green, almond-shaped eyes which occupied most of the face. . . . Gladys . . . [would] feel a tremendous joy at beginning each meticulous copy though toward the middle of each work she'd feel somewhat ashamed for always drawing the same subject"] (31–32). Her drawings are repetitions of "low" images to which she is limited by her own background, until she is introduced as a teenager to the world of "high" culture by her classmate, Fanny (32–34). Although Gladys seems to leave behind, because her work seems to advance beyond, the world of popular art, she remains as a contradictory figure who embodies both currents at the same time, much like Puig's novel itself. While her art would seem to move in one direction, her experience and fantasies seem to go in another: her techniques for creating a personal image, as well as her perceptions of her own "life story," are idiosyncratic, even though they are also clichés modeled on ideas and desires typical of any number of popular culture paradigms. As we recall, Gladys, the serious artist, also fashions herself according to those models: her sunglasses, her make-up, her hairstyle follow and imitate the images of the girls in *Rico Tipo* and, of course, the stars of movies such as those that open each chapter of the novel. (Her hairstyle, for example, fashioned on the model described above, is also the signature of Veronica Lake, the Hollywood actress of the same era as Marlene Dietrich, Joan Crawford, Ginger Rogers, Norma Shearer et al., who appear in those epigraphs' scenes.) Though Gladys seems to start in the world of popular culture, she develops into a "serious" artist, regarded as avant-garde by critics such as Leo. (Perhaps this is what is "predicted" for Toto, in Puig's first novel.) However, she also holds on to her popular origins and predilections. In Gladys—as in the novel as a whole—the one movement does not negate but seems to give new life to the other. See Morino, "Tanghi e pellicole" 402–3, 406–8, for comments on Gladys as an emblem of popular culture and on the text's political relation to its cultural context.

34. The relationship between the verisimilar and the true here is, as noted

above, an inversion that upsets and upholds the very same norms, according
to the conventions of verisimilitude described by Tzvetan Todorov, "An Introduction to Verisimilitude" (1967), in *The Poetics of Prose* 80–88. As we know,
readers anticipate certain events in a detective text partly because of their
knowledge of the popular model. This model is, like any generic form, a set
of laws that determines the structural features and logical conventions of the
text. The degree to which a specific work follows those laws is, in one sense
of the term, the degree to which it is verisimilar (83). In the case of the
detective novel, however, generic verisimilitude can only be established if
verisimilitude as we assume it to operate in the real world is upended: verisimilitude of one sort depends upon anti-verisimilitude of another (85). In
constructing the text so as to confuse appearances with truths, in making true
what appears to be false and false what appears to be true, the genre would,
however, adhere to the conventional rupture between truth and verisimilitude. Puig gives us this rupture, but through a process of inversion that takes
another turn around the characteristic procedures of the genre.

35. At the end of "Mimesis and the Motive for Fiction," *Tri-Quarterly* 42
(1978): 228–49, Robert Alter takes up the case of Puig's novel and argues that
"the compelling psychological reality of the two principal characters" is the
novel's "most salient feature" (247). While this aspect of the novel has its own
power and significance, to separate and privilege it in the manner suggested
by Alter is to suppress in a way the idea of textuality and thus to ignore what
makes the appearance of such a "reality" possible. Puig's novel goes well beyond merely "utilizing" a popular form to "communicate" a psychological reality, demonstrating some of the basic lessons we have learned from modern
criticism—that is, that the novel's "form" is as much an object of invention as
its "content," that the two need to be read as one.

36. See Morello Frosch, "La sexualidad opresiva," for a reading of Gladys
in terms of the fantasies and desires that are "betrayed" or "defeated," much
like those of characters in Puig's other novels.

37. See Echavarren, "Lectura," for a detailed analysis, according to psychoanalytical theory, of these fantasies and their relation to the material scene
from which they emerge.

38. This view of Gladys's relation to that scene also acknowledges that there
is something symmetrical in its relation to the opening scene of the novel. At
the end Gladys reappears in a bed formerly left empty, a bed that she examines for the traces of a mysterious sexual scene she has heard but not seen. It
is a scene that she has imagined herself participating in and has desired to
enter, a scene not unlike others in which she has, in fact and in fantasy, appeared throughout the novel. Moreover, her return to this scene is presented
as a kind of return to a scene of childhood. (This is so because of its suggested

primal qualities and also because of her last moves in the text.) When Gladys returns to the bed, she falls asleep under the watchful eye of the neighbor— a young woman whose own concerns revolve around her family and, at the end, focus on the image of her dead mother. The novel opens with a mother in search of a daughter whose body cannot be found; it closes with the image of both a daughter in search of a mother and a female body that seems to return to the place from which it is originally missed. This scene could be read as closing the text (as opposed to the story) in a way that Leo's final scene is not suited to do. Cf. Robert Alter, rev. of *The Buenos Aires Affair*, by Manuel Puig, *New York Times Book Review* 5 September 1976: 4.

CHAPTER

5

The Politics of Seduction:
El beso de la mujer araña

From 4 April to 8 October 1975 two men share a prison cell in Buenos Aires. One is a twenty-six-year-old political activist imprisoned for his leftist operations; the other is a thirty-seven-year-old homosexual, taken in for "corrupting minors." Limited as they are to the space of their small cell and to one another's company, during at least the last month of their imprisonment together (from about 7 September until 8 October) the two men go about filling much of their time with talk. The "emotional" homosexual, immersed in a world of romantic sentimentalism, likes to narrate his favorite 1940s movies to his cellmate; the "intellectual" revolutionary, dedicated to Marxist principles, wants to teach his prison partner how to think politically about himself and the society in which he lives. By the end of their time together it appears that each manages to seduce the other to his own way of seeing and doing things, that each manages to get the other to play a role to which he initially seems totally opposed. This is essentially how things develop in Puig's fourth novel, *El beso de la mujer araña*.[1]

The text unfolds mainly, as a dialogue between these two prisoners, who seem to incarnate particular features of the novel's primary thematics, which revolve around relations of power and pleasure. Politics and sexuality—to be more precise, leftist politics and homosexuality— are, in fact, the major questions around which the stories told by the protagonists, the discussions and debates held between them, and the authorial footnotes that accompany the text's body revolve.[2] Though issues of this kind circulate in Puig's earlier work, *El beso de la mujer*

184

araña brings them out into the open for explicit consideration, providing as well a theoretical and practical meeting-ground for these disparate models. For example, although *The Buenos Aires Affair* focuses openly, though very briefly, on the political beliefs or actions of its protagonists and *La traición de Rita Hayworth* includes an oblique reference to the political regime in power during part of its story, *El beso de la mujer araña* not only situates its characters within a politically charged historical setting (i.e., recent eras of Peronist and repressive military control) but also sustains a discourse—a mainly theoretical discourse—on politics throughout its pages.[3] Valentín, the imprisoned revolutionary whose thoughts and actions are apparently governed entirely by Marxist precepts, is placed in a situation that allows him time not only to develop further the theoretical basis of his activities but also to communicate his project to an interlocutor who knows virtually nothing about it.[4] Likewise, though *La traición de Rita Hayworth* brings up the question of homosexuality through the story of Toto, that question stands as an issue about which no one seems able to speak openly or with any authority.[5] In *El beso de la mujer araña*, on the other hand, that issue is taken up directly by both the fiction's characters and by the text's apparent author, who offer descriptions of personal experience and authoritative theories of common practice to their respective interlocutors. While Molina, the homosexual prisoner, instructs his listener mainly through his own words and actions, Puig summons the texts of other authorities to explain the case of someone like his fictional character.[6]

These dialogues about politics and sexuality become, moreover, dialogues between two sets of theories and practices (the one political, the other sexual) and between two sets of interlocutors (the one fictional, the other textual), whose relationships develop along parallel lines—lines that, appropriately enough, are not without their own erotic and political patterns. Moreover, what might appear to be clearly distinguishable and disparate positions at the beginning of the novel turn into overlapping and seemingly identical ones at the end. By the end of the novel, when we see the main subjects and theoretical positions come together through an initially unprepared-for switch between the protagonists, we also see that perhaps they aren't so far apart to begin with. What looks like a subject turning toward or arriving at a totally new position is also a subject turning in place.

The novel takes us through those turns by means of the dialogue between [Luis Alberto] Molina and Valentín [Arregui Paz], whose verbal and physical moves appear unmediated by any narratorial subject or textual authority.[7] Though this dialogue dominates the text and gives it the appearance of being composed of homogeneous materials, the novel is in fact composed of several narrative forms. Besides the immediate, direct dialogues of the protagonists, there are direct dramatic dialogues between Molina and the prison warden, some interior monologues, stream-of-consciousness and dream segments produced by each prisoner, a hidden dialogue between the prison warden and his own supervisor, and two unmediated police documents, all situated in the text "above." In the text "below," there is a set of nine authorial footnotes.[8] In at least fourteen of the novel's chapters, the dialogue appears as the privileged narrative form that would seem to control the text, suppressing from view, in a way, the novel's heterogeneous quality. The apparently homogeneous narrative text presents in chronological order the developments in the relationship between the two prisoners, whose story is as much the story of the stories they tell each other as it is the chronicle of the time they spend together, on the margins of the world to which much of their talk would also refer.

The dialogue between Molina and Valentín calls attention to, while also naturalizing and obscuring, the mechanisms that support both their own relationship and that of the text's author and reader figures. The novel covers up—paradoxically, by putting in full view—the strategies designed to keep the text moving, the reader reading, and the characters talking until the end. The talk between the two prisoners is not unlike the "talk" between author and reader, that is, the textual dialogue that runs throughout the novel's body as well as under it, at its feet.[9] In both cases the exercise of power and the experience of pleasure seem tied together through the production of discourse, through language. That discourse as often as not revolves around actions and attitudes, issues and ideas, that are not without their own erotic and/or political designs. That language often originates in or takes everyone toward the world of popular culture, the realm of popular experience, establishing the common ground between these apparently polarized subjects or the theories and practices they suggest. The novel is a set of overlapping exchanges between subjects that differ from yet also identify with one another. These are subjects who are engaged in a relationship in which their own positions cannot be fixed. Each is continually on the move to a place at once "above" and "below," identical to and different from, that of the other.[10] It could be argued that the discourse on sexuality, or the defense of homosexuality, wins out over, perhaps even suppresses in some way, the political discourse by the end of the novel. But the interdependence of the two discourses, the interconnections between their strategies and subjects, is such that that end also seems to open things up and to leave us suspended in their midst, instead of at their end.

At the beginning of the novel we can already see its end coming. Or, rather, at the end of the novel we can see that the beginning already tells us what is to come. Though the dialogue between the two prisoners unfolds in perfectly chronological order, it moves through stories and scenes that repeat and reflect one another, taking things in a kind of circle or spiral whose oscillating pattern forms the path that is also followed by the dialogue's subjects. This dialogue is made up of discursive, thematic, and narrative turns that keep the protagonists moving from one position to another and back again according to a dialectical pattern that remains intact at the end. As Molina and Valentín take turns narrating their fictional and factual tales to one another, the differences as well as points of contact between them are established simultaneously. From the very beginning of the novel, where the question of identification is answered in a significant manner, we see that identity itself is generated through a model of alterity that informs as well the various dialogues that overlap throughout the text.

That Molina and Valentín are partners in dialogue, interlocutors who can only be revealed through their relation to each other, is of course not insignificant. That relational model, with its oscillations and turns, characterizes the way things begin, and later end, here. Molina and Valentín are at first unidentified interlocutors whose identities, or differences, we must work to establish because of the unmediated narrative through which they appear in the text. To begin to read the novel is to try to both identify and differentiate them and the theories or practices to which they seem attached. When these unidentified interlocutors first refer to each other by name (31), the possibility of asserting their individuality begins to present itself—only to reveal, as things move along, that the character designated by a particular name is more difficult to identify and pin down than we might at first think.

When the proper names "Molina" and "Valentín" are disclosed in the text, they tell us nothing in and of themselves. These proper nouns acquire a fuller meaning only as the narrative progresses and the discursive subjects, whose individuality and solidity these nouns seem to represent, continue to define themselves in opposition to one another. At the moment when Molina and Valentín name each other, each provides us with a term that seems to unify within one sign the discursive and thematic networks, as well as the "psychological reality," we would associate with each subject. Each defines and creates himself as a subject whose discourse is at the same time the origin of his subjectivity. But, since each is also an interlocutor named by another subject, each also originates in and is identified through the discourse of the other, by the voice or subject whose "sound" or "image" can be differentiated from his own.[11]

Curiously enough, the moment of mutual nomination occurs at precisely the point where the question of identification is raised by the fictional subjects themselves. When Valentín interrupts Molina's first movie narration to ask him "—¿Con quién te identificas?" ["—Who do you identify with?"] (i.e., with which of the movie's characters) and when, after answering, Molina appropriates his interlocutor's query to turn it back on him ("—¿Y vos Valentín, con quién?" ["—And you Valentin, with who?"]), we see that neither subject can be identified without reference to another fictional entity, another subject, or outside his relation to his interlocutor.[12] Moreover, in that each functions throughout the text as a subject of discourse, and especially as a subject or indirect object of narration (i.e., either as speaker or listener, as narrator or narratee), each can be identified with as well as differentiated from his partner through the turns of their verbal exchange. While the differential or individualizing value of the proper name attached to each speaker would support the notion of identity also through its own negative properties (i.e., the name "Molina" is not the name "Valentín," and therefore each term presumes to mark the distances and differences between the referents), the fundamental instability, the oscillating structure, of the situation of discourse through which they present themselves undermines the apparently immobile and stable identity of each.[13]

The revolutionary discourse of the political activist and the romantic fictions of the homosexual meet within a dialogue that, following this pattern of identification, turns them and their talk against yet into one another, while also turning itself toward and away from the more factual (i.e., "scientific") narrative at its own feet. Several kinds of oppositional discourse and fiction make up the novel. Their polarity is both upheld and put aside by the complex moves plotted by the authors of and the actors in them.[14] The fundamental paradox underlying the interlocutionary relation between the heterosexual political activist seemingly rooted in sociohistorical reality and the homosexual romantic tied to the world of popular fiction and fantasy also finds its parallel in other registers of the novel. Yet the oppositional plays between fact and fiction, between narrative body and authorial footnotes, are also eroded by the strategies of the narrative that makes their presentation possible. Certain discursive, thematic, and textual polarities seem to generate the novel's movement and give it life, but the fictions supporting those oppositions also disclose the precarious nature of their conflictive play.

As the relationship between Molina and Valentín develops, it takes new and unexpected turns toward an ending that seems to upend their original places (i.e., Molina seems to be "transformed" into a revolutionary and Valentín "converted" to a homosexual in the final chapters). Here the question of power is never far from that of pleasure—the novel's fictional and textual partners are engaged in interconnecting plays whose aims are both to control and to cater to each other. Here the strategies of discursive production—that is, the production of discourse within the fiction and around the text as a whole—also make possible the exercise of and resistance to power or the experience of pleasure. The act of narration is at the center of those possiblities within both the fictional world and the novel's text. The production of different narrative sequences allows either subject to potentially dominate or delight his partner, and either fictional or textual figures to be "converted" or "transformed." In a way, to read the novel is to read about how we read as well as about how a story gets told and a text gets written. It is to read about narrative both in terms of the telling and in terms of what is told.[15]

As noted earlier, the narrative is a chronologically ordered set of texts that takes us through a month of conversations between the protagonists. The text of their dialogue has attached to it a mostly logically ordered set of footnotes designed primarily to inform the reader about the origins and nature of homosexuality. In these separate but connected sequences (the one fictional, the other apparently factual) and in the narrative text they form together, the linear movement of things makes it possible for different subjects to seduce and instruct their partners. As in Puig's other novels, the narrative is a play between telling and not telling, between revealing things and covering them up. Moreover, to tell a story in this novel is to move slowly and seductively, through detours and interruptions, toward the end of a narrative mystery that is created by both the deliberate and self-conscious tactics of telling and the material being told.

The narrative sequence is actually a sequence of stories that are embedded in and overlap with one another and the framing sequence of Molina's and Valentín's personal comments. This primary exchange is interrupted by, but itself also interrupts, the fictional and factual tales told by the protagonists. The relation among the sequence of stories in the fictional body is analogous to that between the novel's footnotes and its main text. The novel sets up a play between "horizontal" and "vertical" sequences that both move us forward and stop us from moving on in the text. The insertion of asterisks into the dialogue between Molina and Valentín (66, 88, 102, 133, 141, 154, 168, 209) and the consequent pull toward the feet of the pages where the "installments" of the authorial narrative are displayed serves to advance one sequence while interrupting the other. This eruption of a vertical reading into that of an apparently horizontal sequence is not unlike the relationship between the two main discursive frames and sequences that inform the novel's fictional body.[16] The frame story of Molina's and Valentín's imprisonment and dialogue surrounds but is also composed of the movie stories and biographical narratives, the discussions and debates about politics and sexuality, authored by both of them.

As the novel moves forward, it becomes a sequence of narrative displacements: each story or sequence takes the place of another that leads into it. As each subject speaks or narrates, he displaces and suppresses the voice of the other subject, who will sooner or later emerge to appropriate (even reappropriate) his own place and privilege. Likewise, each story and discourse moves in and out of a prominent position as the narrative schemes of the notes and fictional narrative take hold. Each voice and discourse is, in a sense, pitted against the other in a battle that is also a battle against time and death. In fact, the dialogue itself, as well as the stories and experiences related within it, work together to kill and fill time all at once. The prisoners' talk is an effort to fill with fictional stories a space whose potentially fatal, and certainly repressive, reality they seek to either forget or control. Their main defense against the passage of time and the arrival of death is language. It is the possibility of telling stories and living through, as well as in, a fiction that keeps them alive in the novel.[17]

Of special interest here is the way the two prisoners keep themselves alive by telling stories of death and how, in the end, they also live out the fatal endings against which their dialogue attempts to work. In most of their stories, in fact, we are taken to scenes of death that prefigure the ending that same sequence of stories would seem to prevent. A denial of death is effected by the proliferation of stories and scenes that are all versions of one another. In Molina's and Valentín's conversations—especially in the movie stories narrated by Molina—the fatal ending of one story leads to the beginning of another in which the very same kind of story is again told. Each successive fiction would at once empower and undermine the fatal end that precedes it, for each fiction offers a new beginning to both its author-narrator and listener-reader while also turning them back to the same type of ending.[18]

The power of fictional reprieve is tied to the possibility of textual repetition; to live on and deny death in this text is to live with a text that must also die. The melodramatic endings to the stories told by the fictional characters are thus the prefiguration of the end of the story they live together. The scene of Molina's death (279) and the tortured monologue of Valentín (282–87), left alone at the novel's end, are but repetitions of all the endings to which their own fictional characters have already come.[19] Their own ending would, like the ends of the stories that prefigure it, suggest that things go on, that something or someone (here that seems to be Valentín, whose discourse appears as the merging of their two voices in his final appearance) remains to carry on with another identical story; however, it also presents a violent end to that possibility. The possibility of putting off death—the potential for killing the passage of time—is finally turned around, revealing in its place a tragic and even "romantic" end for these subjects' powers.

Valentín and Molina seem to emerge powerless in the face of the

movement of time and the powers of those who work to control them.
Yet the ending they would seem to resist, but also be powerless to
deny, is the same kind of scene toward which they seem deliberately
to move and to which they appear willingly to surrender. The question
of just what each desires is, from beginning to end, a key issue in the
novel(The question of just how powerful or powerless each is also is
intricately bound up with the question of individual desire. Their dialogue is a complex network of moves that seem generated by, while
also showing the effects of, relations of power and desire.[20] In *El beso
de la mujer araña* each is seduced and controlled by the other; each
seems to be at once more and less powerful than his partner. Throughout the turns in their relations with one another, each seems to design
moves in response to the other subject, with whom he initially or
finally desires to have some kind of relationship. Their dialogue charts
those shifts and displays their effects throughout the novel. Although
it may appear that Molina exercises the most control over the dialogue,
as well as over his interlocutor (we recall that he is finally characterized
by Valentín as the "mujer araña" ["spider woman"] [265] who has
caught his partner in his verbal web), he is also the object of the designs and desires of others. Valentín is of course the most powerful and
provocative subject with whom he deals, for he is his partner in a
dialogue that turns out to be both political and erotic. The delicate
shifts between the novel's subjects give us a model of the kinds of
moves also made together by reader and author. The fictional characters are at once masks for and devices manipulated by the figure of
authority who seems to orchestrate things from above and behind the
entire novel.)

(Molina's narration of movie stories is the main vehicle for the plays
of power and pleasure worked out for both registers of dialogue. These
films carry us forward and away from the reality represented in the
prison cell, but also into the space of that same repressive enclosure.[21]
The stories derived from popular culture might at first seem irrelevant
for the reality at hand, but they turn out to be the means by which
other kinds of truth, at once artistic and political, are revealed. Even
though the movies summarized by Molina are only six in number, his
narration of them fills a dominant portion of the novel's pages. From
the very first chapter, which begins with his narration of the story of
"la mujer pantera" ["the panther woman"], and throughout most of

their dialogue, Molina (this novel's Toto, now grown up, perhaps) tells versions of his favorite, mostly melodramatic and romantic, films to his leftist cellmate.[22] Besides *La marca de la pantera* (*Cat People*, 1942) in Chapters I and II, he summarizes an imaginary Nazi propaganda film about romance and political intrigue in Chapters III and IV; *Su milagro de amor* (*The Enchanged Cottage*, 1944), a sentimental love story, in Chapter V (actually, he silently "tells" this film to himself and not to his partner); an invented film about political conversion and a family romance in Chapter VI; *La vuelta de la mujer zombi* (*I Walked with a Zombie*, 1943), a fantastic and sentimental tale of love, murder, and mystery, in Chapters IX, X, and XI; and a fabricated romantic tragedy typical of 1940s cabaret films in Chapters XII, XIII, and XIV.[23] The films narrated by Molina—or, rather, his verbal renditions of them—revolve mostly around problematic and romantic situations for which there are no perfect solutions.[24] In all but one case (*The Enchanted Cottage*) the main characters seem destined to suffer and sacrifice themselves for passions that cannot be fulfilled and for desires that are not to be satisfied. The scenarios played out and the relationships developed in these tales inevitably involve the meeting of criminal and sexual acts, the suggestion of primal and oedipal conflicts, and the orchestration of romantic and tragic endings. The move from one film story to another takes us toward what, at the end of the novel itself, turns out to be a final encounter between a reality that is violent, even criminal, and a perfect fantasy that is impossible. The stories and endings told by Molina are, in addition, matched by the "true-life" tales related by his cellmate, whose description of the love life of his comrade-girlfriend (48–52), for example, follows the same types of popular models represented by Molina's movies. (In fact, the similarity between their tales is marked openly by Molina, who, led by Valentín to perceive his story as another melodrama, entitles the narrative "*El misterio de la celda siete*" ["*The Mystery of Cellblock Seven*"] [49], underscoring the place in which the story unfolds and the mystery attached to it by Valentín, who refuses to reveal the woman's identity in order to protect her from the authorities.)

The stories told by Molina are, in the end, just like the reality lived by him and his partner-in-narration. Molina's own ending is but another version and verification of the endings of the movie characters who precede and prefigure him in the novel.[25] (His own ending, by the way, is interpreted by his partner as possibly having been set up by him so as to follow the dramatic models offered by the movies he tells and the tragic heroines he adores; see 285.) Moreover, these stories not only repeat but also serve as models for the stories of his prison partner. And they return us to the kinds of stories told and acted out in Puig's other novels. The films provide thematic and generic points of contact among his texts as well as between the novel's two main characters. The film stories are the medium through which they make contact; they are the materials and events through which the homosexual and the revolutionary eventually seem able to reconcile their differences—differences of desire, differences of "destiny." In fact, when the protagonists discuss the question of their artistic value, the films themselves elicit from the interlocutors discussions that pertain directly to the project of Puig's novel, inasmuch as *El beso de la mujer araña* makes statements about literary values and cultural hierarchies. The dialogues about the films are also dialogues about the novel, with the different sides being taken by its own subjects. Their discussions about, as well as their movements around, the question of the relationship between art and politics, for example, is indeed much more complicated than their simple debate would initially acknowledge.

As we might expect, Valentín, the heterosexual, is the subject who draws the line between himself and his interlocutor, while Molina, the homosexual, is the one who works to bring the two of them together. Valentín, the "representative" of politics in their conversation, expounds his theories about the relationship between sensual pleasure and political action, privileging the latter over the former, as dictated by his ideological position (33–34). The hierarchical relation between these categories, as well as the apparent dichotomy of the spheres of activity they seem to represent—that is, work and play, instruction and entertainment; things serious and things frivolous, the interests of men and the interests of women—are underscored by his temporal segregation of the one kind of activity from the other. Daytime is the time for Valentín's political reading and silent study; nighttime is the time for Molina's pleasurable popular narratives and personal talk (see also 15, 23, 63, 85). It is precisely this devaluation of the pleasures produced by popular forms of art and culture that Puig's writing undertakes to overturn. It is precisely this absolute separation of things political and things pleasurable (especially things sexual), between "se-

194

rious" thought and "playful" activity, that their dialogue and his writing erode. What *El beso de la mujer araña* develops is not so much a stable putdown of one side or the other (even though from a certain perspective it might seem that popular art and passion win out over a political ideology and action) but an interplay of and a turning between the poles of an opposition that, by the end of the novel, are brought together.[26] What develops here is a model of how power moves, how positions shift and pleasures change throughout a text in which it is precisely the question of power and the possibility of pleasure that are raised both within the fiction, where some of those issues are openly debated, and around the text, where the complexity of those questions is also put on view.

For example, though Valentín seems to put down Molina's world of popular culture, it is precisely into that realm that Molina seems to seduce his partner. The subject who seems to want to instruct his interlocutor is also turned into the pupil of the person presumed to be taught. Yet to put Valentín only on the receiving end of the novel's strategic turns and Molina's seductive strategies is to stop the text from taking the turns that survive until the end of their story; it is to fix these subjects in places that resist becoming the only places in which to fix them. Although the novel seems to take us all to a place quite different from the one in which we start, that place doesn't really seem to be where things end. Our path, moreover, takes some provocative turns along its seemingly direct route. The turns taken by text and fiction—the shifts in the relationship between the fictional subjects and their textual counterparts—put into question the apparent end to the ups and downs of their dialogue, the finality of their seeming agreement and union. The novel constructs a chain of unpredictable yet perfectly logical moves through a narrative that reveals, but does not resolve, the relations of power and pleasure through which its principal subjects are developed and defined.

The dialogue between Molina and Valentín is just that—a dialogue, a complicitous contractual relation in which the interlocutors are at once opposed to or distinguished from and at the same time at one with each other. Moreover, in this novel to be a speaker is, as often as not, to be a narrator; to be a listener is also to be a narratee. These roles seem to inform almost everything that goes on in the novel, for, as noted above, the exercise of power and some kind of experience of pleasure are mostly tied to language and the production of discourse. However, the dialogue between these fictional subjects demonstrates that the sound of silence may be as powerful, or perhaps even as pleasurable, as the sound of speech. It all depends on the situation, the events surrounding any actual or potential production of discourse, as well as the nature of the discourse produced. This situation reminds us that the relations among discourse, power, and pleasure are ever shifting and unstable; with each new subject and situation the combinations of different categories and the superimpositions of different pairs determine different effects.[27]

At the beginning of the novel (i.e., in Chapters I and II) it might seem that there is a positive correlation between the production of language and the exercise of power. Molina, the one who initially narrates, appears to control the direction of the dialogue and, moreover, to suppress the voice of his interlocutor. Valentín, the listener-narratee, is, by virtue of the silence that "identifies" him, cast in the role of an apparently passive and powerless subject. However, the ostensible dominance of Molina's discourse throughout the novel (his movie stories seem to proliferate within and regulate the appearance of other stories and events) signals instead a precarious, as opposed to stable, contol over the two subjects' exchange. To speak or narrate means not only to control what is said or heard; it is also to lay oneself open to attack and to make oneself vulnerable to the seizure of control by an interlocutor whose silence, therefore, may very well be a sign of a potential instead of a sign of powerlessness. What the two subjects in Puig's novel seem to discover and work with is the potential for any kind of situation of discourse to produce or perpetuate the powerful or pleasurable positions of its individual subjects.

In the novel's initial chapters, where Molina narrates the story of *La marca de la pantera* [*Cat People*], the dialogue turns from one type of power situation to another as each subject plots against and prods, reacts and responds to, the other. Though seductive as a diversionary tale that would allow the prisoners their temporary escape from the hard facts of the situation (see Molina's comments on 85), the film story told here and those later narrated by Molina are not powerful enough to suppress the reality that surrounds them. While these film fictions might for a time obscure from view the facts of the situation in which the interlocutors live, it cannot obscure the fact that another story of power goes on outside their own relationship. The exchange between Valentín and Molina takes us from one frame to the other, alternating and intermixing details of the one with details of and connections to the other. The course of the dialogue therefore forces us to focus as much on the situation in which the dialogue and its constituent narrations occur as on the narratives related by them.

The move between these fictional realms is a dialogue of fictions, a dialogue made possible by the verbal exchange of the characters which, more often than not, seems dominated by large segments of monologic performances. But, precisely because Molina is not allowed to narrate all the time, the dialogue form asserts its hold on the text and its characters. That apparently privileged position of the sole narrator is denied the text's initial speaker not only by the novel's author but also by the other fictional character who empowers him to speak in the first place. Valentín, Molina's sometimes silent interlocutor, works against and disallows that identification, for he, too, desires to be heard and to speak, to direct and to control things. As the two vie for a position of discursive privilege, discussing the film story being told or debating the questions it raises, we see that their dialogue is above all a struggle for control over one another. Each time these subjects reach what appears to be a conclusion or decision about their positions or possibilities, the one who seems to be under the thumb of the other also manages to come out from under the discourse of his apparently more powerful partner.

Though Molina does indeed control the film story as it is told to Valentín, because as its narrator he decides how to tell it, his narration is also controlled, because it is interrupted, by his listener. Valentín is in fact the one who openly points out the pleasures, along with the powers, that accompany the role of the narrator. He clearly states that he wants to share in them, that he prefers to have more time and opportunity to operate as a subject of narration: "— . . . vos te divertís contándola y por ahí también yo quiero intervenir un poco, ¿te das cuenta? No soy un tipo que sepa escuchar demasiado, ¿sabés, no?, y de golpe me tengo que estarte escuchando callado horas" ["— . . . you have the fun of telling it and I just want to chime in once in a while too, see what I mean? I'm not the type who knows how to sit around and just listen all the time, you get what I mean? And all of a sudden I have to sit quiet listening to you for hours on end"] (21); "—

Si vos también ponés tu cosecha, ¿por qué no yo?" ["—If you add things, why can't I?" (trans. mine)] (29). Valentín takes Molina from his privileged place by the very act of interrupting his narration. Thus the silent subject whose voice is suppressed by that of his vocal interlocutor takes over and suppresses that of the narrative partner upon whom he also depends for his own powers, as well as for narrative pleasures. The interruptions of Molina's narration by Valentín do a kind of violence to it and its narrator-author. (We recall that Molina invents as well as reports what he remembers from the films he has seen, and that Valentín takes him to task for taking such liberties with his stories; see 20–23; cf. 170–71.) Valentín's interruptions are also critical interventions that take as their object not only the facts of the story that is told to him but also the person who acts as its knowledgeable and powerful teller.

As the comments and critical assessments made by Valentín are responded to by Molina in the initial chapters, a dialogue of apparent differences is developed. Molina is presented as the uncritical, innocent viewer-turned-narrator who identifies almost completely with the fiction he relates and the characters in it. Valentín, on the other hand, keeps himself at a distance from the stories narrated by his prison partner, responding to Molina's narration of *La marca de la pantera* with critical analyses of its anecdotal content according to theoretical models familiar to him but foreign to his interlocutor. (Psychoanalytic theory seems to govern much of his reading of this film; not surprisingly, he identifies with the film's psychiatrist, while Molina identifies with his patient, the film's heroine. See the already noted exchange on identification, cited above.) Valentín's critical commentary does not stop at the film material itself. It goes beyond the bounds of the fiction to the figure of its narrator. Molina, the subject who provides the material for analysis and who actively controls much of what his listener has to work with, is himself reduced to a passive object of analysis by Valentín. However, the control arrived at by Valentín's critical perspective is forcefully resisted by Molina's narrative performance. Valentín, the critic, is in a way silenced by the silence of his critical object, because Molina seems to regain his privileged position as principal, controlling subject—that is, as primary speaker and narrator— by refusing to say anything at all. His refusal to continue with the film's story at the end of Chapter I, where he cuts it off at a particularly suspenseful moment, constitutes his resistance to the privilege taken over by his partner, his reappropriation of a power he would also attempt to make all his own.

That Molina and Valentín are all too aware of what they are doing and that the ending of Chapter I also "speaks" in the name of the author, whose relation to the reader is both playfully unveiled and potentially masked by the words of the fictional characters themselves, is clear from the last exchange between the prisoners. When Valentín requests that Molina go on with the narration precisely when he wants to interrupt it, Molina replies, "—Un poquito no más, me gusta sacarte el dulce en lo mejor, así te gusta más la película. Al público hay que hacerle así, si no no está contento. En la radio antes te hacían siempre eso" ["—A little bit, no more, I like to leave you hanging, that way you enjoy the film more. You have to do it that way with the public, otherwise they're not satisfied. On the radio they always used to do that to you"] (32). The comparison between the text's techniques and those of popular forms of serial fiction is acknowledged by the very subjects who seem to need to keep their strategies secret (the narrator within and the authorial figure above the text). Moreover, when, after seeming to acquiesce to Valentín's request by telling him a bit more, Molina cuts off the tale once again, refusing to respond to Valentín's "—¿Y?" ["—And?"] with more than "—Mañana seguimos. Chau, que duermas bien" ["—Tomorrow we'll go on. Ciao, sleep tight"], Valentín's final response lays bare some of the rules of the game they are playing. His "—Ya me las vas a pagar" ["—You'll pay for this"] openly declares the powerful economy of their discursive exchange, the payments of pleasure and punishment that each would receive from but also mete out to the other to whom he is, from the start, ever bound in personal exchange.

Molina's decision to regulate his narrative in this manner seems designed as much to tantalize as to torture his cellmate. The revenge he takes for his interlocutor's critical disruptions of his story has a double edge to it, for this vengeful maneuver may turn back on the sender while also moving toward the receiver of its calculated effects. In fact, Molina wants to please as much as punish his listener with his story. His narrative technique, motivated by both of those goals, seems to accomplish that task. By interrupting his own narration and withholding information, Molina makes himself into a disruptive subject who does violence to a story at the moment when that same story also promises us some violence. (Molina stops narrating as a character appears to be stalked by the cat woman/panther one night; see 30–31.) His disruptive technique is an attack on, as well as a defense against, the subject whose attacks on him and his story he once again tries to diffuse and defeat. Valentín's plea for more is proof that Molina knows exactly what he is doing. His strategies prove powerful and pleasurable enough to subvert, even seduce, his critical commentator by turning him into a dependent listener whose own desire for stories helps to keep this narrator in his precariously privileged position.

Valentín's desire to take over the exchange is satisfied, but then again turned around, by Molina's virtual surrender to the end of this story. It is a story that, much like all stories perhaps, also controls the one who tells it. Molina cannot defer indefinitely his arrival at the film's end. It is at that point, when his work as narrator appears to come to a close, that Valentín steps into his narrative place. The end of Molina's film means the beginning of Valentín's own story. As told by Molina, *La marca de la pantera* leads Valentín to tell a "real-life" tale that, in the end, sounds not very different from the one told by Molina about some fictional characters—characters to whom not only Molina but, oddly enough, also Valentín grow very attached. (When Molina's story is finished, Valentín openly says: "— . . . me encariñé con los personajes. Y ahora se terminó, y es como si estuvieran muertos" ["— . . . I've become attached to the characters. And now it's all over, and it's just like they died"] [47].)

Both Valentín's narrative material and his technique of telling turn out to be very much like those of his cellmate. Molina's story serves also as a point of origin for Valentín's factual tale. Though Valentín's story is meant to be a biographical account of his comrade-girlfriend as he analyzes logically and in political terms the development of her life, his presentation of that story transforms it into a sentimental romantic tale not unlike the stories of Molina's films (see 48–52). This story is in a way also co-authored by Molina, who gives his cellmate the chance to speak and to follow the narrative model initially put into question by Valentín's critical comments. Molina also provides his partner's story with a provocative title (cited above) that links it with the tales he himself tells. Valentín tells Molina a story that sounds like a story Molina could have told him; Molina listens to a tale that Valentín himself might have liked to hear.[28]

Having suffered through and been seduced by Molina's tale and techniques, Valentín turns the tables on his listening partner, who, not unlike Valentín before him, still resists being kept in his place. As Valentín assumes the position of knowledgeable narrator who manipulates his narrative material to suit what are at once his narrative designs and his narratee's desires, Molina turns into the inquisitive listener whose questions about potentially significant details manage to direct the dialogue's development as much as his interlocutor's performance (e.g., 50–51). Much like the ending arrived at in Chapter I, and apparently also in response to it, the end of Valentín's tale repeats and returns to the ending of Molina's film. When Valentín's "—Mañana te la sigo, Molina" ["—I'll go on tomorrow, Molina"] is heard by Molina, who, like Valentín before him, wants his interlocutor to go on with instead of interrupting his tale, his reply of "—Sos vengativo" ["—You're vindictive" (trans. mine)] acknowledges, now from the other side, the intricate but always specularly interdependent turns of their plays for power and pleasure inside the cell (52). Moreover, even when they would seem to come to some agreement regarding the moves they would allow each other within their dialogue (e.g., the narrative "pact" or "truce" they form at the very end of Chapter II regarding how they will proceed with each story in the future; see 52–53), they merely establish another ground from and upon which these kinds of moves can be plotted. As their dialogue develops throughout the rest of the novel, they continue to vie for position even as they would come to pleasurable terms with one another. As they move from fictional narrative to political discussion, from disagreements and debates to pacts and mutual promises, they continue to turn around one another while also turning one another around.

Through the development of their discursive performances and personal debates the dialogue of prisoners who are initially strangers turns into a relationship of subjects finally familiar. The familiarity of their relationship is established not only by the way we get to know them but also by the way they get to know each other. Indeed, they become familiar figures also because of the familial roles they play for each other. The familial model they work out together depends upon and provides for the narrative exchange that sustains their dialogue. Within the space to which they are restricted Molina and Valentín reproduce a familial relationship—that of parent and child, mother and son—that has inscribed within it significant relations of power. Their actions and words make increasingly visible and powerful the nature of that relationship. The familial model operates according to the same kinds of complex moves of the discursive exchange with which it develops and on which it is superimposed. Moreover, that private domestic relationship is developed in connection with a public institutional one—that of the prison system within which they have been placed and through which they are isolated from all but each other. Though their cell is a place apart, it is also a place within the larger edifice. It is separated from but intricately bound up in the network of power to which that institution pertains and through which it operates. The moves for power and pleasure within one sphere are not disconnected from those in the other. As places of privilege are secured and subverted in one, so are they set up and put down in the other.[29]

In the dialogues between Molina and the prison warden in Chapters VIII, XI, and XIV we are reminded that the prison cell shared by the novel's protagonists is part of larger power structures, that of this prison in particular and that of the penal system as a whole. Though seeming to be removed from the system, the cell actually manifests the institutionalized exercise of power whose effects are felt far from its apparent source.[30] The verbal exchanges between Molina and the warden reveal the invisible supports of the dialogue between the two prisoners. Their relationship is designed not only by what they desire to do but also by what has been plotted for them from above and outside their cell, both in the fiction they help to form and in the text that forms them. It turns out that Molina has agreed to act as an informant for his superior, the warden, who is himself but an agent of surveillance for those who are above him in the system he works to uphold. (See, for example, his comments about the pressures from his own superiors on 201 and 249–50.)

On the promise of a pardon and early release for himself, Molina agrees to work for the penal system that imprisons him and his partner. He is to extract from his cellmate information about his comrades' identities and activities. Molina, the apparently powerless prisoner outside his cell, is given a chance to exercise a certain power within it. He manages to turn the situation around so as to extend his power beyond its initially limited sphere—to direct things so as to satisfy his own desires while thwarting the warden's designs. Molina's weapon is a fictional one. That is, the art of fiction and fiction-making allows him to subvert the plan that also empowers him. As the artful storyteller, the inventor of tales plausible and powerful enough to seduce his listeners both outside his cell and within it, Molina manipulates his interlocutors into helping him with his own plans.

The plan in which Molina at first agrees to act as a passive agent and collector of information is the plan he manages to appropriate and to redefine as a more active author-director. Hoping to break down Valentín's resistance to revealing information, the prison officials attempt to make him ill by poisoning his food and, thus weakened, willing to tell his secrets to his fellow prisoner. Molina instead convinces the warden that the way to avert Molina's suspicion and even to gain his confidence is to try to please him, instead of punishing him. Molina's visits to the warden's office are to be represented as visits with his mother, whose packages of Molina's favorite foods are to be shared with Valentín as a way of inspiring his trust and their friendship. When Molina winds up dictating the plan, designing its mechanisms and describing its props (he not only dictates the list of items to be purchased by his "mother," but also instructs the warden on how to prepare and present them in a package so as to make them look like the "real thing" [156–57]), he virtually usurps the place of the "Director," whose moves he himself comes to direct. (In Spanish his title is in fact "director.")

The secret plan devised for the purpose of fooling one of Molina's interlocutors (Valentín) turns out to be also a design for fooling the other (the warden). Molina's fiction is authored with an appropriate concern for verisimilitude. Each part of the plan must give the appearance of truth by masking the fictionality of its referent. That is, the packages must give the appearance of his mother's visit; that appearance will at the same time cover up both his talks with the warden and his mother's absence. This fiction is authored and directed with each of his audiences in mind, enabling him to keep both of his interlocutors in the dark about what is really going on before their eyes and ears. Molina thereby manages for a time to exercise a certain amount of power and to obtain a certain amount of pleasure precisely when neither power nor pleasure would seem allowed.

Molina agrees to do for the warden what the warden, with all his power, does not seem able to do for himself. From his own precariously privileged position, Molina exercises a power that is also not his own. He works through a kind of proxy that bestows a privilege upon him while also disclosing that he has very few privileges. As it turns out, though, the "confession" Molina seeks from, and the power he himself desires to exercise over, his apparently less powerful because less knowledgeable partner are of a different but connected order. That is, just when it seems that he is using Valentín to get what he wants from the warden (i.e., his freedom), we realize that he is also using the warden to get what he wants from Valentín (i.e., his affection). Yet, like the other subjects around him, Molina is not in total control of his situation either within the prison at large or the cell he shares. In a way he succeeds with both his romantic-erotic and his political plots, thereby asserting his power over those who would attempt to control him; however, his tragic end (that is, his murder/self-sacrifice) also marks the limits of his powers and pleasures. Those powers and pleasures are destined to be "done in" in his real world, as well as in the films he narrates.

The relationship with Valentín that develops out of the secret plan with the warden is also partly invented by Molina. Showing himself to be a talented improvisor-artist, he manages temporarily to obtain what he wants from each by betraying the one with the other.[31] The packages of food from Molina's "mother," conned as they are from the warden whose power they work to undermine, are the essential props in, as well as links between, these two spheres of action. Moreover, they represent the interconnection between two kinds of institutions, two apparently disparate but in fact not dissimilar relational models developed through Molina's and Valentín's dialogue. Molina seems able to resist for a time the effects of the mechanisms of power for which he and Valentín are objects to be controlled in one institution (the prison itself, the penal system) by generating a strategy for becoming the subjects within another (their "parent-child" relationship, the family unit). In the familial relation that develops between Molina (mother) and Valentín (son), these two prisoners seem temporarily to escape the total control of the ("paternal") authorities who work to monitor, direct, and limit their moves. The ("familial") packages through which institutional power is to be upheld are the means by which it can also be undermined.

However, this resistance to power is also a duplication of the mechanisms they would attempt to evade. Their familial relation implicitly offers itself as a parallel, if not primary, model for the kind of practices institutionalized in the penal system within which they are held. And it is the relationship from which, their own interchange seems to prove, the inherently political as well as erotic relations that develop between either heterosexual or homosexual partners are also derived. The prisoners' return to a seemingly innocent and primary model of relations does not free them from—rather, it shows how much they are inevitably bound by—the erotic and political features of their exchange, the very exchange of pleasures and powers through which they are repeatedly differentiated from and identified with one another. This family model is but a fictional reprieve from the mechanisms of power. It is the means by which each comes to suffer its pleasurable effects and enjoy its powerful evolution. Both power and pleasure are bound to each familial role according to the individual desires and demands of each subject.

When Valentín becomes ill from the poisoned food and loses control over his own body, he follows through on the arrangement by which he is to surrender that body to Molina, who is pleased to control and cater to it. Valentín, reduced to an infantile state of dependency, must look to his partner for nourishment and comfort.[32] Molina, ever the self-sacrificing "mother," feeds him the food sent from his own "mother," cleans him, and tells him bedtime film stories chosen for his "son's" delight (see esp. 118, 123–24, 128, 134–35, 162–63). Molina acts as the maternal servant for the "son" whose well-being he, by virtue of his familial role, wants to control and whose desires he also wants to mold ("— . . . si yo te trato bien ... es porque quiero ganarme tu amistad, y por qué no decirlo ... tu cariño" ["— . . . if I'm nice to you ... it's because I want to win your friendship, and, why not say it? ... your affection"] [206]). Valentín accepts the gifts and care bestowed upon him by his ostensibly selfless partner, yet he resists being kept in the powerless filial position in which that arrangement would place him ("— . . . no me gusta que me manejen la vida. [. . . .] No me digas lo que tengo que hacer, por favor ... [. . . .] ¡Basta! ... carajo!!!"

["— . . . I don't like anybody running my life for me. [. . . .] Don't be telling me what I have to do ... [. . . .] Cut it out! ... Christ almighty!!!"] [197]).

As the cellmates play out their familial relation throughout the major portion of their dialogue, they both certify and contradict some of the characteristics that seem attached to those roles. They reveal that to be either "parent" or "child" means to be situated in a relationship of power with the other, to function as either subject or object of familial authority, and to experience either the privilege or the powerlessness associated with that role. But neither position or role possesses a clearly stable or uniform position, and neither subject is positioned forever above or below the other. While they act out one role, they also seem to desire to play the other. While each looks like either a powerful or powerless figure, he can also be read as the other. Each character shifts also to an identification with the subject in the opposite role so that the possibility of attaching each to only one of them is denied. The paradoxes of their plays for position point up the contradictions inherent in each of their relations to those roles. Molina, who seems to take such pleasure in and works so hard at being Valentín's "mother," is the very subject who reveals that he wants to be mothered by another (see 76, 116, 207). Valentín, the subject who would at times resist his subservient role as "son," comes to accept and take pleasure in it, also pleasing the subject who works at keeping him in that position (e.g., 205–6). The differences that appear to separate these subjects turn out to be the points of contact between them as well.

These provocative contradictions also hold for the other roles, or identities, assumed by Molina and Valentín. Each is a shifting composite of roles and positions that continue to combine with and contradict one another. Molina, the homosexual subject presumably attached mainly to the question of sexuality and concerned only with his quest for pleasure, turns out to be a subject who also knows a great deal about the exercise of power. Molina is the subject who is supposedly innocent of things political (i.e., the leftist theories and practices of his cellmate). Yet in his seduction of Valentín he shows himself to be a powerful subject who, as his partner acknowledges, could teach his interlocutor much about how to dominate or control a situation. (See their talk revolving around the notion of the "mujer araña," 264–65.)

⌐ That exercise of power is not so far from the question of pleasure, for it is precisely that ability to direct another and to lead him to the position he actually winds up in that brings satisfaction to this apparently powerless subject. Their relationship of power is in itself also a relationship of pleasures. Just as the locus of power shifts from one to the other, so does the experience of pleasure. The seduction of Valentín constitutes a success that is as much political as it is emotional and erotic.

That seduction is also a meeting of wills, a meeting of subjects who, not only at the end but also throughout their time together, seem to have much in common. The apolitical homosexual who wants to be a "passive woman" and whose position represents the most reactionary of roles and desires (see 34–35, 68–69, 207, 246–47) is in another way also the more powerful of the two partners, for he is the one who delights in controlling his cellmate so as to satisfy his own desires.[33] The heterosexual political activist who follows the pattern of the "macho" male who would dominate the objects of his desire, and who rebelliously resists the domination of others, is also not strong (or, perhaps, political) enough to deter the plan, to break the "web" of the subject to whom he also surrenders. Yet Valentín also conquers the partner who seems not only to control him but also to cause him to be done away with. In fact, the ends of both protagonists keep them turning away from and yet toward one another.

The novel closes with Molina's death at the hands of Valentín's comrades. Molina becomes caught up in a web of violence from which his artfully powerful skills cannot save him—or from which he seems not to want to save himself. Valentín remains in prison, where he is tortured, and at the very end of the novel finds comfort in a set of fantasies he authors through his final monologue. That interior monologue makes him sound very much like the cellmate who has left him behind and whose own fantasies and discourse Valentín seems to rescue in the end. Molina also remains as a figure or voice inscribed in the discourse of Valentín, as Valentín's identity and image remain bound to his former interlocutor, whose disappearance from the scene this last text would almost deny (see 282–87). The ending, not unlike the ending of the last film narrated by Molina to Valentín (the "Mexican" film from Chapters XII, XIII, and XIV), is "un fin enigmático" ["an enigmatic ending"] that leaves several questions suspended. The end itself turns, as do the last appearances of the novel's primary subjects, toward different readings of its puzzling final scenes.

The ending, along with the confusing superimposition of the images of the two protagonists, is also a return to the kinds of endings that Molina likes to tell. In fact, when he finds out that he is about to leave the prison cell, he chooses to tell his partner the story of a film that ends tragically yet hopefully—that is, "enigmatically." When the young male protagonist of the film dies, the heroine "— . . . sigue caminando sin rumbo, como un alma en pena. Y de golpe se ve grande grande en primer plano la cara de ella, con los ojos llenos de lágrimas, pero con una sonrisa en los labios" ["— . . . keeps walking but with no direction, like a wandering soul. And then suddenly you see a giant giant close-up of just her face, with her eyes flooded with tears, but with a smile on her lips"] (263; cf. 100, 216). In Molina's and Valentín's discussion of the ambiguity of this ending right after Molina finishes his narration, the text provides both a commentary on the endings of the other films that precede and resemble this one and a possible reading of the ending of the novel in which they all appear. While Molina's final comment ("—Qué final más enigmático, ¿verdad?" ["—Such an enigmatic ending, isn't it . . . ?"] [263] provokes Valentín to disagree and attempt to explain his own interpretation of it ("—Quiere decir que aunque ella se haya quedado sin nada, está contenta de haber tenido por lo menos una relación verdadera en la vida, aunque ya se haya terminado" ["—It means that even if she's left with nothing, she's content to have had at least one real relationship in her life, even if it's over and done with"]), it is finally Molina who points out the undecidable nature of the ending. He also explains to Valentín (the novel's "intellectual") the contradictions inherent in his interpretation and in his other theoretical statements. When Valentín reminds Molina that "— . . . habría que saber aceptar las cosas como se dan, y apreciar lo bueno que te pase, aunque no dure. Porque nada es para siempre" ["—It's a question of learning to accept things as they come, and to appreciate the good that happens to you, even if it doesn't last. Because nothing is forever"], Molina undercuts his philosophy and his analysis of the movie by saying, "—Sí, eso es fácil decirlo. Pero sentirlo es otra cosa" ["—Yes, it's easy to say. But feeling it is something else"]. As Molina points out the difference between knowing or believing something rationally and feeling or desiring it emotionally, he presents a defense of his own political, as well as sexual, position against the prior attacks of his interlocutor, whose position he now takes and whose desires, we come to see, may not differ from his own. He articulates a simple but nonetheless powerful observation about the possible difficulties of reconciling psychology with ideology, about the obstacles to controlling desire even when there is a desire to control it.[34]

The film protagonists, who wind up sacrificing themselves for each other, are reflected in and duplicated by Molina and Valentín, who are also allowed to analyze the end to which they all come by the novel's last pages. The film's enigmatic ending closes off a romantic tale about a couple who, faced with innumerable but originally unconnected obstacles to their union, are granted only a brief time together before the hero dies. This is precisely the situation in which Molina and Valentín find themselves; this is precisely the way their story ends. Their discussion of the ending of the film not only prefigures their own endings, but also solidifies their intimately connected appearances and performances. In the interpretive disagreement over the ending of the film, for example, we see that a switch occurs also in their "philosophical" positions. In his comments Molina points out the gap between language and experience, theory and practice. For him the distance between *decir* and *sentir* is fundamentally unbridgeable. In the discussion through which he becomes what Valentín had seemed to be (that is, his interlocutor's critic and commentator), Molina assumes a position that at first might have been thought antithetical to his "nature." It is he who now brings Valentín back to the reality that their fictions (their films, fantasies, and theoretical notions) would cover over and rewrite according to unrealistic designs. And in supporting his own "escapist" interpretation of the film, it is now Valentín who takes the position initially identified with his partner. It is not that either has actually been transformed into the other; rather, the power of each over his partner is such that the lines of demarcation grow less and less visible.

The identification of the one with the other is accomplished in a dramatic way in Valentín's final monologue, where the "voice" of Molina can still be heard.[35] Interestingly enough, this final conflation of images is itself the return to and coming together of other moments of complete identification in the text, moments when the novel turns to raise the question of identity which, as noted above, is one of the first to be openly raised by the subjects themselves. The moment that seems to certify most powerfully the complexities of identification and difference between the two subjects is the moment when the two men finally meet as lovers. The text graphically presents them as if they were not two subjects, but one. They appear to be finally, if not originally, bound up in a situation that would belie their difference from each other. This scene occurs in Chapter XI, after Molina tells Valentín that he is being released from prison.

Oddly enough, it is Molina who seems to be most upset at the thought of his imminent departure and freedom. This turn of emotion puts Valentín in the position of comforter for the interlocutor who has spent so much time comforting him. Moreover, it turns him into the initiator of their physical (i.e., sexual) contact. Valentín's response of action—a response that is also in keeping with his character, since the figure he presents is that of a sexually aggressive male who prefers to control, instead of being controlled by, another—is, however, a response set up by his partner. Only when Molina challenges Valentín to react by insisting that his release and subsequent absence from the cell—even his death—would have no effect on Valentín does Valentín turn guiltily from a gesture of potentially "maternal" comfort to one more appropriate to a lover (219). Molina's apparently passive refusal to speak after making his melodramatic challenge somehow forces his listener to act with an aggressive style, a style originally his own and one that his partner is not uncomfortable supporting.

The image of the two after their physical meeting is that of a subject virtually in dialogue with himself, a subject who sees himself as another whose identity is impossible to separate from his own. After Molina tells Valentín, "—Ahora sin querer me llevé la mano a mi ceja, buscándome el lunar" ["—Just then, without thinking, I put my hand up to my face, trying to find the mole"], Valentín reminds him that it is he, Valentín, who has the mole, and not Molina. Molina, aware of this difference between them, attempts to explain to his silent interlocutor (Valentín's "responses" are represented as ellipses in the text) the contradiction he has experienced: "—Por un minuto solo, me pareció que yo no estaba acá, ... ni acá, ni afuera ... — ... —Me pareció que yo no estaba ... que estabas vos sólo. — ... —O que yo

210

no era yo. Que ahora yo ... eras vos" ["—For just a second, it seemed like I wasn't here ... not here or anywhere out there either ... — ... —It seemed as if I wasn't here at all ... like it was you all alone — ... —Or like I wasn't me anymore. As if now, somehow ... I ... were you"] (222).

This peculiar and paradoxical formulation is an apt representation of their relation to one another throughout the entire text, as well as in this scene and at the novel's end. This instance of dialogue—a dialogue that almost looks like a segment of monologue—inscribes each subject in the place of the other at the same time that it accomplishes a kind of specular self-effacement. Each is posited as a subject by the subject who is and yet is not himself, one who is himself at the same time that he is an other who is supposed to be different from and opposed to him. Molina's fantasy of nonexistence, his perception of himself as having been displaced by and transformed into the subject to whom he speaks but whose voice cannot be heard, becomes a reality of language. The grammatical contradiction of "Yo ... eras vos" displaces his own "I," an "I" that would seem willingly to give up its place to the "you" that also originates in the very subject whose presence is put into question.[36]

The question of who is present, who is the subject of discourse (and whose own identity is also in question), is raised again at the novel's end within Valentín's interior monologue. Like the young man who remains in the Mexican tragedy or the heroine of the Nazi film narrated much earlier, Molina dies a romantic, sacrifical death that leaves behind him the other subject in whom he also remains, the other subject in or through whom his own image is reduplicated. Valentín is left in prison, spinning a mono-dialogic fiction through which his own voice is projected in virtual conversation with another subject who is at once a woman named Marta and his former cellmate Molina. (See esp. 286–87; Marta is not his comrade-girlfriend, but another "classy" woman who, desired by Valentín over his comrade, represents Valentín's "betrayal" of his own politics. See his confession on 147–48; see also 180–82.) Molina's image as a subject is projected onto and intermixed with both of their voices and images. Valentín, apparently ensnared by "la mujer araña, que atrapa a los hombres en su tela" ["the spider woman, that traps men in her web"] (265) who has, appropriately enough, also been ensnared by Valentín, for whom he seems ultimately to sacrifice himself, weaves a recuperative fiction through which he and his favorite interlocutors can be reunited.

The power of Valentín's fiction is such that it might appear to be an exchange between two subjects, instead of a solitary performance. His desire for an interlocutor empowers the voice and image of another subject who turns from one identity to another as it accompanies him, while also certifying the reality of his imprisonment: " . . . *y voy a seguir hablando con vos en el sueño, ¿será posible?, 'sí, este es un sueño y estamos hablando, así que después también, no tengas miedo, creo que ya nadie nos va a poder separar, porque nos hemos dado cuenta de lo más difícil', ¿qué es lo más difícil de darse cuenta?, 'que vivo adentro de tu pensamiento y así te voy a acompañar siempre, nunca vas a estar solo', claro que sí, eso es lo que nunca me tengo que olvidar, si los dos pensamos igual vamos a estar juntos, aunque no te pueda ver . . .*" [" . . . *and I'll just go on talking with you in my sleep, will it be possible? 'Yes, this is a dream and we're talking together, so even if you fall asleep you don't have to be afraid, and I think now that nothing is ever going to separate as again, because we've realized the most difficult thing of all,' what's the most difficult thing of all to realize? 'That I live deep inside your thoughts and so I'll always remain with you, you'll never be alone,' of course that's it, that's what I can never let myself forget, if the two of us think the same then we're together, even if I can't see you . . .*"] (286). Though this final dialogue within his monologue works to deny, even defeat, the reality lived by Valentín, it also reveals his own discursive limits as well as the limits of the linguistic powers of the *mujer araña* (the weaver of verbal and visual traps) from whom he has taken his fictional project.

The "beso de la mujer araña"—both as a metaphor and as a quasi-literal description of an event in the fiction—points up the relation between fiction and power that develops within the protagonist's dialogue and the text that presents them. The narrative strategies of the "spider woman" constitute the principal means by which he can ensnare his prey. Yet this prey is also the subject in whom his power resides. Valentín is not only the subject who enables Molina to exercise his powers by agreeing to listen to him, but also the one who gives him, or allows him to give himself, that mysterious and seductive name. This name, though, also has its origins in a request that the "spider woman" himself makes. After the cellmates end their discussion of the last film narrated by Molina and Valentín confesses his affection for and attachment to his partner, Molina asks him for a kiss: "— . . . querría pedirte algo ... [. . . .] —Un beso. [. . . .] —Pero mañana, antes de irme" ["— . . . I do want to ask you for something ... [. . . .] —A kiss ... [. . . .] —But tomorrow, before I go"] (264). Though Molina makes the request and the kiss thus also originates in his verbal query, he posits himself as its receiver, as the one upon whom it is to be bestowed by his interlocutor. This kiss is a gift that he would receive only by first sending it in another form to the subject by whom he wishes to have it bestowed. This gift is then sent back to its intended receiver. It is a gift that simultaneously marks both the beginning and the end, the origin and destination, of these prisoners' desires.

The "kiss of the spider woman" is not only the kiss that gives life to a set of fictions designed to entrap particular listeners. It is also the kiss of death, the kiss that marks the coming end of things in fiction and text alike. Even though he is taken with the name, this fatal identification is resisted by Molina. He rejects Valentín's initial comparison of him to *la mujer pantera* (from the first film narrated in the novel), after declaring that "Es muy triste ser mujer pantera, nadie la puede besar" ["It's very sad being a panther woman; no one can kiss you"] (265), preferring instead the spider woman metaphor. Nonetheless, he also seems drawn to the kind of ending that could have been set up by that kind of woman—that is, by a *femme fatale*.[37] As noted above, Molina appears to sacrifice himself for Valentín when he agrees to try to pass a message to Valentín's comrades once he is released from prison: he is killed by them when he is followed by the police. (See the police report on his activities and death, on 269–79.) The kiss of death is therefore the kiss to which he succumbs in a plotted scene that he himself could have woven from a movie like those he has told to his partner. The kiss from Valentín is in a way the fatal prize won by Molina. It prepares him for—indeed, also leads him quickly to—his own dramatic ending. Valentín is of course also marked by that kiss and his interlocutor's death. Seduced as he is by the narrative web fashioned by Molina, Valentín finally becomes the subject who fashions for himself the fictions that were once provided by Molina. The spider woman, his comforter and provider until the end (though he seems to

"speak" with Marta, the fantasy she gives him and the voice she uses
are "Molinaesque"), stays with him. She is the figure to whose powers
he would continue to submit and to whose image he would turn his
own voice and gaze.

"El beso de la mujer araña" is, then, an act through which life is
given to a set of fictions that repeatedly lead to death—the death of
the characters who first give them life. This sign of a potentially erotic
relation is, furthermore, the emblem of a powerful and fatal play between two subjects. This sign of seductive contact also leaves its mark
in their play for power. That a political as well as sexual relation is
suggested by the novel's title is rather fitting, since the protagonists
and their "crimes" are originally tied to those spheres of activity, and
the prisoners spend a fair amount of time discussing, as well as acting
out, those same activities and issues during their time together. The
debates they hold and the instructive explanations they give of themselves constitute the explicit thematization of those issues. In the discussions and debates, as well as in their daily activities and talks,
Valentín and Molina establish their different yet identical positions.
There are clashes between words and deeds, between theory and
practice, that both set them up in opposition to each other and bring
them very close together.

If in the activities developed through their "familial" relationship,
for example, Molina seems to come out on top for a while, in the verbal
exchange about matters both theoretical and experiential it looks as if
Valentín manages to gain a privileged position. That is, when the dialogue leads to a consideration of political matters, for instance, and
even when it touches on matters that are also sexual, Valentín emerges
as the more knowledgeable, the more powerful, of the two speakers.
Even when he would admit his ignorance, the pressure he places on
his interlocutor to explain things serves to keep him somewhat ahead
of that other subject who, as we know, is all the while also in control.

For example, when Valentín brings up the question of politics, it is
either to explain to Molina, who seems innocent of political matters,
the theories and ideals that have determined his political activities
(e.g., 33–34, 48, 117) or to try to instruct his cellmate on the political
nature of human relations as a whole (e.g., 69–70, 246–47). In the
end, though, Valentín seems to contradict his speech with his action.
He seems to ignore (perhaps to refuse to see) the similarities between

the practices, maybe even the theories, he calls his own and those he associates with his partner. For instance, Valentín sets up an opposition between Molina's films and his own texts of political philosophy, between Molina, as a subject attached to sentimental fantasy, and himself, as a subject dedicated to theoretical writings (e.g., 15, 63, 77, 85, 103). The contradictions inherent in that oppostion become apparent when, in explaining his use of the texts he reads and the ideals he holds, he unwittingly discloses the analogical relation between the fictions and realities each lives in their cell. Both prisoners imagine themselves to be somewhere else; each transports himself to another realm through his own private fiction. Each uses his particular fictional "text" to deny and also to deal with the reality of his situation. While Molina seeks refuge in film and romantic fantasy, with whose characters he thereby also "lives," Valentín reads his books on politics and philosophy and imagines himself with the comrades whose values and goals he shares (e.g., 48).

There is a tragic connection between the fictions in which each of these subjects seeks to situate himself. It is unveiled and underscored by the fact that it is impossible for either of them to realize what is, at best, a utopian fantasy, an improbable solution, to the reality in which they are trapped during their dialogue. The prisoners reproduce within their own relationship some of the structures of relations that at least one of them desires to abolish. Valentín's blindness to the points of identification between himself and Molina is, for example, what allows or even causes him to reassert some of the roles and structures of power he would in theory oppose. In their final conversation about matters at once political and sexual, they discuss the kinds of relationships that are possible between different types of couples (i.e., either homosexual or heterosexual) and the sorts of roles that each might play (246–47). In this discussion they both support and protest, in either word or deed, the power structure that informs and upholds the "traditional" model of the dominant male/submissive female couple. Though this stereotypical paradigm is in some ways the very model of their own relationship, in their turns with and around one another it becomes an unstable relation of possible pleasures and powers. Their discussion of these matters is also significant because it is when Valentín's discourse on political theory and Molina's descriptions of his sexual preferences converge, entering into a kind of direct dia-

215

logue. It is one of the places where we see how, in turning to consider one of those issues, they (and the reader who follows them) always seem to turn to the other as well.

This last political/sexual discussion—it is the last in a series of brief encounters between those topics in the dialogue—is not unlike others that precede it, in that we receive two different views of things from each of these subjects. Yet this part of the dialogue also develops a significant shift in Molina's attitude and position. From his former resistance to Valentín's exercise of power as the "dominant" male, he turns to reveal his underlying desire to submit. Here Valentín resumes his role as the interrogator, the critical thinker or investigator, while Molina takes on the role of a "native informant." The former asks questions about, and the latter describes, what it means to be a homosexual, what it is that he, Molina, is and desires. What Molina desires for himself, he confesses quite simply to Valentín, is to be a woman who finds the perfect man to whom (s)he can submit (246; see also 25, 35, 65, 68, 72, 133, 207). Though Valentín also shows himself to be powerless because of his lack of knowledge—he is entirely dependent upon his interlocutor for the information he seeks (i.e., information about Molina as a homosexual)—he still manages to dominate, by directing the path of, their discussion through the questions he asks and the advice he tries to give Molina.

In some of their earlier discussions of sexuality Molina deftly maneuvers to escape the position of the critical object and to reestablish his mastery of the situation either by turning back to a film narration or by explicitly refusing his partner's queries and criticisms. Valentín's attempts to dominate, by appropriating through critical analysis, Molina as a sexual or even psychological object are angrily put down in the earlier scenes by the subject who later reveals that he also wants to be dominated. (For example, Molina's "— . . . ahorrame de escuchar consejos porque yo sé lo que me pasa y lo tengo clarísimo en la cabeza" ["— . . . you can keep your advice, because I know what's going on with me and I've got it all very clear in my own head" (trans. mine)] [25] not only resists Valentín's analysis of his sexual practice but also reminds him of the superior knowledge that his partner possesses.)

In their last discussion, however, Molina responds not with rebuttals or protests, but with simple declarative statements about his own desires. When he states that the position which gives him pleasure is that of the ("traditional") woman—the woman who is excited by and desires to submit to the power of the man who dominates her; the quintessentially "unliberated" woman—Valentín tries to prescribe and, paradoxically, to force Molina to accept and identify with another role. Valentín, the revolutionary who would speak in the name of a model of relations free of repression or coercion, presses his interlocutor to make a choice that is not really his own. That is, he tries to liberate sexually and politically the interlocutor who likes being bound: "—Pero si un hombre ... es mi marido, él tiene que mandar, para que se sienta bien. Eso es lo natural, por que él entonces ... es el hombre de la casa. —No, el hombre de la casa y la mujer de la casa tienen que estar a la par. Si no, eso es una explotación. —Entonces no tiene gracia. —¿Qué? —Bueno, esto es muy íntimo, pero ya que querés saber ... La gracia está en que cuando un hombre te abraza ... le tengas un poco de miedo. —No, esto está mal. Quién te habrá puesto esa idea en la cabeza, está muy mal eso. —Pero yo lo siento así" ["—But if a man is ... my husband, he has to give the orders, so he will feel right. That's the natural thing, because that makes him the ... the man of the house. —No, the man of the house and the woman of the house have to be equal with one another. If not, their relation becomes a form of exploitation. —But then there's no kick to it. —Why? —Well, this is very intimate, but since you're asking about it ... The kick is in the fact that when a man embraces you ... you may feel a little bit frightened. —No, that's all wrong. Whoever put that idea in your head? It's absolutely wrong. —But that's the way I feel"] (246–47). Valentín here tries to convince Molina of the correctness of the egalitarian relational model in which he ostensibly believes; in the process, he discloses the opposing moves that support his position.

The clash between Valentín's theories and practices takes us back to the formulation provided by his own seemingly less powerful/political partner: the distinction between, the irreconcilable gap that separates, the verbs *sentir* and *decir*. As in the discussion of the *fin enigmático*, where Molina makes a similar point as a way of resisting Valentín's interpretation of things, here Molina obstructs Valentín's interpretive activity—determined as it is to prescribe an activity for Molina—by resorting to both a declaration that directly refutes the formulations of his interlocutor and a refusal to go any further with the discussion ("—No hablemos más de esto, porque es una conversación que no conduce a nada. —Al contrario, quiero discutir. —Pero yo no" [—"Let's not talk about it anymore, because this conversation isn't getting anywhere. —To me it is, I want to talk more about it. —But I don't"] [247]). Here he would remind his partner, both by what he says and by what he does, that desire is something his theories cannot control. While sexual practice, for example, may be explained *a posteriori* according to a variety of theoretical models, it is not originally generated from or, Molina underscores, necessarily susceptible to change by the knowledge that informs such theories or the discourse that would articulate them. The question of desire remains as a force of resistance that here complicates, even challenges, the relation between theory and practice. It is precisely that question that insinuates itself in the somewhat uncontrollable responses of each subject to the other in their struggle to dominate the situation.

Valentín's apparently sincere effort to save Molina from domination and exploitation recreates, then, the model of power relations to which he himself would also object. When Valentín tries to force Molina to agree with and desire the theoretical relationship he describes, he tries to inscribe within the subject to whom he speaks an image of his own desire, an image that also betrays the "superior" position of the one who proposes the shift. Valentín seems to want to put "down" Molina while also desiring to raise him "up" to a better position. He here asserts his own desire that Molina not only accept theoretically, but practice actively, what he, Valentín, says he should desire to do. When, in a characteristic moment of resistance, Molina cuts off the discussion, he also asserts his right to (refuse to) submit. Molina, the subject who supposedly enjoys being dominated and playing the powerless woman, would, in this return to a resistance to discourse, remind Valentín (and of course the reader) of the power he also enjoys wielding, the control he exerts through the ups and downs of their dialogue. He seems to exercise this power rather carefully in several arenas while also wanting to be—or play at being—powerless. Valentín, the subject who idealizes egalitarian relations and who in seeking revolution seeks liberation for everyone, winds up continuing to try to dominate and control the interlocutor to whom he has also had to surrender throughout the novel.

The conversations about political and sexual relations bring us to much the same kinds of turns that the conversations about and the narration of the popular films develop. They repeat and take a bit further, perhaps, the patterns of shifts that the familial roles played by the cellmates and the institutional models acted out by the warden and the prisoner together construct. These turns of power, as well as the turns around questions of sexuality and politics, establish a network of contradictory stances in both the subjects' statements and actions. These moves put into question a "correct" or "final" reading of these characters. Inscribed in any (or, rather, all) of their discursive, thematic, and narrative positions are the reflections of another figure from whom each is also distanced and distinct, yet with whom each is at once identified. That is, the dialectics of their relationship are not unlike those of another textual dialogue that unfolds near them. The interplay of the novel's primary fictional subjects in fact interlocks with—and offers another model for reading—the graphic exchange of discourse that develops between the text's fictional body and the authorial footnotes. The dialogue between these problematic partners is connected to, even in a way dependent upon, the notes that accompany it. Though their function is presumably to clarify things, those notes at the foot of the text can be seen to complicate matters further.

Though this isn't the first time Puig has used footnotes in his novels (*The Buenos Aires Affair* is of course his first experiment with that type of textual division), *El beso de la mujer araña* offers a significant variation on the technique. Here the notes run on in a relationship between "body" and "foot" that is maintained for the better part of the novel. (They run from Chapter II through Chapter XI, nine chapters out of sixteen.) The main purpose of the notes is to provide information about homosexuality and to fill in what cannot be said directly within the fiction itself. In what seems to be an authorial design to add to the novel material that is clearly derived from and refers as well to the region beyond the borders of its fiction, these notes call into play and put in virtual dialogue a set of distinct authoritative discourses that merge with one another.

The footnotes become the texts through which the figure of the author surfaces most forcefully in the novel. This figure, otherwise suppressed by or willingly hidden under the voices of the characters who are presented "above" it, emerges through the voices of other authors.

It is engaged in a dialogue not only with those authors, but also with the possible readers of the novel within which these notes are situated. In the verbal exchange between Valentín and Molina, the political activist tries to educate the homosexual, upon whom, paradoxically, he must also call for his own education. Valentín's ignorance regarding homosexuals, freely confessed early on in the text ("— . . . yo de gente de tus inclinaciones sé muy poco" ["— . . . I know very little about people with your type of inclination"] [66]), is what seems to make necessary the discourse in the margins of that same text. Valentín may seem more knowledgeable about many things, but when it comes to the question of homosexuality his privilege is undercut. He needs his prison partner to explain things to him. He is thus the model of the textual interlocutor, the innocent or uninstructed reader, for whom the novel's notes seem to be written.[38]

Though the notes concentrate on the question of sexuality, because of some of the theories they present and the strategies used to present them they are also bound up with the question of power. The narrative strategy employed to develop this discussion of homosexuality and to link it finally with a theory of revolution also betrays the political identity of the author's reader-listener and the relations of power through which they can also be read. The play between the figure of the author and that of the reader is set up through a play among a group of authors. The authorial subject who, by virtue of the notes' appearance in the text, seems to desire to put himself on view and demand to be heard and read, is the subject who can only be heard through the voices of other authors. What we see of that figure or hear of its voice are the images and voices of other authorities whose texts and theories are mediated by that same figure. The voices of those other authors, their texts, are at once presented in the names of their original subjects yet kept under the name of the subject who appropriates, by summarizing and repeating, the work of others.

These notes represent an exchange of, a dialogue among, apparently authoritative discourses. This exchange runs parallel to, while also supporting, the play of discourses and subjects above. As the notes sequentially map out a set of theories about the origins and nature of homosexuality, the authorial mediator takes us through a logical summary of the popular and scientifc theories that have attempted to explain the whole matter. The notes devoted to this investigation—notes

1 and 3–9—move from a discusson of various theories about the physical origins of homosexuality in the first and second of the series (66–68 and 102–03) to an extensive summary of the major psychoanalytic interpretations of the question throughout the rest of the entries. Although psychoanalytic theory seems to dominate the notes as a whole, the later discussions (notes 7 and 8) focus on anthropological and sociological theories of the genesis and practice of homosexuality in modern cultures. Moreover, the final note (209–11) is the culmination of all the theoretical models previously summarized. It elaborates a political theory of homosexuality—that is, homosexuality is posited as a revolutionary practice.

This final note appears to be the series' *telos*. The techniques used to arrive at that important end also seem designed to prepare us for, perhaps seduce us into, its propositions. The seemingly marginal commentaries can be read as a kind of serial narrative that parallels the fictional "serial" developing above it. (We recall the techniques used by the author and characters alike at the end of the first two chapters, noted earlier.) As readers are instructed about the possible explanations of a specific sexual practice, we are also engaged in what looks like another playful dialogue with its author. The authorial figure that conceals itself behind, while also revealing its presence through, the footnotes uses the same kind of narrative set-up to sustain the reader's interest in and attachment to the scientific "story" about homsexuality that he uses for the fiction above. By virtue of the ruptures in that story, caused by the interruptions of its theoretical summaries in each note or "narrative unit," the notes seem to constitute a series of installments that lead us to a final resolution. Like the narrator of the films above or the arranger of the text in which those fictions appear, the subject who presents the sequence would lead us straight to, but also delay our arrival at, the end of this authoritative narrative.

For example, in the novel's third note, and the second in the series on homosexuality (102–3), we are offered the beginning of a summary of the most productive and ostensibly "correct" theories on homosexuality (i.e., the theories of psychoanalysis developed by Freud and his followers), after having been shown in a previous note, as well as at the beginning of this third one, refutations of some "incorrect" notions regarding its origins. The turn from incorrect to correct theories is, of course, interrupted as much by the ruptures produced by each note (for example, we have to wait until note 4 for the continuation of the summary begun in note 3) as by the reading process that takes us from the fiction's body to its foot over and over again. The discourse presented to instruct us and convince us that there is some truth to be seen at the end is denied as much as delivered by the authorial mediator who sets us up to see and hear it. The notes instruct us as much about what is presumably not true as about what we ought to be ready to believe, what in the end seems to come closest to what looks like the truth.

The seeming advancement toward truth is, however, questioned in a curious way near the beginning of the sequence of theories. The discourse designed to lead us to the facts is also tied to a discourse that leads us to a fiction. The discourse of science seems to be contaminated by, if not already tied to, a discourse that seems primarily literary.[39] An "extraneous" note is included between the first and second notes of the series on homosexuality. This "disruptive" note uncovers some fundamental connections between fictional body and marginal comments and, in the end, leads us to see how the position of fact is also determined here by the positions of a variety of fictions. In the novel's second footnote (88–94) the authorial subject presents not a continuation of the discussion on homosexuality, but a lengthy addendum to Molina's narration of the Nazi film above (79–100). The note, entitled *"Servicio publicitario de los estudios Tobis-Berlín, destinado a los exhibidores internacionales de sus películas, referente a la superproducción 'Destino'(páginas centrales")* ["Press-book from Tobis-Berlin Studios, for their international distributors of Tobis-Berlin releases, regarding the superproduction entitled *Her Real Glory* (middle pages)"] (88), pretends to offer us information, some of which is historical (there are quotes from Hitler and Goebbels), about a film that is supposedly made within the film Molina narrates to Valentín.

The juxtaposition of this note with those that develop the ongoing discussion of homosexuality has a curious effect. The thematically homogeneous and quasi-scientific discourse of the theoretical discussion is disrupted by a discourse that is more closely tied with the realm of fiction. Though the discourse on homosexuality, which is itself in a way homogeneous, seems to determine the identity of the notes as a group because it dominates the set, the historico-fictional publicity notice, itself a mixture of discourses, contradicts that uniform appearance through its fundamental heterogeneity. This juxtaposition upsets and puts into question the differentiation of the thematic material and the modes of discourse—the textual hierarchy—that the deployment of authorial footnotes also sets up.

The relation between this second note and the others surrounding it follows in the steps of and parallels the play between the main characters' voices and the move between the major divisions of the text. The second note is, in the first place, a contradictory meeting of fiction and fact. Its documentary nature suggests its proximity to historical fact. (It is presented as a "real" set of pages from a press release and makes reference to, sometimes by quoting directly from, speeches made by leaders of the Third Reich.) But the narrative to which it is connected and which, oddly enough, is also carried on within the text of that same note establishes it as an artifice. This "document" provides "historical" information about the fictional actress-protagonist of the very film narrated by Molina, who is himself a fictional character whose discourse is invented by another author.

Though the difference between Molina and the subject of the note about the German character is theoretically not difficult to establish (this is the difference between a subject outside and another within the novel's fiction; it is the difference between two different subjects within the same text), the resemblance between the stories told and the voices that tell them in both fictional body and marginal note also denies it. The narration through which we learn the details of the time the actress spends in Berlin and of her relationship with her lover follows the very same patterns developed by and within the narrative created by Molina above (see esp. 92–94). The note that would appear to take us outside and beyond, or even above, the fictional dialogue between the novel's main characters also takes us back into it, into a discourse and story that cannot be distinguished from those found in the fiction. The possibility of distinguishing between the subject of the discourse in one part of the page and that in the other is put into question.

Though the note turns out to appear more fictional than factual and we thus are unable to accept it as a historical account of things, its proximity to and placement among the other, nonfictional commentaries about homosexuality somehow give it a truthful appearance. Yet those summaries of scientific theory also have connections to some realm of fiction with which they might also be identified in the end. That is, the historico-fictional discourse of the one note that seems so different also has much in common with the scientific-theoretical discourse of the notes that surround it. Their common ground is established both through the manner in which each type of discourse is produced—that is, mediated—by an invisible author and by the nature of what each refers to. Although the discourse of scientific theory would take as its referents objects whose status clearly differs from that of fictional entities, for example, it is in its own way also a kind of artifice. The theories that constitute that type of discourse are in their own way fictions, too. Moreover, Puig's footnotes on homosexuality are offered as fictional approximations of facts that still exist as a body of coherent fictions. They are rewritings and summary reconstructions of other written texts that are, we must remember, not explanations of proven facts but formulations of theoretical models in terms of which the phenomenon of homosexuality might yet be understood. These authorial summaries of the writings of other authors therefore repeat and reconstitute models of explanation, theoretical systems, invented to explain observations of certain facts whose origins and true nature cannot yet be definitively determined.

The representations of theories from outside the world of the novel's characters are set up to look like and produce effects that seem not much different from the fiction that develops above them. These scientific fictions or theoretical facts are authored (better yet, re-authored) by a figure whose plan seems to take into account how the theories of other authors might best be read. They are organized in such a way that the reader might be convinced of and lured forward by the logical progression of the "story" they tell. In fact, they seem set up to render powerful and entirely credible a final fictional note in which not one author but two come into view. In all but the first two paragraphs of the novel's last footnote the authorial mediator presents a summary of the work of a Dr. Anneli Taube, best represented, we are told, by her book *Sexualidad y revolución* (209–11). Her work, the note informs us, brings together a number of theories at once political and sexual, as the title cited clearly implies. She supposedly characterizes the homosexual as a nonconformist revolutionary, analyzes the bourgeois relational models of heterosexuals which homosexuals seem mostly to have followed, and postulates the ultimate liberation of both homosexual and heterosexual relationships from that bourgeois paradigm of oppression and submission.

What is most significant about this theory is that it turns out to be invented (instead of summarized, like the others) by the novel's author.[40] The note provides a summary of nonexistent texts whose theoretical contribution to the existing field of study appears as a logical, verisimilar development from, as well as conclusion to, the notes that precede it. Once we know what is behind it, though, we see that this quasi-borgesian maneuver keeps under cover the work of an author whose position it also reveals. The authorial figure's turning positions are uncovered, then, both above, in the fiction where Molina and Valentín turn around each other within the space they inhabit together, and below, in the margins where the homosexual and the revolutionary are bound by a theory designed to support them. The subject who seems to give up his place of privilege to all the other authorities whose voices his mediating summaries would partially respect also reasserts his own position of authority, albeit from under the cover of another author's name. The subject who lurks behind or outside the theories of other authoritative subjects unveils another authorial impulse at the end. He who would appear merely to present and remain behind the theories of other authors also manages to situate himself among them. That position is revealed as much as it is veiled by the appearance of another author whose name and gender mask his own: here, the identity of a male author is finally (un)masked by the name of a female doctor. In turning from one gender and identity to another, this authorial figure also follows a model already developed by both of the novel's fictional characters. Their positions are finally united and upheld by another sexually ambiguous and ambivalent subject.

The authorial figure works throughout the text not just as an organizer and appropriator of the discourse of others, not just as the arranger-translator of texts not his own, but as an apparently original subject. This subject turns from summarizing theories of other authors to constructing a theory of his own. This theory follows from, and thus seems authorized by, the theories of those whose names already bear a certain authority. It is a theory that would conclude their work, as well as that of the protagonists above, whom they underwrite. This meeting of homosexual and revolutionary at the foot of these pages is a prelude to, a kind of theoretical preparation for, their meeting in the novel's body. (This last note comes in the middle of Chapter XI; the characters' sexual encounter takes place at the end of that same chapter. Molina, acting as a kind of revolutionary, is killed in Chapter XV, while Valentín, sounding at times like his homosexual partner, rambles on in Chapter XVI.) The note seems to explain and legitimize the story that appears above it, though it is also explained and illustrated by that same fiction. Although the lines between body and footnotes, like those between the novel's fictional subjects, can in a way be drawn (certainly the graphic separation of notes from text and the division of the fictional discourse according to the conventions of direct dialogue draw those distinctions), they are also put into question by what each says and does.

These notes seem to turn things around by also incorporating into their own body the image of the subject (i.e., the revolutionary, Valentín) whose ignorance of and even resistance to the issue of homosexuality they are designed to overturn. That the homosexual can work in the name of revolution might also mean that the revolutionary can uphold the cause of homosexuality. That the homosexual can be a revolutionary means that the revolutionary can also be a homosexual. By identifying the one type of subject with the other, the end of the notes' essentially didactic narrative posits its own "happy ending." It potentially brings to a close the struggle that the physical, emotional, and discursive unions above it also undercut. The battle between opposing political or sexual positions, the clash between distinct discursive practices and cultural values that are developed within as well as between fictional body and textual notes, is also turned into a somewhat surprising, but nonetheless internally logical, conciliatory play in Puig's novel.

In the meeting of the discourse of politics or science and that of popular fiction or film, in the confrontation between or merger of the will to knowledge and the will to pleasure, *El beso de la mujer araña* raises questions that circulate throughout Puig's writing. The discourse of the fictional characters is not tied absolutely to either pole of any such pair—indeed, as the novel unfolds it establishes each subject's turns between disparate and intersecting positions. Yet, as noted, they also act in the name of one or another position at different moments in their dialogue, raising "up" or putting "down" the other to whom each is related, questioning and supporting the models that each would appear to represent. That much of this happens through the deployment of a popular form of fiction (i.e., films or film stories) characteristic of the cultural models with which Puig's work is concerned, and that one of its protagonists is cast as defender of and the other as detractor from those models, is not insignificant. If in the voice of Valentín we hear the parodist and in that of Molina we hear the stylizer of popular models, we also see and hear how all of this becomes turned around by these same subjects.[41] While Valentín would initially criticize and devalue the popular models offered by his interlocutor, Molina would attempt to present them as stories to be valued and taken seriously. Valentín assumes a critical distance from the models, as well as from the interlocutor, above which he implicitly situates himself. But Molina identifies with his popular fictions, taking care to praise them and protect them from his interlocutor's attacks. Yet, as we know, Valentín is also drawn into the fictions he would first put down and winds up telling similar stories of his own. And Molina, taken as he is with the fictions he tells and the life that Valentín describes, is finally caught both by his popular model and by the political subject that also controls him.

In a way, parody is itself both put "down" and raised "up", and stylization seems to dominate and be done in at the novel's end. Valentín's critical voice is certainly given its place in the text, even though he is also won over, so to speak, to the other (that is, Molina's) side. Molina's discursive allegiance to and identification with the fictional world of Hollywood films is carried along throughout the novel and, in a way, holds everything together. Nevertheless, his death comes at the hands of a group of revolutionaries whose position his own performance, as the dialogue emphasizes, would certainly seem to oppose. His faithful, stylizing performance is cut off by the forces of those to whom he seems to want to switch his attachment. Yet this turn against him is also a turn toward his popular desires. As earlier comments suggest, Molina's end might also give him precisely what he wants—a tragic and thus happy ending. In the encounter with the revolutionaries he can act in the name of power (that is, for a political cause and subject) and in the name of pleasure (that is, for his film fantasies of a romantic and tragic death). Though he is violently eliminated from the text, we recall that he is also allowed to survive in his partner's monologue. The defeat of stylization of popular fiction (now brought from the realm of narration to that of action) also turns itself into a triumphant event in Molina's final "scene." Likewise, in Valentín's final appearance we might read the simultaneous defeat and critical survival of the parodist's powers. In his drugged ramblings Valentín does not in fact lose the perspective from which he can analyze part of Molina's—and even the novel's—ending. When he suggests to himself, as well as to his reader, that Molina dies like a movie heroine (285), he transforms his former prison partner into a perfect parody of the popular model. That is, if, from Molina's perspective, that ending is just right, from Valentín's it is more than a bit too much, and thus fit for critical comment.

But this isn't the only way things end, as we know. In Valentín's final interior monologue things continue to turn around. Though Molina dies, he also remains alive; though Valentín remains imprisoned, he also sets himself free. Each turns from one situation and position to another; each helps the other to restore yet put aside either the parodic or stylizing effects of his performance. As in Puig's work as a whole, in *El beso de la mujer araña* it is not so much that the protagonists' positions and identities can or cannot be determined, or that the "true" nature of the text through which they appear is impossible to identify. Rather, the performances in fiction and text alike lead us to read things now one way, now another. In the end, we see that things keep turning away from and then toward the very positions in which we might think either the fictional character or the authorial figure is finally fixed. The novel represents, and thus returns us to, the problematic moves of Puig's writing as a whole. At the same time it returns us to the sorts of questions that pervade modern fiction and criticism alike. If the tradition of reflexive writing, carried on by Puig's work, is understood as a tradition grounded in the kinds strange and familiar critical turns that we have come to associate with it, then *El beso de la mujer araña* brings into view the way in which that tradition has been turned in our times. Indeed, in this novel Puig explores, in a popular and provocative way, how contemporary writing has gone about giving new life to a variety of old fictions and forms.

NOTES

1. Manuel Puig, *El beso de la mujer araña* (Barcelona: Seix Barral, 1976). All quotations are from this edition; hereafter page references appear parenthetically within the text. The novel has also been published in English as *Kiss of the Spider Woman*, trans. Thomas Colchie (New York: Knopf, 1979); quotations in English are from this edition, unless otherwise noted. A shortened version for the stage appears in Manuel Puig, *Bajo un manto de estrellas: Pieza en dos actos; El beso de la mujer araña: Adaptación escénica realizada por el autor* (Barcelona: Seix Barral, 1983); in this version the homosexual is forty-one years old (87).

2. Like the previous novels, this one is composed of sixteen chapters divided equally between the text's two parts. (Of the later novels, *Pubis angelical* is the only one that follows this pattern.) Accompanying the fictional body are nine unnumbered footnotes; these are connected to the text by asterisks at specific points in the characters' dialogue in Chapters III through XI. In dealing explicitly with questions of politics and sexuality, the novel also seems to challenge the characteristic discursive prohibitions surrounding those very issues. On such prohibitions, see Michel Foucault, "The Discourse on Language" (1971), trans. Rupert Swyer, in *The Archaeology of Knowledge* (1969), trans. A. H. Sheridan Smith (New York: Harper & Row, 1972) 215–37. See also Roberto Echavarren's comments on this aspect of the novel in "*El beso de la mujer araña* y las metáforas del sujeto," *Revista iberoamericana* 44 (1978): 65–75 (hereafter cited as "Metáforas"), and Rodríguez Monegal's related observations about Puig's first novel in "Myth" 60–62. See also Michèle Débax, Milagros Ezquerro, and Michèle Ramond, "La marginalité des personnages et ses effets sur le discours dans *El beso de la mujer araña* de Manuel Puig," *Imprévue* 1 (1980): 91–112 (hereafter cited as "Marginalité"), for a helpful discusssion of how this text addresses these and others issues of marginality.

3. See Chapter 2, note 30, and Chapter 4, note 28. Further suggestion of Puig's possibly anti-Peronist stance is revealed in the novel's focus on the era surrounding Perón's return to power (1973) and, particularly, on the years after his death (1974), when his wife Isabel took over and was later deposed by the military (1976). Clearly, the prison cell is a powerful model of repression; its inhabitants in Puig's novel help to reveal the direction that such authoritarian exercise of power has often taken.

4. According to Efraín Barradas, "Notas sobre notas: *El beso de la mujer araña*," *Revista de estudios hispánicos* 6 (1979): 177, Valentín should be read as the expounder of pseudo-Marxist and pseudo-Freudian clichés.

5. See Puig's comments in Christ, "Puig" 26.

6. The notes on homosexuality refer to the following authors and titles in Spanish (titles are here given only in English; publication dates have been added): Dennis Altman, *Homosexual: Oppression and Liberation* (1971); Norman O. Brown, *Life against Death* (1959); O. Fenichel, *The Psychoanalytic Theory of Neurosis* (1945); J. C. Flugel, *Man, Morals and Society* (1945); Anna Freud, *The Psychoanalysis of the Child* [*The Psycho-Analytical Treatment of Children*] (1946); Sigmund Freud, *The Interpretation of Dreams* (1900), *Three Essays on the Theory of Sexuality* (1905), *Character and Anal Eroticism* (1908), *On Narcissism: An Introduction* (1914), *Instincts and Their Vicissitudes* (1915), "Letter to an American Mother" (1935); Herbert Marcuse, *Eros and Civilization* (1962), *The One-Dimensional Man* (1964); Kate Millet, *Sexual Politics* (1970); Otto Rank [*Myth of the Birth of the Hero* (1909)]; Wilhelm Reich, *The Function of the Orgasm* (1927); Theodore Roszak, *The Making of a Counter Culture* (1969); J. L. Simmons, *Deviants* (1969); [Gordon] Ratray Taylor, *Sex in History* (1953); J[oseph] D[aniel] Unwin, *Sex and Culture* (1934); D. J. West, *Homosexuality* [cited in Spanish as *Psychology and Psychoanalysis of the Homosexual*; title corrected in the English version of the novel] (1955), 4th ed. (1977) entitled *Homosexuality Re-examined*. The 1977 (London: Duckworth) edition of the West book contains a complete bibliography on the subject, and in it the studies of other researchers cited in the novel (i.e., Barahal, Foss, Gibbons, Kallman, Lang, Lewis, Money, Pare, and Swyer) are also listed. The English version includes all of the above, except where noted otherwise. However, sections of the note dealing with Freud's theories of the Oedipus complex are excised from that text. See Puig's explanation of his use of the notes in Christ, "Puig" 27–28, and Marcelo Coddou, "Seis preguntas a Manuel Puig sobre su última novela: *El beso de la mujer araña,*" *American Hispanist* 2.18 (1977): 12 (hereafter cited as "Preguntas").

7. The protagonists refer to each other only as "Valentín" and "Molina" and make no reference to their other names. The prison document presented at the beginning of Chapter VIII is where their complete names are revealed (151). The suppression of Molina's given names (i.e., Luis Alberto) and Valentín's surnames (i.e., Arregui Paz) already sets up the possibility of reading their dialogue as produced by a divided, yet individual, subject named "Valentín Molina"—something not so far from what the novel suggests in several ways. (See Borinsky's comments in *Ver* 40, 60.) In our personal interview, Puig stated that the difference of nomination marks the distance between the two characters within the fiction. That is, Valentín calls Molina by his surname precisely because he wants to keep intact the formal nature of their relationship—he wants to keep his cellmate at a distance. As we know, that is precisely the distance that remains in question throughout the text.

8. More detailed discussion of the novel's heterogeneous discourse and nar-

rative techniques can be found in Marcelo Coddou, "Complejidad estructural de *El beso de la mujer araña*, de Manuel Puig," *Inti* 7 (1978): 15–27 (hereafter cited as "Complejidad"), and Frances Wyers, "Manuel Puig at the Movies," *Hispanic Review* 49 (1981): 163–81 (hereafter cited as "Movies").

9. See Coddou's discussion in "Complejidad."

10. In *The History of Sexuality* Foucault states: "Pleasure and power do not cancel or turn back against one another; they seek out, overlap, and re-inforce one another. They are linked together by complex mechanisms and devices of excitation and excitement" (40). This statement, included among other observations about the interconnections between power and sexuality (or, rather, the discourses of power and sexuality) underscores that the two areas and questions are indeed related; that certain political issues surround both sexual theory and practice; that those theoretical and practical concerns are also governed by a network of power relations that are not without their own erotic components, as the above emphasizes. The complex relations of power and pleasure developed by Puig's novel might help us to understand some of those connections, just as Foucault's discussion helps us to turn in another way toward this fictional text.

11. See Benveniste, *Linguistics* 195–204, 224–30.

12. This structure of identification might also imply some psychoanalytic readings along the lines of Freudian and Lacanian theory. Some such notions are taken up to focus on a variety of the novel's features in the following: George Yúdice, "*El beso de la mujer araña* y *Pubis angelical*: Entre el placer y el saber," in *Literature and Popular Culture in the Hispanic World* 43–57 (hereafter cited as "Placer y saber"); Echavarren, "Metáforas"; and Stephanie Merrim, "For a New (Psychological) Novel in the Works of Manuel Puig," *Novel* 17 (1984): 141–57 (esp. 148–57).

13. See Ferdinand de Saussure, *Course in General Linguistics*, trans. Wade Basking, ed. Charles Baley, Albert Sechehaye, and Albert Riedlinger, (New York: McGraw-Hill, 1966), for the basic discussion of the differential and oppositional features constituting linguistic value. See Benveniste, *Linguistics* 200–4, 218–20, 224–27, and Mukařovský, "Two Studies in Dialogue" 86–91 and 96–99, for discussion of the situation of dialogue. Their work reminds us that interlocutors are, by definition, always switching positions as they move from one pole of a correlation of subjectivity to the other, from the role of speaker or addresser to that of listener or addressee. To be engaged in a dialogic exchange means to occupy one or the other discursive position while also being on the verge of moving to the other. It is to reflect within one's own linguistic position the other toward which one is always about to turn.

14. See also Francine Masiello, "Jail House Flicks: Projections by Manuel Puig," *Symposium* 32 (1978): 15–24 (hereafter cited as "Flicks").

15. See, for example, Roland Barthes, "Introduction to the Structural Analysis of Narrative" (1966), trans. Lionel Duisit, *New Literary History* 6 (1974–75): 237–72, and Genette, *Narrative Discourse*.

16. See also Coddou, "Complejidad" 18–19.

17. The Scheherazade metaphor, implied here, is also used by Borinsky, *Ver* 76, Débax, Ezquerro, and Ramond, "Marginalité" 97, and Daniel R. Reedy, "Del beso de la mujer araña al de la tía Julia: estructura y dinámica interior," *Revista iberoamericana* 47 (1981): 109. On the relation between life and death and narrative as exemplified by the *Arabian Nights*, see Tzvetan Todorov's "Narrative-Men" (1967), in *The Poetics of Prose* 66–79 (esp. 73–76).

18. See Masiello, "Flicks," and Oviedo, "Exposición," for discussion of the film stories' narrative patterns and their function in relation to and within the relationship between Molina and Valentín, and also in the author-reader dialogue. Frank Kermode's *The Sense of an Ending: Studies in the Theory of Fiction* (New York: Oxford UP, 1967) has suggested ways of seeing the relation between endings and beginnings for this discussion.

19. See also Coddou, "Complejidad" 21, and Masiello, "Flicks" 17–19.

20. Yúdice reads the novel in terms of the question of desire, and sees it as an "allegory of the will to pleasure" not unconnected to the issue of power, in "Placer y saber."

21. What goes on in the cell and what goes on in the text itself may be read in terms of the notion of repression, as pointed out in the related discussions of Borinsky, *Ver*, and James Ray Green, Jr., "*El beso de la mujer araña*: Sexual Repression and Textual Repression," in *LA CHISPA'81: Selected Proceedings*, ed. Gilbert Paolini (New Orleans: Tulane Univ., Louisiana Conference on Hispanic Languages and Literatures, 1981) 133–39 (hereafter cited as "Repression"). Their positions are in agreement with related points made here, except where otherwise noted.

22. The Toto/Molina connection is also commented on by Echavarren, "Metáforas," 65; cf. Barradas, "Notas sobre notas" 181, note 12.

23. In the Coddou interview, "Preguntas," Puig distinguishes between the three cited films and the imaginary ones he invented from memories of similar movies or, as is the case of the Nazi film in Chapters II-IV, with the aid of historical documents. Except for the title of the zombie film, which is provided in the novel's text (163), the Spanish titles are taken from Puig's statements. See also the Christ interview, "Puig" 26–27, for other details regarding the sources for the film narratives, and especially his research on the Nazi materials. The space devoted to and the time spent narrating the films is also part of the novel's plan. The first two films are narrated in two chapters each, the third and fourth appear only in one chapter each, and the fifth and sixth in three chapters each. Though the move from two to one chapter per film

would seem to keep things moving toward and even accelerate the arrival at various endings, the use of three chapters apiece for the last two film stories seems to slow things down again and, perhaps, to negate as well as defer the deadly endings toward which each story moves.

24. See Wyers, "Movies," for the most helpful discussion of Puig's "special kind of visualized form" (167) and the play among narratives at once visual and verbal.

25. See Puig's comments on Molina's death, chosen by the fictional character, he emphasizes, not the author, in Christ, "Puig" 27.

26. Cf. Green, "Repression" 137–38.

27. This view of things draws on Foucault, *The History of Sexuality* 44–49, 92–102, and *Discipline and Punish* 202–7.

28. Parallels can also be drawn between the story of Valentín's relationships with his girlfriend(s), as he describes them in Chapters III and VII, and Molina's story of his desire for Gabriel, a young waiter with whom he is infatuated (Chapter III). Both of those stories are also analogues of the sentimental and "tragic" songs of love, like the bolero "Mi carta," which Molina's comments, and later Valentín's emotional confession, connect to the "Dear John" letter Valentín receives from his comrade-girlfriend (137–40). As these connections are made within the fiction itself, Valentín comes around to admitting that life and popular art have much in common.

29. Borinsky focuses on related points in *Ver* 38–41, 48–49.

30. See Foucault's description of the panoptic model of surveillance in *Discipline and Punish* 195–228. This is precisely one of the functions of power exercised through forms of surveillance in the prison—to be everywhere invisible, yet to see and control all those who are enclosed within its walls and line of vision.

31. Echavarren reads both the novel's characters and its author as practitioners of *bricolage* (as defined by Lévi-Strauss in *The Savage Mind*), in "Metáforas" 67–70.

32. Their familial relation seems to make possible their adult sexual union. It is as if, in order to seduce Valentín (that is, in order to provoke a sexual response, another type of desire in him), Molina had to take his adult interlocutor back to an infantile state in which sexuality, according to Freud (i.e., *Three Essays on the Theory of Sexuality*), has its origins in order to change his "orientation." By becoming Valentín's only source of food and comfort, by functioning as the protector upon whom his "child" is totally dependent, Molina seems to reprogram the original relation between his sexual drive and his nonsexual, vital functions (e.g., feeding), causing him to make what might be called anaclitic as well as narcissistic (love) object choices. See Jean Laplanche, *Life and Death in Psychoanalysis* (1970), trans. Jeffrey Mehlman

(Baltimore: Johns Hopkins UP, 1976) 8–24, on Freud's notion of "propping" and the relationships between the vital function, need, and instinct and the sexual drive in infantile sexuality. From that perspective, Molina's strategy could be read as a misreading of Freud's theories, as explained by Laplanche, even though it seems to work on Valentín.

33. Cf. Green, "Repression" 136–38.

34. If we were to read the novel as a defense of the homosexual whose politics leave much to be desired (that is, from the standpoint of the revolutionary), Molina's statement could become part of that defense, for it could serve as a critique of a political ideology that fails to take into account and contend with personal psychology.

35. The monologue is set up as a kind of interior mono-dialogue within Valentín, who, drugged after being tortured, "talks" with Marta, one of the women about whom he speaks to Molina while they are together. Both Marta's responses to Valentín and Valentín's description to her of a hallucination he lives as he is taken back to his cell and through the monologue itself bear within them the marks of Molina, now ostensibly absent from the scene. Marta's reassuring words to Valentín, his movie-like fantasy escape to a tropical isle with a beautiful woman (cf. Toto's fantasies) that is "narrated" to his imaginary interlocutor, contain not only thematic but also stylistic echos of Molina (see esp. 283–84) and, moreover, references to (even verbal repetitions of) parts of their earlier conversations and scenes together (cf. 181–83, 222).

36. See also 146 and 181–84 for analogous scenes of specular superimposition of the two subjects. The first involves Valentín's projection of himself into the role of the "mother," through a memory of a scene from his own life, while he is also playing that of "son" to Molina. The second occurs when Valentín dictates to Molina a letter he never actually sends to Marta and in which he remembers and fantasizes an erotic scene with her. There is a complex conjunction of images and voices as Valentín dictates and Molina writes, receives, and reads the letter back to its sender, while also playing all the roles within its erotic fictional scene with Marta. The identities superimposed in these scenes are at once thematic and discursive, and have to do as well with sexual relations and relations of power.

37. See also Echavarren, "Metáforas" 73–74, and Borinsky, Ver 61–63, 71–72. While the image of the deadly black widow spider (i.e., the female spider who entraps and kills her mate) might suggest itself as a source for the novel's title, a possible connection to a 1940s film would also fit rather well here. In the 1944 Sherlock Holmes movie *Spider Woman*, starring Basil Rathbone, Nigel Bruce, and Gale Sondegaard, the famous detective comes up against a cunning *femme fatale* (Holmes himself describes the Sondegaard character in those words) in whom he seems to meet his match and with whom he vies for

power. He manages to catch her even though she thinks she has caught him. That this film might serve as the title's source is also proposed by Oviedo, "Exposición" 619–20.

38. The series of footnotes is cast as a kind of response to the implicit query of Valentín's statement, cited above. The first asterisk that directs the reader to the bottom of the page is placed precisely at the end of that declaration. See Christ, "Puig" 27–28, for Puig's comments regarding the "violent" suppression of the material that he here consciously works to provide for his reader. He claims that the slight difference between the Spanish and English editions (some material is excised from the translated version; see note 5) has to do with the differences between the kind of information available to readers in the United States and in Latin America.

39. See Roland Barthes, "Science versus Literature" (1967), in *Introduction to Structuralism*, ed. Michael Lane (New York: Basic Books, 1970) 410–16, on the relationship between scientific and literary discourse.

40. Unlike the titles cited and the authors mentioned in note 5, no amount of research would discover either the work mentioned or the author named in this note. Puig admits not only to constructing "paraphrases" of the work of existing authors, but also to authoring a theory of his own; see Christ, "Puig" 28. In our personal interview, he virtually admitted to being Dr. Anneli Taube.

41. Cf. Gustavo Pellón, "Manuel Puig's Contradictory Strategy: Kitsch Paradigms *versus* Paradigmatic Structure in *El beso de la mujer araña* and *Pubis Angelical*," *Symposium* 36 (1983): 186–201 (hereafter cited as "Strategy").

CHAPTER

6

In the Author's Place:
Unfinished Business

"Le tenía miedo a la tercera persona"; "¿Usar una tercera persona?
¡Jamás! No podía asumir esa responsabilidad" ["I was afraid of the third
person"; "Use the third person? Never! I couldn't assume that responsibility"].[1] In these statements regarding the writing of his first novel,
Puig confesses his difficulty with the traditional, but not entirely dis-
carded, notion of what an author does in writing narrative fiction, what
a traditional author is supposed to do and be. Much of his novelistic
practice—that is, his choice of narrative techniques in all of his texts—
seems to circumvent such conventional authorial "responsibilities."[2]
The persistence of forms of unmediated discourse and of naturalized
texts throughout his novels (from *La traición de Rita Hayworth*
through the more recent *Pubis angelical*, *Maldición eterna a quien lea
estas páginas*, and *Sangre de amor correspondido*) works against the
emergence of a more or less conventional (i.e., realist) authorial voice
or image.[3]

This feature of Puig's writing is, of course, not unique to his work.
Indeed, in recent decades there have been some radical shifts in the
practices of fiction writers, a fact of which Puig himself has become
aware. Though his resistance to such traditionally authorized forms of
narration could be described as an idiosyncratic gesture or "symptom"
(viewed according to the virtual dictates of conventional narrative
practice, such a resistance might be read, in Puig's words, as "una
debilidad de carácter" ["a weakness of character"], a kind of authorial
"failure" to measure up to the laws governing works of fiction), it is,

236

he reminds us, also a practice consistent with and representative of "la crisis del narrador" ["the crisis of the narrator"] within modern fiction.[4]

At issue for Puig in much of this is the idea of objectivity. In question is the image of the author as an unchallenged authority whose omniscience and omnipotence seem to be asserted and perpetuated by more or less traditional narrative texts. (The qualities of omniscience and omnipotence, we must remember, are often ascribed to the authorial figure through the performance of its apparent surrogate, the powerful and knowledgeable narrator behind whose third-person narration the images of both these controlling subjects often seem to mingle and meet.) Such an image implies a subject with both the responsibility and the power to put things not only correctly but also completely in a text. The position of this authorial subject bears with it the kind of privilege and authority that Puig claims to have resisted in theory, if not to have refused in practice. In place of this magisterial figure he would himself authorize another type of author—the self-effacing author, the authorial subject who disappears behind or who is absorbed into the discourse of all the other subjects that are made to surface in his text. This author would let everyone else speak for him or herself, while he, as the author, would remain silent and invisible behind, beneath, and above all those other subjects. Absent as he would seem to be from the text, and overpowered as his voice would seem to be by the voices of the fictional subjects who dominate each work, this author would seem deprived of, because he would seem willingly to give up, a voice or an image that could properly be called his own.[5]

This virtual disappearance of the author seems to characterize much of Puig's writing, especially those novels in which, for the most part, there is no third-person narration (i.e., *La traición de Rita Hayworth*, *El beso de la mujer araña*, *Maldición eterna a quien lea estas páginas*, and *Sangre de amor correspondido*). That is, the absence of an apparently authoritative narrating subject whose voice and vision would seem to point toward, if not actually to reveal, the presence of an authorial subject capable of empowering such a narrator seems to place the figure of the author somewhere else, out of sight and out of mind. By doing away with this kind of narrator in these novels, Puig's writing seems to deny the authorial subject his "proper" place, his "responsibilities." Moreover, even in those texts where third-person narration figures as an important, even dominant, narrative method (i.e., *Bo-quitas pintadas*, *The Buenos Aires Affair*, and *Pubis angelical*), Puig's deployment of this device seems also to turn it against itself. It could be read as a critique, instead of a certification, of the convention's proper powers. Instead of reaffirmimg the possibility of saying and seeing everything objectively, the playful manipulation of this technique might put those same effects into question. It could undercut the objectivity supposedly represented by the narrator's performance.

This turn to a conventional device is part of what Puig terms his "búsqueda formal" ["formal search"]. However, it is also a critical commentary, even an attack, on the conventions of narrative fiction. In fact, this author claims that when he turned to that technique in *Bo-quitas pintadas*, what interested him was precisely "llevar la crispación de esa tercera persona—del deseo, del ansia, del afán de esa tercera persona—, llevarla a su última consecuencia, para demostrar su falsedad" ["to take the tautness of that third person—the desire, the anxiety, the eagerness of that third person—, to take it to its ultimate consequences, in order to demonstrate that it's a lie"].[6] The exaggeratedly "objective" reports supplied by the omniscient narrator in each of those novels could be seen as turning the convention around by taking it to its limits and forcing it to establish the impossibility, or even absurdity, of such seemingly absolute objectivity. Instead of legitimizing the "voice" and "vision" traditionally supported by this narrative method, Puig's writing could undermine—even make laughable—the idea that this kind of practice possesses any power at all.[7]

Puig's resistance to this narrative norm is also a reminder that the convention probably is no longer all that dominant. In modern Spanish American fiction, for instance, it is difficult to find novels that follow, even if only to lay bare the precarious powers exercised by, this conventional model of narration.[8] Puig's statements, along with the narrative practice developed by him and his compatriots, also remind us that to speak of writing a text in either the third or the first person is, as modern narrative theory has begun to show us, not necessarily to speak of putting things in such radically different ways. We have come to understand that the way things are told is also bound up with the way things are seen, and that a variety of relationships determine the apparent authority of any narrating subject.[9] Nonetheless, Puig's declaration also points up that a certain amount of authority still rests with the type of narrating subject he has put into question. An author's authority (or, rather, the appearance of authority) is as often as not tied to the performance of other narrators who, though actually masking them, would also seem to put that author's powers on display. Puig's statements also reveal the hold that that image of the author—the author as knowledgeable and powerful, the author as master and controller and authoritative origin of a text—has over us. His desire to resist this hold is, according to his own comments, a product of both fear (fear of what an author must take charge of and be accountable for) and dissatisfaction (dissatisfaction with the assumptions underlying such conventional devices).

This turn away from the role of the author is, of course, another kind of turn toward it. Puig's writing seems to elude the conventions of authorial practice (that is, its "responsibilities") because it demystifies the image of authority that is projected by the narrating subject (i.e., the invisible, omniscient narrator who is his surrogate) who speaks not about himself but about others (i.e., the fictional characters who are referred to in the third person). However, to engage in this sort of narrative subterfuge is to inscribe within the text the image of another type of author—or, rather, another type of image of the author—albeit that of the "modern writer" who emerges as simultaneous with, not anterior to, the text through which it appears.[10] The refusal of conventional authorial practice and the overt questioning of its powers challenges the traditional image of the author, putting in that author's place another kind of image. But this image possesses its own kind of authority. It, too, hovers over while also emerging from the text. This textualized author is a figure that haunts any text of fiction—Puig's writing allows us to see it as that kind of haunting figure and to read it in a uniquely critical way.

We understand that to move away from the image of the author as an all-knowing, all-seeing originator and master of the text is not to banish the author as a figure—and especially as a figure of authority—from that text. To leave the biographical author behind, as well as to disempower or disassemble the authoritative narrating voice that might seem to stand in for the authorial subject, is not to strike from the text either the signs of a textual authority or the image of a governing subject who might even be viewed as coincident with, as opposed to anterior to and separate from, the text in which that same figure

239

moves. Indeed, the author may very well be "dead," but the ghost lives on. Though that ghost may be read as the image left behind by the empirical authorial subject, it is, more precisely, both a disembodied textualized figure and a self-constituting suspended fiction that manages to revisit, as another type of subject (indeed, as a subject with a certain amount of authority), every text we read. Puig's writing brings this figure into view. Along with this figure come questions of authority and truth, power and knowledge—the kinds of questions around which Puig's writing revolves. This figure emerges in each of his novels and, consequently, from among them. It turns now one way, now another, taking things now toward, now away from the authorial fiction itself. Curiously enough, then, though Puig's writing proposes to circumvent traditional models of narrative authority and to undercut the idea of the author as an all-powerful subject, his novels wind up sustaining (though in a radically critical way) this very image of authority.

As the earlier discussion of Puig's fiction has emphasized, every text implicates an authorial figure through the provocative, because manipulative yet unstable, maneuvers orchestrated in it. From *La traición de Rita Hayworth* to *El beso de la mujer araña* and then on through the most recent novels, many curious moves are made by the authors figured in these texts. These figures come together in Puig's writing to form the unfinished image of an author who is suspended above and within the total, yet incomplete, text through which it is constituted. From each text the figure of a plotting subject surfaces. This subject resists being turned toward any single end. Such figures take us from one model of authorship to another, from one manifestation of authority to another. Such authorial moves produce no final figure or system of authority, no fixed view of where an individual or overriding authorial figure stands in Puig's fiction. What we see instead is the turning of such figures and fictions, such issues and questions, themselves. To move through Puig's novels is to turn with each figure of the author and with the shifting fictions—fictions that suspend things and fictions that are themselves suspended—through which that figure comes into view.

As we recall, *La traición de Rita Hayworth*, the novel through which Puig originally seems to resist using any conventional narrative strategy, calls up the image of the author not only in its chapter divisions and headings, but also in the temporal inversion through which Berto, the partially hidden father, presents himself to us. The figure of the author emerges not as a voice of authority, but from around the voice of a father figure whose place coincides rather significantly with his own. In finally writing himself into the text Berto reveals his problematic position of authority. In seeming to position that revelation in a place where things finally get turned around, the authorial subject implied by that maneuver is also kept on the move. This structural play is, of course, the sign that another subject "above" controls the text and determines how it might be read. Precisely this kind of image is inscribed within most of the novels that follow. It is most blatant in *Boquitas pintadas* and *The Buenos Aires Affair*, where each text's structural complexity and discursive heterogeneity openly assert its presence. Yet in *La traición de Rita Hayworth* this figure's place, if not its power, is problematic because, much like the father in the fiction, the "father" of the text seems to turn away as much as toward the position of mastery and control to which the inversionary procedure points.

As suggested earlier, the place in which these two figures emerge is in a way not the proper place for either of them. Placing the author at the end of the text that he would presumably precede, the temporal displacement of Berto's letter turns both figures away from their traditionally "proper" positions as originators or creators.[11] But that displacement also questions what is appropriate for and proper to each of them. It rewrites the routes they may take and the angles from which they may be positioned in both fiction and text. Each of these figures has a filial as well as paternal role to play here. Each is recognized in both of the positions between which he would seem to move and in neither of which, in the end, he can be fixed. This is precisely the situation that is created by the text's simultaneously, yet alternately, parodic and stylizing moves. The author "behind" the text seems to take now one position, now another, in relation to the popular discourses and traditions with which the novel engages in dialogue and the fictional entities through which they are presented. That is, given the stylizing and parodying turns taken by the discourse of each of the novel's subjects, the text, and thus the authorial figure "behind" it, resist being fixed in relation to those same traditions. Here and in all the novels that follow, the authority of popular culture is both sustained and called into question by an authorial subject who would place himself above, but also remain within, the very traditions around which the novel revolves.

These kinds of textual and authorial moves take us through *Boquitas pintadas* and *The Buenos Aires Affair*. As we recall, these novels develop in a more complex fashion the mystery structure implied by Puig's first novel. *The Buenos Aires Affair*, of course, openly takes up the most popular mystery genre, the detective novel. In each the question of knowledge and, consequently, the notion of truth surface as central issues around which the implicit dialogue between authorial and readerly subjects is formed. The figure of the author is that of a manipulative veiler and revealer of facts, a seductive partner and adversary whose apparent desire for control seems both to succeed and to fail. This appearance of control—that is, the image of omniscience and omnipotence—derives not only from the complex narrative structure and the heterogeneous array of discourses that this masterful subject utilizes to confound yet carry along his partner in textual intrigue. It also emerges from the performance of a (not so) traditional narrative surrogate—an omniscient narrator. In both novels the image of the author is also figured through the appearance of a narrating subject whose knowledge of anecdotal and textual matters would draw the two of them together.[12] But, as Puig's comments begin to suggest, this turn to a convention of narrative fiction may also turn the text and its author away from the conventional assumptions underlying that type of text. Nonetheless, this turn also brings with it some of the relationships and laws it seems to leave outside its practice.

Though the omniscient narrator may also look like an authorial subject in these novels, we see that, when that same subject's apparently unlimited knowledge is displayed, its authority is also put into question. That is, in underscoring the inherently conventional (i.e., fictional) nature of this figure's omniscience and by rendering comically false the presumption of objectivity that underlies the nature of the narrator's knowledge, the ground upon which the presumably omniscient subject stands would be eroded, if not entirely destroyed, by Puig's writing. However, this "put-down" of the powers and the position of such a subject would at the same time imply the superior knowledge and perspective of another subject who positions himself above, and thereby also reasserts his proprietary relation to, the place where

this seemingly knowledgeable and powerful narrator-author is suspended. The possibility of reading that narrator's full access to knowledge also as a sign of the limited nature of that knowledge derives from
the possibility of reading through the text the traces of the superior
position held by another, "truer," authorial figure who works behind
the scenes. It is to consider that authoritative subject as in a position
to "see" the limitations of the subject "below" and to undercut, in a
way, the exaggeratedly conventional views of that subject within the
text over which his authority seems to be held and within which it is,
in the end, difficult, if not impossible, to establish any real authority.
Or, seen from another angle, the authorial figure produced by the text
shifts from one position of authority to another, now seeming to know
all, now seeming to show that not all can be known. These shifts take
us from one narrative level to another, from one level of knowledge
and authority to another, and back again, as they figure a subject of
authority who turns in place while also turning from one place to
another.

In *Boquitas pintadas* such authorial moves draw the figure of a masterful, manipulative designer of seductive plans, plans that might seem
also to ensnare their own author. The curious ups and downs of the
protagonist, Juan Carlos, and, consequently, the contradictory turns
taken by the cultural and literary models he implicates through his
traditionally rebellious and seductive moves, appear to be the work of
an author whose own unstable position vis-à-vis those models comes
into view as well. The play among maneuvers designed to subvert
authority in fiction and text alike (that is, the maneuvers designed both
by the novel's fictional characters and by its textual authority) and
those that reinstate some of the traditions and laws presumably put
down in the novel suggest a figure not quite in control. This is a figure
whose desire to control must, of necessity, confront the controlling
powers of other systems and subjects of authority with which that same
figure is also bound through the text in which it appears. The play
between the novel's parodying and stylizing effects signals a text or an
author whose "intentions" are finally contradictory. Whatever or
whoever seems to be put "down" here is also turned around and made
to rise "up", and whatever seems to rise "up" also appears to be put
"down."

That the possibility of reading a stable authorial position into or from

243

the text of *Boquitas pintadas*, or other of Puig's novels, is put into question does not necessarily negate the narrative powers displayed by such a figure. In both *Boquitas pintadas* and *The Buenos Aires Affair* the development of the author-reader dialogue produces the image of an authority who always seems to be on top and ahead of the interlocutor-accomplice whose image, totally bound to that of the author, is simultaneously produced by each text. That the authorial subject knows more than the reading subject is repeatedly underscored in each. That the reader's goal is, in a way, to learn the truth of the matters at hand, and that the author plays on a hermeneutic desire inherent in the reader's role, is implied by every narrative tactic of each authorial figure. In *The Buenos Aires Affair*, moreover, it is precisely the desire for truth (the desire to hear it named or to see it written or acted out) that seems to permit and promote the exercise of those powers. Much as those powers are contingent upon this kind of desire, the desire itself, it seems, is strengthened by the exercise of those powers.

The authorial figure produces, yet is but the specular image of, the reading subject already in the text. The truth that is sought out by the reader is but the creation of the powerful subject who gives the illusion of its presence, only to reveal it as a fiction at the end. It is the illusion of a mystery, transformed into a fictional truth, that the novel's reader-spectator seems to desire and that the authorial subject seems ready and able to provide. The simultaneous impostures of textual authority and fictional protagonist finally render elusive, though still powerful, the idea of the truth. They also undercut and support the image of an authority whose privilege and position would certify his access to such a truth in the first place.

In *The Buenos Aires Affair* the authorial figure reveals that the genre's conventional notion of truth and the powers of its author are upheld by playful deviations from convention. In doing away with the detective and dispersing that figure's functions among other fictional characters and/or readers, the authorial subject reminds us that the genre's chief investigator—the detective, the conventional criminal authority who investigates, reveals, and explains the relation between mystery and truth—is but a mask for the text's higher authority. It is precisely this position of authority, this figure apparently privileged with the possession of the truth, that this novel winds up highlighting instead of hiding. Indeed, *The Buenos Aires Affair* signals the death of the detective as a conventional figure at the hands of the only other authority capable of depriving him of and then usurping his place.

The detective's murder, as it were, constitutes the visible consolidation of the author's powers, as opposed to the effacement of his privilege and position.[13] This figure authorizes both mystery and solution. In this subject presumably originates the (un)conventional design of the set-up into which the novel's disparate readers are drawn. To that figure, it would appear, the text's reader has more "direct" access, since the conventionally authorized mediator for the authorial figure has been eliminated. The heterogeneity of the text's discourse and narrative techniques would bring that figure into view, just as it would allow the figure a variety of places to hide. The moves from one language and device to another (even to third-person narration, wherein the authorial position seems openly figured) keep that figure always on the move. That figure does not and cannot move alone. Its partner, its accomplice in criminal fiction, is bound to it in the textual relationship that follows so seductively that of the fictional figures around which they move. The author's figure turns against, yet with, its conventional and criminal interlocutor. The authorial designs are at odds with, yet promote (by working in the name of), the popular models from which they are also derived.

Whatever the "intention" apparently displayed by the text or its authorial strategist, the novel calls everyone's attention to the popular traditions to which Puig's name itself has become attached. Moreover, it takes up the "cases" of two characters who, because of their pathological and popular patterns of behavior, might otherwise be left behind, along with the kinds of traditions and tales that make up the stories that inform and circulate in this novel, as well as in, for example, *La traición de Rita Hayworth* and *Boquitas pintadas*. The authorial figure that surfaces in *The Buenos Aires Affair*, then, is also a subject who grants a place of privilege to the "low" characters and stories, the "trivial" discourses and genres, that appear in its text. Though that authorial subject can be seen to shift position around the popular models with which the text works and to exist in an ambivalent relation to them, it is significant that these are the kinds of traditions and texts around which that figure also chooses to move, albeit according to an uncontrollable and contradictory design. The politics of these choices for which this figure also seems to be responsible are inherent in and form a good part of the provocative turns of each work. Indeed, each parodying and/or stylizing move legitimizes a "higher" position for the figures and fictions brought from "below," even when, as each textual turn reveals, they would also be put "down" by those same moves.

La traición de Rita Hayworth, *Boquitas pintadas*, and *The Buenos Aires Affair* produce the figure of an author who appears to act in the name of certain traditions and texts that otherwise seem to find little or no support from other authors. If an authorial voice is discerned along with or through the voices of the subjects whose fantasies and fictions are democratically given their own space within which to be seen and heard in these novels, it is not that of a subject who speaks "his own mind" directly about the politics inherent in these popular choices. In *El beso de la mujer araña*, on the other hand, the authorial subject appears to make a discursive space for himself in the footnotes. This space, reserved as it is by convention for a discourse of authority (or, rather, marking as it does the authority of the subject whose discourse fills it), is where the figure of the author emerges to address, in his own "voice," it seems, some of the questions raised by the fictional characters that move above it. At issue in *El beso de la mujer araña* are the activities of homosexuals and revolutionaries, as well as the place of "low" forms of art. The question of homosexuality, the issue of political activism, and the problem of cultural or artistic value are addressed openly by the characters in the fiction, laying bare, it seems, a set of authorial mono-dialogues on topics that might otherwise be dismissed as either too trivial or too taboo for "serious" concern.

The explicit thematization of such questions (this kind of thematization also informs a good portion of *Pubis angelical* and *Maldición eterna a quien lea estas páginas*, which follow) seems to bring the authorial subject out into the open, out from under the fiction and from behind the invented figures who, in speaking for themselves, also speak for the authorial figure that seems to empower them. In the footnotes, however, that figure's presence is most visible. There, at the edges of the fictional body, the author's apparent desire to take a position in the text is revealed. In the notes, what sounds like a discrete authorial voice surfaces to authorize a set of views on the question of homosexuality, and thereby to offer support to the figure who incarnates that issue in the fiction. The status of this voice, however, remains in question. Its place is a precarious one, situated between the discourses of fiction and fact within the notes themselves and in the text as a whole.

Unlike in the other novels, where something like an authorial voice might surface in the guise of an omniscient narrator, here that voice is "heard" as the discourse of a subject who openly mediates the discourse of other authors. The authority of the novel's authorial subject is built on and upheld by the authorities whose discourse that same subject appropriates for his own use. Given this discursive relation among authorial discourses, this subject can be viewed as an author inasmuch as he seems to bind together the discourse of other subjects of authority; however, he is also an originator or inventor of theories not held by any of those existing authors.[14] That is, although the theories, whether "real" or "invented," have an equally fictional status in the text, the biographical author's virtual confession of total responsibility for one of the theories also puts things in a slightly different light. As suggested earlier, the fact of the last note's testified "fictionality" both differentiates its author from and identifies him with the authors of the other theories offered by the novel.

The questionable status of this authorial figure is, as we recall, grounded not only in the layering of authorial discourses that impedes the identification of an original discourse or author, or only in the recognition of the fictionality of the final theory that masquerades as the work of yet another author. It is also generated by their juxtaposition with and "contamination" by the discourse of fiction that fills one of the notes and by the fictional author suggested by it. These texts and their author(s) are thereby turned in several directions at once. Of course, these turns are supported by, as they are also figured in, the moves of the fictional entities in dialogue above. There, above the notes, the text develops the images of two subjects who speak almost as one and one subject who speaks almost as two. These fictional and authorial subjects are put into peculiar positions, positions through which they would at once challenge and consolidate the forces of traditional or radical authority according to which they all operate. Clearly, the open discussions of homosexuality and leftist politics, as well as the incursions into the field of popular culture, constitute a more direct encounter with the kinds of problems of authority that circulate in all of Puig's novels. Though the authorial figure that emerges from the text seems to take a position designed to aid the position of a specific subject within it, the moves made by each of those figures disclose the difficulties of fixing authority behind any single figure.

Such turns are also taken in *Pubis angelical*, *Maldición eterna a quien lea estas páginas*, and *Sangre de amor correspondido*, where questions of authority and power, as well as truth and knowledge, continue to circulate. In *Pubis angelical*, and more so perhaps in the two novels that follow it, the authorial subject once again seems to recede behind the text, never seeming to speak directly, as it were, through a specialized discourse or in a single place. This figure seems only to show itself through the fictional subjects in and the narrative designs of each text. *Pubis angelical* is the novel whose narrative designs are the most complex of the three. Its authorial subject surfaces as the manipulator of two apparently interrelated stories, one of which its knowledgeable narrative surrogate (i.e., an omniscient narrator) appears to control from a place far enough "above" the narrative so as to suggest that it is also where we might find the author.[15] Yet the author figured by the narrator's work is an authority who, as in *Boquitas pintadas* and *The Buenos Aires Affair*, would undercut as much as support the powers of the narrating subject heard and seen "below" in the text.[16] In *Maldición eterna a quien lea estas páginas* and *Sangre de amor correspondido* the authorial figures seem to emerge only between the lines of the unmediated dialogues and monologues that make up most of those texts, as well as from around the thematic concerns of the subjects whose discourse fills and forms each fiction.[17] In both of these works the authorial subject seems to work entirely "behind the scenes" of the direct discourse that fills the novel's pages. The self-effacing authorial subject maintains the appearance of power as each text creates the impression of a truth soon to be seen, though difficult to arrive at, and ultimately, we discover, impossible to locate.

In each of these novels the reader-author dialogue develops around and through the dialogues of texts and fictional characters whose relation to one another follows the dialectical patterns set up in the earlier novels. The stories that each tells, the characters about and through whom those stories are presented, and, in two cases, the published texts we are presented are situated mostly in unclear and curious relation to one another. For example, though we know that at least two stories are being told in *Pubis angelical*, their connection is not entirely clear. Though there are only two protagonists of *Maldición eterna a quien lea estas páginas*, their identities are often confused and confounded both by what they do and say (or do not say). And though we come to understand the story of seduction and betrayal that is told in *Sangre de amor correspondido*, we don't always know who is telling it, or whether what is told is originally true or eventually invented by the subjects from whom we learn about things from one moment to the next.[18] Though the authorial figure presumably knows and controls all that the reader cannot quite grasp or resolve, and each text presumably would construct some kind of image of an authority that appears to move above or behind it, each text would also figure a subject that seems conscious of the possible limits of the knowledge or power of such a subject. These novels seem to turn the authorial figure from a position of mastery over each text to a position where no such mastery is possible, and back again.

In these three novels the suggestion of a knowledge held yet out of reach, the idea of a power exercised yet not controlled, comes in part from the unresolved debates and discussions, the inconclusive memories and unverifiable fictions, and the original yet reinvented texts that structure them. Such problems arise especially in the continued thematization of cultural, social, and political issues and concerns in *Pubis angelical* and *Maldición eterna a quien lea estas páginas*, and in the problem of textual authority posed both by the latter and by *Sangre de amor correspondido*; here the figure of an author still on the move, or even suspended between contradictory positions, suggests itself. Moreover, the figures from each of these texts together construct the image of a subject ever more self-conscious about the politics and problems of the fictions authorized by each novel and about the positions that might be taken, or not, through them. This is especially so in *Pubis angelical* and *Maldición eterna a quien lea estas páginas*, where the authorial subject turns things around over discussions of matters that touch on the novel's own thematic concerns. However, these discussions underscore that such questions can be read now one way, now another. They repeatedly remind us that two sides or positions can be taken around any one of them, two sides or positions between which these authorial figures move, along with their own fictions.

For example, in *Pubis angelical* the protagonist openly addresses questions about the political and cultural realities of her time: she considers the state of affairs in Argentina, she tries to analyze the power structures inherent in male-female relations, and she attempts all the while to situate herself in relation to these key issues as she either engages in verbal disputes with her political activist and feminist interlocutors or self-consciously dialogues with herself in her diary.[19] At the same time, in the "Hollywood" and "science-fiction" tales that parallel both her diary discourse and the discussions or debates with her two partners, similar issues are raised—not so much through what the narrator says about what the characters do or think as through the situations in which the female protagonists find themselves struggling.[20]

Likewise, in *Maldición eterna a quien lea estas páginas* the two male protagonists whose dialogue fills the novel's pages circle around and switch places as they explore relations of power and knowledge, questions of politics and art.[21] These interlocutors engage in a dialogue that differentiates each from and identifies each with the other. Each manipulates the other through the willful construction of fictions or the uncontrollable fluctuations of memory that, along with their discussions of irresolvable issues, deny access to truth and undercut the idea of an apparently final authority. These two novels suggest that the authority that might appear to move behind the text is not necessarily an authority on the issues raised in them. The author's powers seem to consist of setting things up so as to explore what cannot yet be turned toward a single solution. The authorial figure seems to become merely another subject whose powers are, paradoxically, at once greater and limited, much like those of the other subjects around which he makes his moves.

That the author is a figure who seems to know and, moreover, to organize things so as to control what we can know is again brought out in *Sangre de amor correspondido*. That such a knowledgeable and powerful figure actually has access to such complete knowledge—the apparently absolute and original truth about everything that matters—or that such knowledge even exists to be grasped by such a figure is put into question by the very same text. The author figured by *Sangre de amor correspondido* can be read as a subject who knows but will not divulge the truth about the story or set of scenes presented by the novel's discursive subjects, or as a subject who has no more power over things than the reader, no more power to get at the truth of the tale than his admittedly less knowledgeable partner. Such a subject's authority becomes doubly problematical as the very text that that subject seems to author becomes involved in another question of authority. The monologues and dialogues that form *Sangre de amor correspondido* set up an ambiguous route around a set of scenes and figures that presumably pertain to the same familiar story (i.e., the story of a small-town Don Juan) but that, nonetheless, always retell things differently.

The contradictory versions of the story's sequence and setting, the repeated revisions of and returns to different scenes by the same subjects, take things in disparate directions. One sort of truth first seems to be told, and then another. The self-effacing authority who moves behind those turns seems to work only as a transmitter, a recorder of conversations about which not only that seemingly knowledgeable figure, but also the subjects of the novel's discourse itself, could not discover the truth. The illusion here is that not even those who seem in a position to certify the truth are originally, or any longer, in possession of it; there is no authority who can distinguish among what emerge as equally authoritative stories and subjects. This question of authority that develops and takes over the discourse of the fictional subjects seems also to repeat and refigure a similar question that revolves around the novel as a whole, for another play of shifting authority surfaces between different versions of this text. The novel has been published simultaneously in Spanish and Portuguese. The Spanish edition thus turns out to be a text that is both an original and a copy, a unique or singular and an unoriginal or repetitive work.[22] Through this double set of turns, the figure of the author seems to displace itself, taking the place of one or the other author and turning from one image of authority to another. The place of *Sangre de amor correspondido*'s author is, of course, at once within, above, behind, and also between each version of the novel. It is now here, now there, in what seems to be one or another place of authority.

The authors figured by each of Puig's novels also construct, or come together to suggest, the image of another author, one who moves among them and whose movements work against any idea of closure. This figure's place remains open, of course, while Puig continues to write. It will also remain open, and his figure suspended, even when his writing has ended.[23] The place of the author—the place that belongs to no real subject but to the figures of an author—is opened up by the turns taken by all the subjects of authority apparently placed in it. In Puig's novels that is at once the place where such figures seem to shift position and the place from which all plots of authority seem to be designed. It is the place where such figures might be renewed; it is the place that seems closed to the possibility of closure. Puig's writing shows us that the "death of the author" always entails another authorial return. In his work, as in modern Spanish American fiction as a whole, that return has been orchestrated in necessarily paradoxical and provocative ways. Oddly enough, at the very moment when we might have thought that the author had been done away with and that another figure (i.e., that of the reader) had emerged to take its privileged and "proper" place, Puig and other Spanish American writers have come along to turn things around—to turn the author into a radically modern figure of (in)visible authority.[24] Puig's writing also reminds us that this figure does not stand alone, that it is always dependent upon the textual partner moving with and bound to this apparently primary figure. To read the maneuvers of the author is to read the maneuvers of his partner. Puig's novels bind those figures in provocative and political play.

In Puig's novels the author is figured as a subject who is openly engaged in a variety of complex relations not only with those texts' readers, but also with certain cultural and literary traditions, and even critical practices, through which that same figure—or Puig's text itself—is turned first one way, then another. Questions of cultural or political authority, issues of literary or artistic value, are opened up and turned around through his writing. Puig's apparent challenge to our notion of what is "high" and what is "low," his apparent attempts to resituate a variety of discursive and generic models, establish not so much a finally identifiable or closed position as a place where notions such as these might be put on critical view. Precisely this sort of critical current turns things around—indeed, keeps things open and suspended—in Puig's novels. Precisely this sort of critical position marks the possibilities of narrative fiction today.

NOTES

1. Puig makes the first statement in Sosnowski, "Entrevista" 72; the second set of comments is in Corbatta, "Encuentros" 614. Translations are mine.

2. See related notions of "responsibility" in *MLN* 91.5: *Responsibilities of the Critic* (1976); see esp. Samuel Weber, "The Responsibility of the Critic: A Response" 814–16.

3. The discusssion that follows refers to these editions of Puig's novels: *Pubis angelical* (Barcelona: Seix Barral, 1979); *Maldición eterna a quien lea estas páginas* (Barcelona: Seix Barral, 1980)—this novel has also been published as *Eternal Curse on the Reader of These Pages* (New York: Random House, 1982); and *Sangre de amor correspondido* (Barcelona: Seix Barral, 1982)—the English-language edition is *Blood of Requited Love*, trans. Jan L. Grayson (New York: Vintage, 1984).

4. Corbatta, "Encuentros" 614.

5. See Sosnowski, "Entrevista" 71–72.

6. Corbatta, "Encuentros" 614.

7. Ibid., 615.

8. Cited earlier as examples of an apparent return to traditional forms of narration and representation are García Márquez's *Cien años de soledad* and Donoso's *Casa de campo*. Each of those texts, however, self-consciously points (the former implicitly and the latter explicitly) also to the distance between the assumptions underlying its own narrative procedures and those that characterize, on the other hand, realist or mimetic fiction. See especially *Casa de campo* (Barcelona: Seix Barral, 1978) 53–54, 404–5, 490–93, for the author-narrator's self-referential analysis of precisely those differences.

9. See especially Genette, *Narrative Discourse* (e.g., 161–211), and Mieke Bal, "Narration et focalization: Pour une théorie des instances du récit," *Poétique* 29 (1977): 107–27. For a summary of the development of modern theories of narration and focalization, see Shlomith Rimmon-Kennan, *Narrative Fiction: Contemporary Poetics* (London and New York: Methuen, 1983) 71–116.

10. See Barthes, "The Death of the Author."

11. This notion of the author is taken up by Said in "Molestation and Authority in Narrative Fiction." See also the discussion of Spanish American narrative by Jean Franco in either "Narrador, autor, superestrella: La narra-

tiva latinoamericana en la época de cultura de masas," *Revista iberoamericana* 47.114–15 (1981): 129–48, or "Memoria, narración y repetición: La narrativa hispanoamericana en la época de cultura de masas," in *Más allá del Boom* 111–29.

12. The second part of each novel is opened by a "Recapitulación" (*Boquitas pintadas* 127–28; *The Buenos Aires Affair* 158) that implicitly acknowledges this textual division about which the authorial subject would, by definition, have knowledge and of which the narrator here also seems to be aware. The position and authority of the one would approach and potentially coincide for a moment with that of the other, since the responsibility for the term "recapitulación" seems to rest with either or both of them.

13. This conventional generic authority is not the only powerful figure that is "done in" by Puig's writing. Throughout the novels all kinds of figures of authority, especially father(ly) figures, seem to be done away with or deposed—that is, killed off, forgotten, rendered powerless or entirely absent—from their powerful positions. Though the fact that so many characters are left fatherless and many models of power and authority seem to be brought down is of interest here, what seems perhaps most provocative is that the authorial movement against such figures, or even the laws that support them, is itself a design that certifies the powers of one figure of authority. The challenge to these various forms of conventional authority is effected, it seems, by another subject who would himself usurp the places left vacant by those figures apparently kept down. That subject, at once fictional and textual, would challenge certain laws whose authority such "rebellious" action would also keep alive, in fiction and text alike.

14. The idea of the author as a binder of discourses is suggested in Chapter VI of the Fourth Treatise of Dante's *Convivio*, trans. and ed. Philip H. Wicksteed, 3rd ed. (London: J. M. Dent & Sons, Aldine House, 1912) 251–58. There Dante talks about the author as one who ties or binds words together and whose work is figured in the verb from which the term itself, he claims, is derived (252; cf. trans. note, 257).

15. *Pubis angelical*'s sixteen chapters, equally divided into two parts, develop two parallel and alternating stories whose female protagonists seem to be linked. The "main" story focuses on Ana, an Argentine woman hospitalized apparently for cancer in Mexico City in 1975. Her dialogues with two interlocutors (Pozzi, a political activist and Argentine lawyer, and Beatriz, a feminist) and with herself in her diary form the text of that narrative sequence. This story alternates (sometimes within chapters, sometimes from chapter to chapter) with another that is itself a combination of two seemingly interconnected and continuous stories narrated entirely in the third person. This "second" story—second only in that it might appear to derive from the other as a

contingent narrative of the secret fantasies or desires of Ana; it is also "first," since Chapter I opens with this story and then moves to the 1975 setting—develops, in chronological order, two other stories. It moves from a tale about "la mujer más hermosa del mundo" ["the most beautiful woman in the world"] (9; this character and her story appear to be modeled on Hedy Lamarr as described in her *Ecstasy and Me: My Life as a Woman* [New York: Bartholomew House, 1966]), on whose life from 1936 to the mid–1940s it focuses, to a story about "W218," a young woman who was born before the "Gran Vuelta de Página" ["Big Turn of the Page"] when the "era polar" in which she lives began (151) and who seems to be the other's descendant (see, e.g., 211–12). The contemporary narrative focuses on topics at once political and sexual, public and private, as its protagonist moves through a series of discursive encounters with herself and with others during the time of her hospitalization, paralleling at the same time, it seems, some of the thoughts and actions of the protagonists of both the "Hollywood" and the "science-fiction" sequences. Nonetheless, the precise relationships among these figures and between the two principal narrative sequences are never clearly or finally delineated by any textual authority. On this and other issues raised by the novel, see Yúdice, "Placer y saber"; Pellón, "Strategy"; and Marta Morello Frosch, "Usos y abusos de la cultura popular: *Pubis angelical* de Manuel Puig," in *Literature and Popular Culture in the Hispanic World*, 31–41 (hereafter cited as "La cultura popular").

16. The texts of the "Hollywood" and "science-fiction" stories are narrated in much the same way (that is, by a subject distanced from and far "above" the fiction that is presented) as those sections of *Boquitas pintadas* and *The Buenos Aires Affair* over which the omniscient narrator presides. Moreover, the "objective" reports of events seem to be at once serious or totalizing and comical or limited. (See, for example, the novel's opening pages, where the narrator, following not only Hollywood movie paradigms but also the narrative procedures and discourse of popular fiction, such as serials, tells us every detail of the "opening scene" where we first "see" the protagonist. On the popular paradigms and language reworked in this novel, see Morello Frosch, "La cultura popular.") The narrator is, indeed, on top of it all, yet under the direction of another authority whose work merges with and turns against that surrogate subject.

17. *Maldición eterna a quien lea estas páginas* is in two parts. The first contains twelve unnumbered texts akin to chapters that are composed of dialogues between the novel's two protagonists: Larry, a thirty-six-year-old former teacher of history, works as a companion for Ramírez, a seventy-four-year-old Argentine in exile in New York City. The second part of the novel has eleven similar divisions, the first ten of which continue the protagonists'

dialogues and the last of which contains written texts that follow up on the month or so they spend together. In that last text are six letters, Ramírez's last will and testament, and a job application filled out by Larry. The novel focuses on the relationship that develops between the two men as Larry takes the wheelchair-bound Ramírez for walks around Greenwich Village or visits him in his room at a nursing home and a hospital. In their verbal exchanges the two characters relate and at the same time seem to invent the stories of their own lives or to try to author scenes in the life of the other. They argue about political or cultural issues with which they are each concerned and play out "family dramas" through which the thematics of power and desire, for example, are also developed. The two subjects identify with and violently oppose one another. They seem to invent or lie about their own lives and thoughts; yet they also confess and try to analyze some of their most intimate feelings. Larry and Ramírez support while also doing verbal violence to one another. Their voices are revealed in a dialogue through which neither is able to resolve the issues of concern to himself or the novel as a whole.

Sangre de amor correspondido, also in two parts, has twelve unnumbered and untitled chapters that are equally distributed between those sections, plus a final unnumbered "Epílogo." These narrative units are composed of immediate, direct, and hidden dialogues and monologues from which the story of Josemar, the main discursive subject and apparent center of the fiction, and his girlfriends is constructed. The dialogues and monologues revolve around and keep returning in contradictory fashion to the relationship of Josemar and Maria da Gloria, whose "deflowering" scene is revised over and over by each of them. Several conflicting versions of that scene and its consequences emerge from the characters' discourse. These distinct but related versions of the story make it impossible to establish exactly what happens between the two characters, or even when or where it may have happened. Throughout the novel's "spoken" texts we "hear" these same subjects contradict themselves and each other. We "hear" them doubt what they themselves say, as well as what their interlocutors assert. Everything appears as a different version—a kind of revision or rewriting or rerecording—of a narrative sequence whose truth cannot be fixed by anyone inside or outside the fiction, and whose "facts" seem to turn things one way and then another at any moment of the text. For an introduction to the novel and some helpful comments on the equivocal nature of its text and story, see Emir Rodríguez Monegal, rev. of *Sangre de amor correspondido* by Manuel Puig, *Vuelta* November 1982: 34–35.

18. In *Pubis angelical*, see, e.g., 17, 26, 34, 131, 138, 161, 262; cf. 41 and 59, 94 and 158, 134–35 and 154, 138–39 and 149. In *Maldición eterna a quien*

lea estas páginas, see, e.g., 41–45, 71–73, 81–83, 97–103, 132, 139, 165–71. In *Sangre de amor correspondido*, see, e.g., 24, 27, 33, 91; cf. 9–15, 21–22, 109–13, 204–7.

19. See, e.g., 19–21, 38–40, 52–54, 57–59, 78, 85–95, 114–24, 192–97.

20. For example, the story of "la mujer más hermosa del mundo" (or "la mujer más bella del mundo," e.g., 76) and that of "W218" can be read as sequences in the quest for, first, a male protector-liberator and, ultimately, the "man of her dreams." The first part of the quest is suggested by the former's relationships with men who control and totally dominate her, her "escapes" with the aid of another, preferred partner, and her eventual destruction at the hands of the powerful men who seem to "do her in." The second is seen through the latter's explicitly posited quest for "un hombre superior" ["a superior man"] or "el hombre de sus sueños ["the man of her dreams"] (e.g., 158, 180–81, 259), which is similarly doomed to failure. Cf. Ana's consideration of this problem of desire on 20–21, 94, 190–91, 226.

21. See, e.g., 48–56, 150–55, 218–25.

22. The novel has also been published as *Sangue de amor correspondido: Romance de Manuel Puig* (Rio de Janeiro: Nove Fronteira, 1982). Though the edition published in Brazil also indicates that it is "Revisão de original" by Luiz Otávio Barreto Leite, the simultaneous publication of both editions, as well as the reworking of conversations that originally were carried on in Portuguese, suggest this question of textual identity. See the review cited in note 17 for Rodríguez Monegal's brief discussion of the problematic relationship between this text and the one in Spanish, referred to here and below. (See also *Maldición eterna a quien lea estas páginas* and *Eternal Curse on the Reader of These Pages*, for related issues raised by the prior publication in Spanish of the supposedly original English-language version of the novel.)

23. This author is another fiction, a textualized subject, that emerges from and is identified with the body of writing produced by an individual subject, as the signature appearing on each text asserts. The name of that subject stands not for the biographical author, not for any one of the authorial figures produced by each text, but for a set of texts and discourses that is, in a way, never closed off or finally defined by that subject. See Michel Foucault, "What Is an Author?" (1969), in *Language, Counter-Memory, Practice*, trans. Donald F. Bouchard and Sherry Simon, ed. Donald F. Bouchard (Ithaca: Cornell UP, 1977) 113–38, for this view of the author, the author's name, and related comments.

24. The individual studies and collective volumes that seem to represent the recent developments in "reader-oriented" criticism and theory include the following: Eco, *The Role of the Reader*; Wolfgang Iser, *The Implied*

Reader: Patterns of Communication in Prose Fiction from Bunyan to Beckett (1972) (Baltimore: Johns Hopkins UP, 1974) and *The Act of Reading*; Susan R. Suleiman and Inge Crosman, eds., *The Reader in the Text: Essays on Audience and Interpretation* (Princeton: Princeton UP, 1980); and Tompkins, ed. *Reader-Response Criticism.*

Index

Alegría, Fernando: 19n
Alter, Robert: 17n, 19n, 20n, 21n, 182n, 183n
Altman, Janet Gurkin: 77n, 125n
Alurista: 129n
Andreu, Alicia G.: 126n
Arenas, Reinaldo: 1, 3
Asturias, Miguel Angel: 2
Author: as paternal figure, 38–41, 241; as filial figure, 40, 241; textual signs of, 76n; as powerful, 84, 88, 97–98, 242; as manipulative strategist, 92, 97–98, 149, 242; as agent of justice, 111; Don Juan-like performance of, 115, 121–22, 133; as mobile figure, 115, 240, 243, 252; as detective's "murderer," 159, 245; as criminal figure, 171–72; and final truth, 171–72; as mediator of other authors, 219–20, 247; as turning figure, 225; as originator, 225, 239; disappearance of, 237; objectivity of, 237; self-effacing, 237, 248, 251; resistance to authoritative image of, 238–39; as textualized figure, 239, 252, 257n; empirical, 240; as ghost, 240; as agent of authority, 243; subversion of authority by, 243, 254n; as binder of discourses, 247, 254n; as specular image of reader, 244; limited knowledge and power of, 249–50; suspended image of, 249; con-

cept of, 253n, 254n, 257n. *See also* Author-reader dialogue
Author-reader dialogue: 50, 89–90, 116–17, 242, 244, 248–49; and temporality, 135–36; as contract of accomplices, 136; and characters' dialogue, 186, 192, 199; in footnotes, 220. *See also* Author; Reader
Authority: of European tradition, 2; of realist fiction, 5; and Berto, 33–35, 37–38, 40–41; and the author, 40–41, 239, 243, 250–51; of voices and styles, 54; Esther's reverence for, 78n; suspended, 115; image of, 172, 240; and the narrator, 238–29; authorial subversion of, 243, 254n; instability of, 248
Azuela, Mariano: 3

Bakhtin, Mikhail: 19n, 21n, 22n, 23n, 74n, 129n, 179n
Bal, Mieke: 253n
Barradas, Efraín: 229n, 232n
Barth, John: 17n
Barthes, Roland: 23n, 125n, 232n, 235n, 253n
Bécquer, Gustavo Adolfo: 176n
Benveniste, Emile: 76n, 77n, 130n, 231n
Berto: identified with Rita Hayworth, 30–31; as betrayer of Toto, 30–31; as figure of authority, 33; as object of be-

Index

bivalence, 56; theory of, 76–77n; as contractual partners, 117–19; Puig's explanation of, 128n, 182–83n; as authorial masks, 192

Choli: language of, 43–44; fantasies of, 70–71

Christ, Ronald: 74n, 76n, 78n, 79n, 123n, 124n, 126n, 128n, 179n, 229n, 230n, 232n, 233n, 235n

Clara Evelia: as investigator, 140–44; and parody, 176n; as curious reader, 176n

Closure: 37, 38, 40–41, 61, 80, 93, 134, 137, 174n

Cobito: language of, 42–43, 44; fantasies of, 71

Coddou, Marcelo: 230n, 231n, 232n

"Concurso anual de composiciones literarias *Tema libre*: 'La película que más me gustó', por José L. Casals, 2.° año nacional, Div. B": 63–66

Corbatta, Jorgelina: 176n, 253n

Cortázar, Julio: 1

Crime, scene of the: as spectacle, 138–39, 177n; as set-up, 145; described, 145–46; as narrative unit, 146–49; as artifice, 149, 157; original, 150-51, 163–65; and repetition, 154–55, 170–71; displacement of, 166–67, 178-79n; as scene of seduction, 157–58, 179n

Culler, Jonathan: 77n

Dante: 254n

Débax, Michéle: 229n, 232n

Defamiliarization: 93, 125–26n, 131

De Quincey, Thomas: 178n

Desire: 57, 63, 136, 162–63, 182n, 192, 209, 217–18, 257n; imitative, 29–30; mimetic, 75n; and reader, 84, 92; mediation of, 106–7, 128n; and social order, 128–29n

Detective: and reader, 137; as agent of justice, 159; as "victim," 159, 245; as "murderer," 180n; death of, 244; and author, 244

Detective fiction: and *La traición de Rita Hayworth*, 39–40, 76n; and *Boquitas pintadas*, 124n; closure in, 134, 174n; teleology of truth and justice in, 136,

175n, 180n; and reader, 136–37; relation to "high" and "low" culture of, 167; verisimilitude in, 167–68, 181–82n; studies of, 172n, 173n; narrative structure of, 173n; temporality of, 173–74n; and Aristotelian categories, 174n, 177n; and reading time, 175–76n; and primal scene, 176–77n; proliferation of crime in, 180n

Dialogue: as privileged narrative form, 186; as contract, 195; as dialectic of power, 196–97, 201, 202–4; and monologue, 211; theories of, 231n

Díaz, César, E.: 173n

Don Juan: Héctor as, 71; as legendary model, 94–95; parodied and stylized, 96; Juan Carlos as, 98–99, 127n; "salvation" and "damnation" of, 99–101; as mediator of desire, 106–7; Puig's views on, 124n; studies of, 126n, 127n; and social order, 128–29n; as "(in)consumable" figure, 129n

Donoso, José: 3, 17n, 153n

Double-voiced discourse: 10–15, 22n, 23n, 52, 55, 97

Echavarren, Roberto: 175n, 177n, 182n, 229n, 231n, 232n, 233n, 234n

Eco, Umberto: 125n, 129n, 257n

"En casa de los padres de Mita, La Plata 1933": 46–48

Epple, Juan Armando: 172n, 173n, 178n

Epigraphs: 123n, 132, 153, 173n

Esther: language of, 43; diary text of, 48–49; fantasies of, 70

Family: relationships within, 33–37, 75–76n, 201–2, 204–6, 233–34; "romance" of, 73n

Felman, Shoshana: 128n

Fernández Moreno, César: 20n

Films: titles of, 79n, 193; textual placement of, 232–33n

Folletín: as generic model, 80, 83, 126n; as subtitle, 80; and reader, 92; structure of, 92-95; parody and stylization of, 96. *See also* Serial fiction

Footnotes: 170, 186, 219–26, 229n, 230n; as serial narrative, 189–190, 221;

Index

the crime," 147; as criminal, 150,152, 162, 178–79; as political prisoner, 151–52; as victim, 152, 162; as perfect partner for Gladys, 153; and authorial figure, 155, 157; as criminal author, 155–57; logic of, 156; with psychiatrist, 159–60; as"detective," 162, 180n
Levine, Suzanne Jill: 123n, 128n
Loveluck, Juan: 19n
Luraschi, Ilse Adriana: 79n

Mabel: hidden identity of, 91–92; as Pancho's accomplice, 107; "rewards" and "punishments" of, 114–15
Mac Adam, Alfred: 75n, 125n
Maldición eterna a quien lea estas páginas: author-reader dialogue in, 248–49; authorial figure in, 248–50; narrative structure and story in, 255-56n
María Esther: as reader-witness, 155; as accomplice-actor, 156, 158; criminal seduction of, 158, 179n
Markiewicz, Henry K.: 21n, 23n
Martínez, Z. Nelly: 23n
Masiello, Francine: 231n, 232n
Merrim, Stephanie: 231n
Mita: language of, 51; fantasies of, 70; reality of, 71
Molina: compared to Toto, 193, 232n; as teacher, 195; as controlling narrator, 196–99; identified with film characters, 198; as passive object of analysis, 198; narrative techniques of, 199–200; as disruptive listener, 200; as agent of surveillance, 202; as manipulative author-director, 203–4; as maternal figure, 205–6; as seductive, powerful subject, 206–7; as critic, 209; as passive figure, 210; as ensnared by his partner, 212; as "native informant," 216; as "traditional" woman, 217; resistance to cellmate, 218; as revolutionary, 226; as stylizer, 227
Morello Frosch, Marta: 75n, 78n, 128n, 182n, 255n
Morino, Angelo: 125n, 172n, 181n
Mukařovský, Jan: 78n, 231n
Murch, A. E.: 173n

Narration: first-person, 48–49; third-person, 132, 236, 237–28; as description, 147; unmediated, 186; tied to power and pleasure, 189, 197-200; theories of, 253n
Narrative fiction: authorial duplicity in, 19n; and critical vocabulary, 20n
Narrator: absent, 24; omniscient, 83–84, 117, 132–33, 139–40, 146, 148, 170, 238–39, 242, 248, 255n; as authorial surrogate, 132–33, 239, 242; objectivity of, 238; authority of, 238–39, 242–43
Nené: letters of, 88–89, 118–20; in final scenes with Juan Carlos, 99–101; as "savior," 100–101; "rewards" and "punishments" of, 111–12
Neruda, Pablo: 1, 2

Oviedo, José Miguel: 76n, 232n, 235n

Pancho: as reader-rival of Juan Carlos, 105–7; as parodist and stylizer, 108-9; and Don Juan tradition, 108–9, 128n; subversion of social order by, 109; "punishments" of, 113
Parody: politics of, 6, 13–14; structure of, 11–12, 22n; and reflexive literature, 12–13, 21n; and stylization, 12–13, 15, 53–56, 64–66, 95–97, 103, 108–9, 168, 241, 243, 246; as subversive, 13; in Latin American literature, 21n; studies of, 21n; varieties of, 22–23n; and related terms, 23n; and *La traición de Rita Hayworth*, 54–56, 64–66; and Peronism, 78n; and *Boquitas pintadas*, 95–97, 103, 108–9, 126n, 243; and *The Buenos Aires Affair*, 138, 150, 152, 167–68, 176n, 177n; and *El beso de la mujer araña*, 227–28
Paz, Octavio: 1, 18n
Pederson-Krag, Geraldine: 176–77n
Pellón, Gustavo: 235n, 255n
Pérez Firmat, Gustavo: 127n
Peronism: 78n, 179n, 229n
Piglia, Ricardo: 75–76n, 79n
Popular culture: and Puig's writing, 3, 8; language of, 51, 53; as model for Gladys, 180–81n; as narrative source,

Index

A Note on the Author

Lucille Kerr teaches Spanish American literature at the University of Southern California. She continues to write about modern Spanish American fiction.